# The Fleurs de Lis of the Kings of France
## 1285–1488

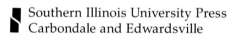 Southern Illinois University Press
Carbondale and Edwardsville

# The Fleurs de Lis of the Kings of France
## 1285–1488

William M. Hinkle

Copyright © 1991 by the Board of Trustees, Southern Illinois University
All rights reserved
Printed in the United States of America
Designed by Katherine E. Swanson
Production supervised by Natalia Nadraga
94   93   92   91      4   3   2   1

Library of Congress Cataloging-in-Publication Data

Hinkle, William M., 1905–
    The fleurs de lis of the kings of France, 1285–1488 / William M.
  Hinkle.
      p.      cm.
    Includes bibliographical references.
    1. Fleur-de-lis. 2. Capet, House of. 3. Heraldry—France.
  4. France—History—Medieval period, 987–1515. I. Title.
  CR41.F6H56 1991
  929.7′4—dc20
  ISBN 0-8093-1676-5                                                    90-34030
                                                                           CIP

The paper used in this publication meets the minimum requirements of
American National Standard for Information Sciences—Permanence
of Paper for Printed Library Materials, ANSI Z39.48-1984. ∞

# Contents

Contents

vi

# Plates

Plates

viii

Plates

ix

# Preface

This study of the fleurs de lis of the kings of France does not pretend in any way to cover all aspects of the subject, but in the ensuing pages, I have tried to trace what I consider to be the major developments of this theme within the general time limits of 1285 to 1488. As an art historian my own interest in these royal emblems initially centered around the numerous pictorial illustrations of the legendary origins of the fleurs de lis that also, as it turned out, happened to be largely confined to the fifteenth century. I soon discovered, however, that in order to do justice to these works of art I was obliged to acquaint myself with the earlier literature that dealt with the royal emblems and to take into acount the various numismatic and sigillographic aspects of this theme that were also linked to some of the major problems in which the arms of France were involved. Much of this material, in turn, pointed to a close connection between these heraldic emblems and contemporary historical events, ranging from the last flourishing period of medieval France at the turn of the fourteenth century, through the long dark days of war and defeat that followed, and to the final emergence of a new and militant nation with the advent of Charles VIII in the fourth quarter of the fifteenth century.

As my research progressed, conducted in a more or less chronological order, to my surprise, in spite of the intricacies of the material with which I was dealing, a lucid if complex story unfolded itself, the story of the fleurs de lis, whose ramifications and dramatic highlights I have attempted to convey to the reader in the following chapters. But in order not to obstruct the involved flow and continuity of the historical connections, pictorial developments, and literary allusions that make up the major portion of this story, I have relegated much additional information and some of my own comments, as well as most controversial matters, to the notes, in which I have also taken the opportunity to correct the not infrequent errors that appear in the relevant and often recent bibliographical items. And since some of these errors occur in well-known publications or in works by reputable authors, it is all the more necessary to point them out before they become part of the accepted record. I can only hope that my own errors in this present study are few and minor.

Among the many to whom through the years I am indebted for their contribution to this work and from whose suggestions I have benefited, I wish in particular to express my gratitude to Professor Elizabeth A. R. Brown and to Patricia Danz Stirnemann for providing me with a great deal of the essential documentation.

Genealogical chart showing the descent from Louis IX of the Dukes of Burgundy and the Kings of France and England through Charles VIII and Henry VI

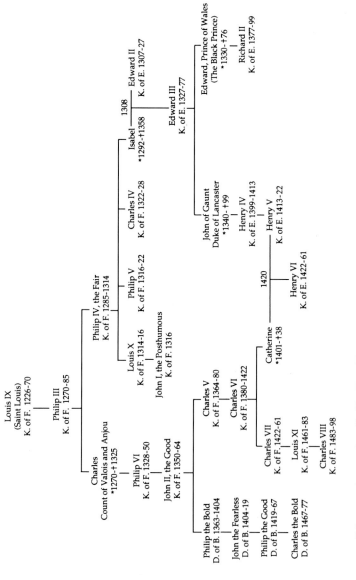

Only regnant dates are given. K. of F. = King of France; K. of E. = King of England; D. of B. = Duke of Burgundy; * = born; † = died

# The Fleurs de Lis of the Kings of France
# 1285–1488

# 1

# The *Signum Regis Franciae*

hen heraldic emblems first came into extensive use in western Europe during the second half of the twelfth century, they largely served the practical purpose of identifying the combatants in warfare and in the tournaments that were already in vogue. By the beginning of the thirteenth century, when armorials were no longer exclusively reserved for purposes of combat, they were adopted by all of the European nobility, and soon thereafter, they spread to all classes of society as well as to civic and religious communities.

So it was with those perennially favorite devices, the fleurs de lis. Spread far and wide during the first half of the thirteenth century, they not only appeared in a variety of heraldic colors on the escutcheons of the nobility and on the borders of the royal Scottish coat of arms, but also on the seals of the Norman peasantry, and they were likewise chosen as the insignia of towns and cities, notably Florence and Lille.[1] Independently of these many and varied usages, however, the fleurs de lis were known above all as the heraldic emblems of the kings of France.

Beginning shortly after 1285, for almost a century and a half the royal fleurs de lis were the subjects of a surprisingly extensive literary activity. Well-known poets, scholars, and historiographers, as well as anonymous writers, were all engaged in elaborating on their arcane symbolism, in creating intricate allegories to explain their presence on the royal escutcheon, and in relating the legends that told of their supernatural origin. And in the course of this same long period, the arms of France with the fleurs de lis were also credited with a uniquely influential role in that seemingly endless dynastic struggle between France and England known as the Hundred Years' War.

Before we proceed with these historical and literary matters, however, a short summary of the more immediate antecedents of the royal fleurs de lis, as well as a brief analysis of their pictorial features, is essential for a fuller understanding of these later developments and the problems in which they were involved. Although the name itself, fleur de lis, first occurs in its plural Latin forms, *flores lilii* or *liliorum*, shortly after 1214 and in a strictly armorial sense,[2] this heraldic motif, as it emerged in its maturity toward the end of the twelfth century from earlier representations of a three-petaled flower, was only one of several related configurations, including the ornamental finials on scepters and crowns, that have also come to be known as fleurs de lis.

The common characteristics of all of these variants are a tall pointed central petal and two lower ones curving outwardly on either side. In the heraldic emblem the three petals are clearly separated, while the lateral ones assume ever more graceful curvilinear contours (figs. A, B). Their organic character is in turn contrasted with the abstract silhouette of a straight horizontal bar by which they are united below. Sometimes the bar is slightly curved, suggesting a solid three-dimensional ring that holds together the separate petals (fig. C). Two ways of terminating the nether portion of the heraldic fleur de lis can also be distinguished. In one case the thin stems of the petals continue below the horizontal bar (fig. A). In the second and more usual category, a small inverted trilobe with pointed ends projects beneath its center (figs. B, C).

Although there was general agreement among the later writers that the botanical prototype of the fleur de lis was the white lily, the *lilium album* or *candidum* of the herbals, admittedly in none of its variations does this floral motif bear any visible resemblance to the flower of any known member of the lily family. Moreover, its very name, "flower of the lily," seems redundant, but not, however, when it is understood to mean the flower of the lily plant. According to the medieval herbalists, basing their therapeutic lore on the late classical and Arabic authors, the flower, leaves, and root of the lily plant were all regarded as curative, a reputation that was recalled in the title *Lilium medicinae* chosen in the opening years of the fourteenth century by Bernard de Gordon of the University of Montpellier for his popular medical treatise.[3] Later in Digulleville's allegorical poem on the floral emblems, the therapeutic properties of the plant were transferred to the heraldic flower itself when Sapience says of the fleur de lis, "elle est medicinable à maint mal dont on est malade."[4]

## The *Signum Regis Franciae*

3

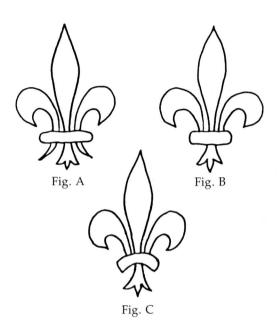

Fig. A

Fig. B

Fig. C

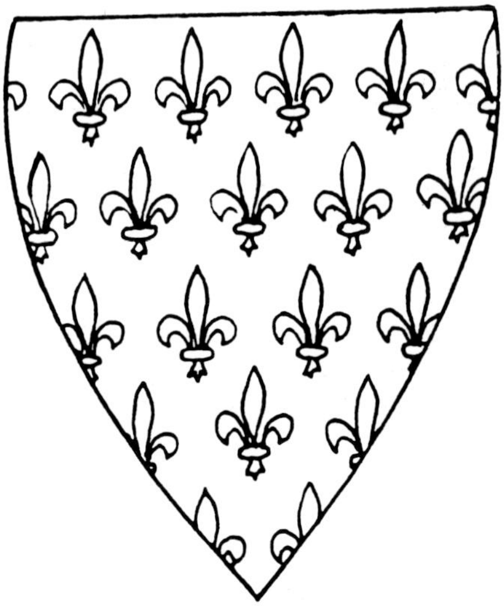

Fig. D

Of crucial importance, however, for the later history of the arms of France was the problem of the number of the lilies on the shield. For long after the leopards on the English coat of arms had been permanently established as three by Richard I in the 1190s and the arms of the other major reigning houses of Europe had also been consolidated, the number of the emblems on the French coat of arms continued to be a matter of personal preference. Though in a few instances reduced to three, the number of the heraldic flowers as officially represented on the royal seals and on the coinage is generally in excess of three, usually six or more. And to add to the indeterminate nature of the French armorials, instead of being composed entirely of whole fleurs de lis, the design of the shield is sometimes conceived as a continuous overall pattern so that some of the flowers along the edges are partially cut off (fig. D).

In spite of the unresolved problem of the number of the flowers, the French royal arms nevertheless shared the practical usages common in this early period to armorial shields in general at a time when they were still an intrinsic part of the new military equipment that had evolved in the course of the twelfth century. As is graphically illustrated in the equestrian figure of Prince Louis, the son and heir of Philip Augustus, on his seal of 1211 (plate 1), the shield bearing his coat of arms not only constituted a warrior's major protective armament, but since his features were completely concealed beneath the visor of his helmet, the emblems also provided the only means by which he could be identified by his fellow combatants in the melee of the battle. This dual role of protection and identification on the battlefield, which was of major importance in the origin and early usages of the armorial shield, later inevitably led to the frequent association of the emblems of the kings of France with martial themes and with the politics of warfare.

Whereas the shield on Prince Louis' seal of 1211 is the earliest surviving example of the French coat of arms,[5] it was probably not on a shield that the arms of France made their initial appearance but rather on the king's personal banner. In another equestrian portrait of Prince Louis in a small clerestory rose of Chartres cathedral of around 1220, the king's banner, displaying his arms in their heraldic colors of gold for the fleurs de lis and azure blue for the ground, took the form of a rigid upright rectangle, so that even when it was held motionless near the king on the battlefield, the royal arms were always completely visible on its surface (plate 2).[6] Thus it served primarily to locate the king's exact position during the battle, however confused the fighting might be, and in this way, it functioned as an instrument of identification similar to that of the armorial shield.

Known to have existed in the time of Philip Augustus, the king's banner with the fleurs de lis may already have come into use sometime before 1180 during the long reign of his father Louis VII.[7] There is good reason to conclude, moreover, that long before the appearance of the very first armorials of any kind in the second quarter of the twelfth century, the Capetians had already chosen a single stylized lily as their particular attribute.[8]

On the seal of Robert the Pious, who reigned from 996 to 1031 and who was the son of Hugh Capet, the founder of the dynasty, the little half-figure of the king, seen in frontal view, holds in his right hand a small floral motif (plate 3a).[9] By 1035, on the seal of Robert's younger son Henry I, the motif in the king's right hand has now taken on the more distinct form of a three-petaled flower (plate 3b), while Henry's full-length seated portrait, however primitive in design, can also be said to have established that most prestigious of the French royal sigillographic types, the so-called seal of majesty, comparable to what might be termed the great seal of France.[10] Moreover, all of the *sceaux de majesté* of Henry's successors through Philip IV (1285–1314) continue to display the flower in the king's right hand. And that it was indeed meant from the beginning to represent a stylized lily is confirmed by the fact that the flower on the later seals gradually assumes the unmistakable features of a fleur de lis (plates 3c–e).[11]

In contrast to the manifold symbolism that was later to be ascribed to the fleurs de lis, no text of any kind survives to inform us of the particular symbolic significance that may originally have been attached to these floral emblems or to explain why Robert the Pious, near the very beginning of the dynasty, chose a lily as his personal attribute.[12] As it turned out, however, the fleurs de lis, whatever their original symbolism may have been, were particularly fitting in their innocuous appearance as the devices and attributes of these early Capetians. Not for them were the aggressive carnivores favored by other reigning houses. Living unpretentiously on their little island in the Seine, at a time when the royal domain over which they exercised direct rule did not extend beyond a small area immediately surrounding their capital city of Paris, they were also faced with rebellious vassals whose feudal territories and potential resources were sometimes far greater than theirs. Against such challenges, what could be more disarming than these inoffensive flowers?

Well aware of the appropriateness of the lilies as the emblems and attributes of these early kings, Gerald of Wales, writing around 1217 during the latter part of the reign of Philip Augustus, compares the unostentatious pleasures of Philip's father, Louis VII, with the luxurious living of Henry II of England and matches the modest simplicity of Louis VII with those simple little flowers, the fleurs de lis.[13] But under the harmless exterior of the lilies that seemed to threaten no one there also lurked a formidable power. "In our own day," says Gerald of Wales, "we have seen these simple flowers conquer the leopards and the lions," a direct reference to the battle of Bouvines of 1214 when Philip Augustus overcame the combined forces of the Plantagenets and the Guelphs.[14] But even before Bouvines, Philip's earlier victories had already created a turning point in the fortunes of the Capetians, not only by furthering the unity of the French state under the crown, but also by fostering the precipitous rise in the prestige of the French monarchy. This process in turn culminated during the reign of Philip's grandson Louis IX (1226–70) when after 1250, with the extinction of the imperial Hohenstaufen line, the king of France became in fact, if not in title, the emperor in the west.[15] And a little over a decade after the death of Louis IX in 1270, there appeared the very first known references to the symbolism of the emblematic lily.

Not unexpectedly, these earliest literary allusions emanated from the royal abbey of St-Denis that was conveniently situated in the immediate vicinity of Paris and that had links with the monarchy extending back into early Merovingian times. Although the abbey had failed to wrest from Reims the rights to the coronations, during the second half of the thirteenth century the ties between St-Denis and the monarchy had been increasing in a rising crescendo. Whereas in former times the kings were wont to deposit their regalia in the abbey, this custom had been ignored by Louis VIII and for a time by his son Louis IX as well. But in 1261 the king officially designated St-Denis as the permanent repository for all of the regal crowns and other ornaments used during the ceremony at Reims.[16] Beginning in 1231 the abbey church, which had long been favored as a royal necropolis, was rebuilt on a much expanded scale in order to accommodate an ambitious program of dynastic tombs, a project finally completed in the 1260s with the king's direct assistance.[17] And with the canonization of Louis IX in 1297 his own tomb in the new church became in turn the active center of his cult.[18]

The many benefits that the alliance with the crown had brought to St-Denis were reciprocated by the inmates of the monastery who ever since the time of the abbot Suger in the middle of the twelfth century had been furnishing the monarchy with its historiographers. In the period immediately following the death of Saint Louis, the abbey's two outstanding historians were the monk Primat, who in 1274 completed the first redaction of that ever-popular Bible of French monarchical history, the *Grandes Chroniques de France*,[19] and Guillaume de Nangis, whose Latin *Life of Louis IX*, begun in 1285 and completed before the canonization of the king in 1297, contains the very first of the commentaries on the symbolic significance of the heraldic flowers (appendix 1).[20]

The author has just been describing a serious fracas that erupted between the students of the University of Paris and the townspeople early in the reign of Louis IX. In the subsequent dispersal and emigration of the scholars and students from the city the king, says Guillaume de Nangis, grieves that their departure has also resulted in the loss of the study of learning, along with the practice of chivalry, both of which had formerly been transmitted from Athens to Rome and from Rome to France. And should this precious treasure of learning, he says, be utterly banished from France, the emblem of the lily, the sign of the king of France, will also remain permanently disfigured (appendixes 1, 2, 4).

Before proceeding further one should immediately note that the author is here concerned only with the single emblematic flower, and not with the number of times it is reproduced on the king's escutcheon and on his banner, both of which de Nangis also mentions. And furthermore, de Nangis has portrayed Louis IX in his grief over the loss of learning and chivalry as identifying himself with his own emblem of the fleur de lis that through this same loss runs the risk of lasting damage and that he names, in formal terms, the *signum regis Franciae*. Inevitably, too, we are reminded of the single flower in the hand of the king on the *sceaux de majesté*. And since the royal seal itself, when attached to a document, was the most personal mark of the king's authority, the equivalent of his own signature, the flower in his hand could even more fittingly be called the sign of the king of France. There is, moreover, some reason to believe that Saint Louis himself had a particular preference for the single lily as his personal device. Following an unusual precedent established by his grandfather, Philip Augustus, each of Louis IX's counterseals of 1240 and 1256 bears only one large fleur de lis (plate 4).[21]

In mentioning the loss of learning and chivalry due to the exodus of the students from Paris, Guillaume de Nangis reminds us that both of them had formerly been introduced into France from Athens and Rome, a theme, however, which he was far from being the first to have propounded. As Edmund Faral has pointed out, the idea of the migration of chivalry from Greece and Rome had often been sounded before, beginning with the late twelfth century *Cligés* of Chrétien de Troyes and extending to the prologue to the *Grandes Chroniques de France,* whose first redaction, as we have seen, was completed in 1274.[22] The key source for the migration of learning, however, occurs, not in Chrétien de Troyes, but in another chronicle, of which only fragments remain, composed in the opening years of the thirteenth century by Helinandus, a monk of the Cistercian abbey of Froidmont in the Beauvaisis.[23] And according to the monk of Froidmont, the Carolingian scholar Alcuin under Charlemagne had transferred the study of learning from Rome to Paris after it had been introduced to the Romans from Greece. The relevant passage has been preserved by Vincent of Beauvais in his *Speculum Historiale* and thus would probably have been known to Guillaume de Nangis, who borrowed material from this same *Speculum* for the earlier portions of his *Life of Louis IX*.[24]

In spite of the fact, moreover, that the concept of chivalry only began to emerge in the Late Middle Ages, these references to the migration of learning and chivalry were by no means entire fabrications of Helinandus and Chrétien de Troyes, but had genuine roots in the much earlier idea of the transfer of culture from the ancient classical world to northern Europe, a theme that in the ninth century had become an integral part of the whole concept of the Carolingian *Renovatio*.[25] In adopting this concept, however, Guillaume de Nangis has credited this cultural migration not to the ninth century but to the very beginning of the Christian era and has applied the terms *Sapientia*, that is, learning, and *Militia*, the usual medieval Latin name for chivalry, to none other than the fleur de lis itself. For *Sapientia* and *Militia*, he says, are also represented by two of the three petals of the lily, both of which had followed Dionysius the Areopagite from Greece to France, where these two petals had then acted as the defenders of the third petal, *Fides* (appendix 1.6). For faith, according to the author, is governed by learning and guided by chivalry, that ideal code of combat that we know from other medieval sources sought to enlist the raw militancy of the age in protecting the defenseless and in defending the church.[26]

Before attempting to elucidate these admittedly cryptic references concerning the significance of the petals, it should first of all be pointed out for the benefit of those unacquainted with Dionysian lore that the Athenian Dionysius the Areopagite, who is mentioned in the Acts of the Apostles as having been converted by Saint Paul, had long been identified, however unhistorically, with that other Dionysius, Saint Denis, who was not only the patron saint of the abbey that bore his name, but also of the monarchy and of France itself, and who in the middle of the third century had brought Christianity to the inhabitants of Lutetia, the Roman colony that was later to become Paris.[27] And the symbolism of the three petals, in which the two representing learning and chivalry had followed Dionysius the Areopagite from Greece to France, where they became the defenders of the third petal representing faith, is thus not only an allegory of Saint Denis' journey to the distant city on the Seine, but also presents him as the one who in the apostolic age had first introduced into France the ancient culture of the now Christianized classical world.

Reverberations of Guillaume de Nangis' comments on the fleur de lis can be detected far into the future. Their more immediate impact resulted in several later versions of his commentary that were also produced at St-Denis, one of them being an amplified Latin discourse on the symbolism of the petals composed by Yves, a monk of the abbey, who introduced it into his extensive three-volume *Life of Saint Denis* that was offered in 1317 to Philip V by Gilles de Pontoise, the abbot of the monastery.[28] Included in the third volume of Yves' work that comprises the later history of the French rulers, his short chapter on the fleur de lis is not, however, incorporated into Yves' account of the university riots in the reign of Louis IX, but it has been inserted into a long section devoted to the legendary exploits and reputed erudition of the emperor Charlemagne.

Some effort to establish a link between Charlemagne and the patron of the abbey, however implausible from the point of view of historical chronology, might nevertheless be expected in any work featuring the lives of both Saint Denis and the later rulers of France by an inmate of the monastery that prided itself on its many associations with the emperor. The monk Yves, moreover, has managed the transition from Charlemagne to Saint Denis with considerable ingenuity.

Since, as we have seen, Guillaume de Nangis had portrayed Dionysius the Areopagite as the bearer of the Christianized classical culture symbolically represented by *Fides, Sapientia*, and *Militia*, a parallel could be drawn between the accomplishments of this first-century disciple of Saint Paul and Charlemagne's ninth-century renaissance, as Yves has intimated in the heading to the chapter immediately preceding that on the symbolism of the fleur de lis, in which he states "how in the time of Charlemagne the study of letters increased in France and how through Saint Denis France excelled all other kingdoms in faith, learning and chivalry."[29] And since Helinandus of Froidmont, whom Yves had obviously consulted, had ascribed to Alcuin the introduction of learning from Greece and Rome to Paris in the time of Charlemagne, and since Yves himself in this same chapter claims that Alcuin, among other scholars, had fostered the *studium litterarum* after it had been introduced to Paris along this same route,[30] it would seem indeed as though the monk of Froidmont had provided Yves with a convenient bridge between the saint and the emperor that also allowed him to insert among the chapters devoted to Charlemagne an allegorical account of the missionary journey of Saint Denis; for as Dionysius the Areopagite he had also brought the culture of the classical world to France long before it was introduced into Paris by the Carolingian scholars.[31]

In the chapter on the symbolism of the fleur de lis that follows, however, Yves has confined his own observations to the merits of faith, learning, and chivalry (appendix 2.1, 2). For the allegory of Saint Denis and the three petals, he has relied on yet another offshoot of de Nangis' comments on the fleur de lis, a little Latin poem of five verses that he credits to an illustrious, though nameless, writer:

> Flos duplex Achaie, sophos et milicie,
> Sequens Dionysius, servit regno Francie.
> Fides summa specie florem facit tertium.
> Trini floris folium effigiat lilium,
> Signum regis Francie.

The five verses may be freely translated as: "The two petals of the flower of Achaia, learning and chivalry, following Dionysius, watch over the kingdom of France. The third petal, representing faith and which is taller in appearance,[32] completes the flower. The triple petals of the flower form the lily, the sign of the king of France" (see also appendix 2.3).

Though one might suspect that the illustrious writer of this little poem was de Nangis himself, the words *sophos* for *sapientia* and *Achaia* for Greece are certainly alien to his Latin vocabulary. Although the identity of the author remains perforce unknown, additional information concerning the poem is provided by Thomas of Ireland, one of the contemporary luminaries of the University of Paris. After quoting the verses in a short tract, *De sensibus tribus sacrae scripturae,* which he composed between 1316 and circa 1321, he also informs us that they were written "super tomba Sancti Dionysii . . . in Franciae."[33] From this we can assume that the verses were probably inscribed on a parchment scroll or placard, and from what is known of the tomb of Saint Denis itself, the location of this placard over the tomb can also be approximately determined.

Situated immediately to the west of the apsidal hemicycle in the abbey church of St-Denis, the *tomba Sancti Dionysii* was not, however, a tomb in the usual sense of the word but rather took the form of an elaborate shrine consisting of three distinct parts. On the west side of the shrine was the altar of the martyrs dedicated to Saint Denis and his two companions, Rusticus and Eleutherius, all three of whom were said to have been beheaded on the heights of Montmartre. Behind the altar a small chamber encased in black marble contained their relics. Directly above this reliquary chamber was a wooden tabernacle in the form of a diminutive three-aisled nave. In each aisle was placed an empty rectangular coffin. All three coffins apparently once contained the remains of the three martyrs in the *confessio* of the earlier Carolingian church and were thus also objects of veneration. The wooden coffins, as well as the whole exterior of the tabernacle, were sheathed in precious metals and colored enamels and studded with jewels, carved crystals, and antique cameos.[34]

Although the shrine was partially destroyed by the Huguenots in 1567 and finally demolished in the seventeenth century, some idea of the west front of the tabernacle can be gained from a miniature by Jean Fouquet in a copy of the *Grandes Chroniques de France* illuminated shortly after 1461 that illustrates in a somewhat fanciful fashion the inhumation of Philip the Fair in the sanctuary of the church (plate 5).[35] In the background, the tabernacle's three-gabled facade rises like a triptych above the altar of the martyrs, which is here presumably hidden by the laymen and prelates assembled in front of it. Beneath each of the three gables of the tabernacle is a relief of one of the martyrs. The round Romanesque arches framing the lateral figures of Rusticus and Eleutherius suggest that at least these two reliefs may have stemmed from the time of the abbot Suger himself, who commissioned the original shrine around 1140.[36]

According to the Comte de Montesquiou-Fezensac a similar three-gabled facade terminated the east end of the tabernacle.[37] And since it was the east end of the shrine that was frequented by the pilgrims who came to venerate the three martyrs and to gaze through the gilded openwork screens at their silver reliquaries hanging in the black marble chamber, we may assume that it was on this same east end of the tabernacle, where it could be easily read, that was posted the little Latin poem celebrating the journey of Saint Denis and the symbolism of the three petals.

The poem, however, was not the only reminder of the lily of the kings of France on the tabernacle. In a codicil to his will, drawn up in 1314, Philip the Fair bequeathed a gold fleur de lis to each of four of the most revered shrines of the age. And among these four shrines, as one might expect, was that of "the blessed Dionysius, our most glorious patron."[38] The accounts of the commandery of St-Denis for the years 1329 to 1330, cited by Montesquiou-Fezensac, indicate that Philip's fleur de lis was affixed to the central gable of one of the tabernacle's facades, along with two other votive lilies.[39] Three more silver gilt lilies from the tabernacle are recorded in the 1634 inventory of the abbey, though whether or not two of them may have been identical with those that accompanied Philip IV's golden flower cannot, of course, be determined.[40]

With the poem on the petals exposed on the tabernacle for those versed in Latin to read and the votive lilies attached to one of its gables for all to see, the abbey was now well on its way to claiming the fleur de lis of the kings of France as its own. But the intractable problem of the number of the emblems on the royal escutcheon still remained unresolved. Whereas the four votive offerings of Philip IV may be taken as a further indication of the attachment of the Capetian rulers to the single lily as their particular emblem, this preference, in turn, may account, at least in part, for the indifference that continued to be shown as to the actual number of the emblems on their coat of arms, an attitude that is reflected in Yves' comments at the conclusion of his chapter on the fleur de lis. Noting that not only one or three, but a plurality of lilies is depicted on the eight-penny coins of the realm, he leaves it up to the diligent reader to discover for himself any hidden meaning their numbers might convey (appendix 2.6).

The single emblematic lily, as the *signum regis Franciae,* was soon, however, to take a secondary place among the literati when its three petals were transformed into three entire flowers that for the later writers became henceforth the acknowledged number of the emblems on the arms of France. An early phase in this process of transformation, which in time was to become so crucial in both its literary and historical implications, can already be observed in Yves' chapter on the symbolism of the petals. His own awareness of what can be called the problem of the numbers is already evident in the passage just quoted, when he notes that not only one or three, but a plurality of lilies is found on the coins. Earlier in this same chapter he concedes that the triple meaning of the single fleur de lis has sometimes been applied by others to three separate lilies as well (appendix 2.5). And finally, in the vernacular version of his third book of the *Life of Saint Denis,* that was not, however, the work of Yves himself but of an anonymous translator who was far from being literal-minded, not only have the petals in Yves' Latin text been consistently replaced by three independent flowers, but three fleurs de lis are now also said to be the number of the emblems on the royal escutcheon.[41]

# 2
# The Trinitarian Symbolism of the Three Fleurs de Lis

 t about the time that Guillaume de Nangis was at work on his *Life of Louis IX*, another major line of development in the literary history of the royal fleurs de lis was inaugurated, one that owed nothing to the Dionysian authors but that sprang from that rich allegorical exegesis on the Biblical lily whose outstanding exponents in the twelfth and thirteenth centuries were Bernard of Clairvaux and that renowned master of the spiritual life, the Franciscan Bonaventura, who began teaching at the University of Paris in 1248. Among the later writers stemming from this same exegetical tradition can be counted the unknown composer of the *Vitis mystica*, an extensive work of a Bonaventurain character that François Chatillon has tentatively dated toward the very end of the thirteenth century.[1]

With the eye of a botanist, though lacking the botanical terminology, the author of the *Vitis mystica* has devoted a long section of his tractate to the lily and not only to the flower but to the entire plant as well, to each part of which he has given a mystic meaning.[2] Starting with the root and proceeding to the stem and its two tiers of surrounding leaves, he finally comes to the flower itself, whose white exterior perianth identifies it as the *lilium candidum* of the herbals and the medieval medicinal tracts. Its six floral leaves, says the author, are divided into two groups of three each that can be said to correspond to the three petals and the three sepals that alternate to form the actual floral envelope of the lily flower (the three-petaled fleur de lis is perhaps not so unlike its botanical counterpart after all).

From the white floral leaves, whose two groups represent respectively the present earthly life and the life hereafter, the writer progresses to the interior of the flower, whose six golden *flosculi,* or florets, can be recognized as the stamens, here equated with the six acts of mercy. At the very center of the flower is a single tall *flosculus,* the pistil. Rising higher than the other *flosculi,* that it dominates, it thus becomes a symbol of divinity that is above all other things. The head of the pistil is a triangle, the form of the Trinity that is one in substance but whose three angles, each distinct from the other, are the three persons who together make up the indivisible Godhead.[3]

Echoes of this botanical *lilium mysticum,* as it might be called, can immediately be detected in a work of an otherwise totally opposite nature, the *Dit des Alliés.* Composed by that lively Parisian versifier, Geoffroy de Paris, sometime between the end of 1316 and the very beginning of the following year, this colorful vernacular poem was thus probably finished only a few months before Yves' *Life of Saint Denis* was presented to Philip V.[4] Although no contemporary records exist concerning the poet, from his writings it can be assumed that Geoffroy was possibly a cleric, probably a member of the royal chancellery and certainly, as the poem reveals, one of Philip V's most ardent supporters.[5] Completed during the first critical months of Philip's reign, this best known of Geoffroy's works was likewise dedicated to the king.

Unlike the historiographers of St-Denis, who drew their material largely from the deposits of the past, Geoffroy de Paris also dealt with some of the major political issues of his own day. So it was with the *Dit des Alliés.* Ever since the end of the reign of Philip's father, Philip IV, various leagues of provincial nobles, the allies of the title, were vociferously demanding an end to the reforms the king had imposed upon them, and above all to the taxes that, they claimed, were reducing them to poverty.[6] Although at first only wishing to return to the *bonne coustoume* of former times, says Geoffroy, the rebellious barons are now nothing but conspirators attacking the sacred crown their ancestors had glorified. But they shall regret their audacity, for they are no better than an animal brought to bay by the hounds and shall be made to pay for the mess they have made.[7]

Having vented his indignation against these disloyal subjects of the king, Geoffroy then reminds Philip of the heraldic emblem of his house, and in so doing, the poet's indebtedness to the author of the *Vitis mystica* begins to manifest itself in the white lily that is its model:

> Roys, la flour de lis esmerée (pure)
> Blanche est comme la nof negée
> Mais en la teue a dorement,
> Roys, ta flour de lis est dorée;
> Dont charitez t'est demoutrée,
> Et qui vivre doiz chastement,
> En tes .V. senz sensiblement.[8]

The snow-white flower of the lily is thus contrasted with that other flower, the golden fleur de lis, the gold signifying the charity and chaste living, which is expected of a conscientious king. In the very next verses, on the royal shield in martial array, the fleur de lis is now tripled as a sacramental sign of faith in the Deity, who is three persons in one:

> En ton escu de parement,
> Trible à flour de lis en armée,
> C'est de la foy le sacrement,
> Une en déité simplement,
> Et en personnes est triblée.[9]

Here for the first time in the extant literature the three heraldic lilies on the arms of France are associated with the three persons of the Trinity. And then, in verses that strikingly recall the triangulation of the head of the pistil in the *Vitis mystica*, the analogy with the Trinity is applied to the triangular form of the shield itself:

> Roy, telle est la fourme fourmée
> De l'escu qu'elle est trianglée,
> Et par ceti disposement
> T'est il la Trinité notée.[10]

That Geoffroy may well have had the text of the *Vitis mystica* directly at hand is further suggested by the general similarities in the progression of the colors and the forms—in the *Dit des Alliés*, beginning with the white flower and proceeding to the golden fleurs de lis and finally to the triangular shield; in the *Vitis mystica*, starting with the white floral leaves, then continuing with the golden *flosculi*, and ending with the triangulation of the head of the pistil, the symbol of the triune God. And in the *De Alliatis*, the slightly earlier Latin version of the *Dit des Alliés*, in direct emulation of the *Vitis mystica*, Geoffroy has also devoted a whole stanza to the symbolism of the lily plant from root to flower.[11]

It should be pointed out, however, that while in the *Vitis mystica* the triangle was held up as the ideal representation of the Trinity, denoting at once the unity of the deity and the separateness of the three persons, the three identical flowers on the royal shield remained an imperfect Trinitarian symbol, since they failed to express the unity of the Godhead.[12] Nevertheless the religious significance with which the triple fleurs de lis were now endowed was in time to further enhance the sacred aura surrounding the monarchy and allowed the later writers to ascribe to the royal emblems a supernatural and benevolent influence on the fortunes of France and its kings. Such indeed seems to have been implicitly the case in Geoffroy's own invocation of the heraldic flowers on behalf of Philip V, who in this first year of his reign was struggling to assert his rights to the throne. As though the arms of France entitled the king to assume a more determined and optimistic attitude, after the verses that have just been quoted Geoffroy assures Philip that victory is awaiting him.[13] In conclusion he exhorts his sovereign to be as durable as stone and as firm as a spear or a sword. For he must keep to what he holds, since the crown is his.[14]

The poem indeed was composed at a crucial moment in the affairs of the monarchy. The death of Philip V's elder brother Louis X on 5 June 1316 had precipitated a crisis in the matter of the succession. For the first time in the long history of the Capetian dynasty, a king had died without male issue. And for the first time the throne of France was claimed by a female heir, his seven-year-old daughter Jeanne. Although on 13 November 1316 a son was born to the widow of Louis X, the child, known as John I, lived only for a few days. Philip, who had been the regent, lost little time in having himself crowned at Reims on 9 January 1317. Although all but two of the secular peers of France stayed away from the ceremony and some of the disgruntled "allies" continued to regard Philip V as a usurper, in February a grand convocation of representatives of the three estates and doctors from the University of Paris, as well as delegates from the principal French cities, ratified his coronation.[15] According to the testimony of two chronicles they also solemnly declared that "no woman succeeds to the throne of France," thus anticipating the later application of the Salic law.[16]

And so, as Geoffroy had urged him, the king held on to the crown that was his. As Geoffroy had also predicted, the "allies," overcome as it were by the subtle power of the fleurs de lis administered through the king's commissioners, soon ceased their protests.[17] Another crisis, however, one with far graver consequences, occurred in February 1328 with the untimely death of Philip's successor, Charles IV. Like his brothers Louis X and Philip V, the youthful Charles left no male heir. This time the nearest blood relative of the deceased king in direct line to the throne was not a French princess, as had been the case at the death of Louis X, but the son of Charles IV's sister Isabel. And this son was none other than Edward III of England.

As in 1317, an assembly was convened in April 1328 to decide on the matter of the succession. Since the precedent established in the case of Philip V had debarred a female from ascending the throne, Isabel, in the judgment of the assembly, could hardly be said, as the widow of Edward II, to have transmitted the succession to her son. The choice, therefore, fell on Philip of Valois, the first cousin of the three last Capetians and their nearest relative through the male line (see genealogical chart).[18]

The transition to the new Valois dynasty was accomplished without any internal opposition and, for the time being, with little cause for apprehension in regard to external dangers. What indeed could France, ostensibly the richest and most powerful realm of continental Europe, fear from the little island kingdom across the Channel? Young and untried, Edward III was not yet ready to use his claim to the crown of France as a pretext for gaining by force of arms direct sovereignty over Aquitania, that vast fief for which the Plantagenets, as vassals of the French kings, had for so long paid ignominious homage.[19] Edward even went so far as to ally himself momentarily with Philip VI in drawing up plans for an ambitious crusade against the Seljucid pirates of the eastern Mediterranean and the maurauding Mamelukes.[20] And even before Philip took the cross on 25 July 1332, Edward appointed an embassy to arrange a meeting between the two kings.[21]

Soon, however, Edward withdrew from the project, leaving Philip VI as its sole leader. Shortly after 1332, in celebration of the preparations for this grandiose crusade that was being preached throughout Europe, one of France's foremost lyricists, Philippe de Vitri, composed a lengthy allegorical and didactic poem of some eleven hundred verses. Entitled *Le chapel des trois fleurs de lis,* it was completed some time before 1335, the year set for the departure of the crusaders, and it is thus the first major work in French that is largely devoted to the theme of the mystic lilies.[22]

Counselor to the French king and friend of Petrarch, who hailed him as "poeta nunc unicus Galliarum," Philippe de Vitri was a man of many parts. Acquainted with the Roman authors of antiquity, he was known to have composed motets in his youth and acquired a reptuation as a mathematician and philosopher. And in spite of the conventional religious moralizing that encumbers much of *Le chapel des trois fleurs de lis* and the many borrowings from other sources, here and there one can detect something of the ardent nature that was ascribed to the author. Above all, his love of France, for which Petrarch, enamoured of Italy, was later to reproach him, is already evident at the very beginning of the poem.[23] Echoes of Geoffroy de Paris and the Dionysian authors, whose works would have been familiar to him as a member of the French court, are immediately apparent in the opening stanzas,[24] while throughout most of the poem, in true poetic fashion, the distinction between the natural flower and the heraldic lily is often blurred.

Referring to the "chapel" of the title, France, says de Vitri, is crowned by the chaplet of the three fleurs de lis. These three flowers that have rendered France honored and strong are called "Science, Foy et Chevalerie,"[25] the same familiar attributes, with only a slight difference in substituting "Science" for "Sapience," that had been applied to the three lilies by the anonymous translater of Yves' chapter on the petals of the flower. There then follows the Trinitarian symbolism previously proposed by Geoffroy de Paris:

> Diex qui est treble en unité
> A fourmé une trinité
> En ces .iii. fleurs dessus nommées.[26]

The verses can be aptly compared to those of the *Dit des Alliés* already cited:

> Trible a flour de lis en armée,
> C'est de la foy le sacrement,
> Une en Deité simplement,
> Et en personnes est triblée.[27]

The ensuing dissertation on the virtues of "Science, Foy et Chevalerie" and the abridged translation of *The General Rules of Warfare* by the classical Roman author Vegetus serve as a prolonged introduction to the central theme of the poem, the reconquest of the Holy Land, when the three mystic lilies, advancing together, are to retake the lost heritage.[28] The enthusiasm that the prospect of the crusade seems to have engendered throughout France is reflected in Philippe de Vitri's reference to the date set for the embarkation. Paraphrasing a verse from the Book of Daniel, "Blessed indeed," he exclaims, "are those who will be living in the year thirteen hundred and thirty five!"[29] Integral to the concept of "Chevalerie" is the ideal of the chivalrous crusader that the author then invokes. Having paid all his debts and renounced all mundane luxuries, the crusading knight, says de Vitri, shall bid farewell to wife and children and with a contrite heart shall take up the cross, for God himself has ordained that the three flowers are to recover the sacred land wherein he is to find his salvation.[30]

In a passage of major significance in the evolution of the theme of the fleurs de lis, Philippe de Vitri then accepts unreservedly the Dionysian origin of all three of the flowers that, he claims, Saint Denis and his two co-martyrs Rusticus and Eleutherius had brought to France from Athens:

> Et Jhesuscrist, le roi de grace,
> De ces .iii. belles fleurs dus face
> Les .iii. tressains martirs d'Athenes
> Qui ces fleurs en France aporterent.[31]

No longer couched in merely allegorical terms, the migration from Greece of all three of the lilies is now stated as an unadorned, quasi-historical fact. Out of the figurative language of symbolism and allegory the basis for a true legend was finally established. In the next two stanzas, in likening both the three saints and the three flowers to the Trinity, the author cannot resist indulging in that favorite literary exercise of the latter Middle Ages, the play on identical numbers:

> Diex qui est treble en unité
> Si voult par une trinité
> De saint Denys, Rust, Eleuthere,
> Envoyer ou regne de France
> La noble foy et la creance.
>
> . . . . . . . .
>
> Ces .iii. saints, ces .iii. fleurs de France,
> Nous font une signifiance
> Que la souvraine trinité
> A singuliere affection
> A la françoise region.[32]

In the concluding section of the poem, de Vitri returns to the theme of the "chapel" admonishing the young scions of the royal house to study carefully the significance of the lilies that adorn the chaplets they wear and to emulate their virtues. For the white lily, with its curative powers, is earth's noblest flower:

> Belle et blanche est, d'oudeur habonde,
> Fleur douce, fleur de medicine.[33]

In a final passage reminiscent of the contrast between the natural lily and the king's heraldic emblem in the *Dit des Alliés,* the white flowers are replaced by those others emblazoned in gold on the azure field of the royal escutcheon.

Whatever merits *Le chapel des trois fleurs de lis* may have as a literary work, as a historical document it is of some importance as an expression of the contrasting tendencies of the period. In seeking to revive the fervor of the earlier crusaders, the author, like so many of his compatriots, including the king himself, indulges in a romantic nostalgia, unaware of the fact that the great era of the crusades had long since come to an irrevocable and tragic end in 1270 with the death of Louis IX in Tunis.[34] But the poem also testifies to a new national spirit that had already begun to emerge during the reign of Philip IV. For the fleurs de lis are here preeminently the lilies of France, that favored realm beloved by the triune God and that is destined to reign in power while her enemies are execrated.[35] In a different vein, however, Philippe de Vitri urges the knights to be ready to shield the people against rebellions at home and from invasions from abroad, and he calls upon Saint Denis to defend the kingdom and to deliver it from its errors, ending with the prayer that God may bring peace to the people of the land.[36] Underlying the optimistic dreams of retaking the Holy Land, a note of anxiety can be sensed that was not without its justification. Although in May of 1333 a brief attempt was made at settling the disputes between Edward III and the French king,[37] it was precisely in the years between 1332 and 1335 during the preparations for the crusade that the relations began to deteriorate ominously between Philip of Valois and his adversary across the Channel, both of whom were fearful of a general war neither of them seems to have wanted. Eventually the Pope decided that if the conflict was to be averted, the date set for the departure of the expedition would have to be postponed, and in March 1336, the crusade that had been so fervently heralded was finally called off.[38]

Though a monument to a lost cause, in condensing and concretizing the literary traditions concerning the fleurs de lis the poem can nevertheless also be regarded as the final stage in a development stemming from both the Dionysian historiographers and from Geoffroy de Paris. Beyond the particular subject matter with which each of them deals, however, one may well ask what prompted these authors to elevate the "simple flowers" of Gerald of Wales to the status of potent symbols of France and the monarchy until, sanctified by the Trinity, they have now become the basis for a true legend.

In large measure the answer lies, not only in the new national spirit celebrated by de Vitri, but also in that intensification in the cult of the monarchy that had its genesis in the reign of Louis IX, he who incarnated the ideal of Christian kingship and whose aura extended to all of his successors.[39] As the symbol of the king's virtues and holiness, the fleur de lis can indeed be regarded as an image of major significance in the legacy that Saint Louis bequeathed to his descendants. It is thus through no mere accident that the first symbolic interpretation of the emblematic flower should have occurred in the *Life of Louis IX* by Guillaume de Nangis. And when the monk Yves in his *Life of Saint Denis* transferred the symbolism of the petals to the chapters on Charlemagne, he was careful, in dealing with the insurrection of the students during the minority of Louis IX, to retain a reference to the indissoluble ties that bound the king to the emblem of the lily, the *signum regis Franciae*.[40]

Around 1300 the royal banner with the mystic lilies is invoked in a sermon by the Dominican Guillaume de Sauqueville, when it is exalted as the banner that appeared at the first coming of Christ, who is the king of the Franks.[41] In another sermon the Dominican monk says that the heir of France, by virtue of the healing powers that he derives from his anointing and crowning, can be called, like Christ, the son of David.[42] In much the same vein, Henri de Mondeville, surgeon to Philip the Fair, compares Christ, the archetype of the surgeon, to the French king who through the touch of his hand cures the scrofulous.[43]

In the eyes of his countrymen such Christological analogies were particularly applicable to Philip the Fair who had worked hard to secure the canonization of his grandfather[44] and who, in emulating the stringent ascetic practices of Saint Louis, had earned, in addition to his title of *Pulcher,* that of *Pius,* bestowed upon him by both Henri de Mondeville and Yves of St-Denis.[45] The piety of the king in turn was matched by the religious devotion that ever since the middle of the thirteenth century was attributed to the nation.[46] Just as the king of France held a unique position among the sovereigns of Europe, so the French came to be regarded as occupying a special place among the peoples of the continent. In his bull *Rex Glorie,* addressed in 1311 to Philip the Fair, Clement V went so far as to claim for France a divine mission in declaring that "the French, like the children of Israel, are a peculiar people especially chosen by God to carry out the mandates of Heaven."[47] In terms of the fleur de lis, the preeminence of France had already been underlined by Guillaume de Nangis when he stated that the king of France adorned his arms with the lily as if to say to the whole world that the faith, learning, and chivalry that its petals represented flourished more abundantly there than in any other realm (appendix 1.5). In Philippe de Vitri's poem, the three lilies were said to signify that particular affection that the sovereign Trinity had for France, while as the flowers of the chaplet they became the crown whereby France was endowed with honor and power.[48]

# 3
# The Celestial Origin
# of the Three Fleurs de Lis

n his *Chapel des trois fleurs de lis,* as has been seen, Philippe de Vitri's literal reference to the introduction of the three lilies into France by Saint Denis and his two companions had finally established the basis for a genuine Dionysian legend. It would seem, indeed, only fitting that the patron saint of the monarchy, whose relics were kept in that same abbey church that was the burial place of French royalty and the repository of the regalia and the oriflamme, the sacred battle standard of the French armies, should also have been credited with bestowing upon the kings of France their armorial emblems. What was still needed, however, was a more extended and detailed account than that given in Philippe de Vitri's poem of just how this transfer of the heraldic flowers from Athens was accomplished. What form did the three lilies brought by the three martyrs assume? Were they painted on a shield or on a parchment scroll? Or were they the natural flowers, each carried separately, perhaps even in the guise of three potted plants? To whom were they given, under what circumstances, and precisely where? And where, when, and from whom did the three martyrs acquire the lilies in the first place? These are questions that any legend purporting to elucidate the mystic source of the armorial emblems of Europe's most prestigious monarchy might be expected to answer, however miraculous or improbable the story might be.

It so happened that at about the time Philippe de Vitri was at work on his poem, or slightly earlier, another account of the origin of the fleurs de lis that gave abundant answers to all such questions was being composed in the small Premonstratensian monastery of Joyenval situated not far from Paris near the confluence of the Oise and the Seine, on the edge of the vast forest of Marly.[1] The work of more than one of the anonymous canons of the monastery, this versified Latin legend was nothing less than a complete recasting of the traditional story of the conversion of the Merovingian king Clovis I who, according to the sixth-century *Historia Francorum* of Gregory of Tours, was thus the founder of the Christian monarchy.[2]

As related by Gregory, during a battle against the Germanic tribe of the Alemanni, Clovis, the pagan king of the Franks, fearing that his army is on the verge of defeat, calls for assistance upon the God of his Christian wife Clotilda. Whereupon the enemy is vanquished, their king killed, and Clovis, now converted to the true faith by the miraculous victory, prepares himself under the tutelage of Clotilda for his baptism at the hands of Saint Remi, the bishop of Reims. A northern counterpart of the victory of Constantine at the battle of the Milvian Bridge, as Gregory of Tours was well aware in calling Clovis a new Constantine,[3] the conversion of the Frankish king during the battle is given its most dramatic pictorialization in a grisaille copy of one of the lost miniatures of Yves' presentation manuscript of the *Life of Saint Denis* (plate 6). In the lower register of the two-part illustration, while the king of the Alemanni lunges threateningly towards him, Clovis, mounted on his charger, lifts his hands in prayer toward Clotilda's God whose blessing hand, like Constantine's vision of the cross, emerges from a cloud in the sky. In the upper register of the drawing, the tables are now turned. Clovis suddenly thrusts his sword like a bolt of lightning at his adversary, who reels backwards in the saddle of his faltering horse.[4] The two battle scenes are followed in the upper right-hand corner by a small illustration of the baptism of Clovis and the miracle of the holy ampulla.

In the Latin poem from the abbey of Joyenval, Gregory's account of the battle has been drastically refashioned. Clovis is now demoted to the rank of a petty chieftain who resides in the castle of Montjoie, and the host of the Alemanni has been reduced to the single figure of a more powerful local tyrant named Conflat who has been terrorizing the surrounding region from his neighboring stronghold at Conflans.[5] One day Conflat challenges Clovis to meet him in single combat. Preparing himself for the encounter, Clovis asks for his shield. When it is brought to him, however, he finds that instead of the usual crescents it is adorned with three golden fleurs de lis.[6] In spite of his distaste for these novel decorations, he is forced to accept his arms in their present state in order to keep his appointment with Conflat. But in the midst of the combat he suddenly finds his strength unaccountably redoubled, and he is able to overcome his stronger adversary.

Thus the battle between the two armies in Gregory of Tours has been replaced by a duel between two local chieftains, and the victory of Clovis is accomplished, not by his appeal to the Christian God but as a result of some mysterious power whose nature he cannot fathom. After the encounter he asks his Christian wife, Clotilda, if she can shed some light on the unexplainable presence of the three fleurs de lis and on the unforseen outcome of the combat. "It is the Holy Trinity," she tells him, "that has given you this victory so that from now on the unity of the triple flowers shall be on your shield as a sign of your strength and your right to rule."[7] Then, as in Gregory of Tours, Clovis renounces his pagan idols, embraces the faith of his wife, and is finally deemed ready for baptism.

As Francois Chatillon has demonstrated in his detailed analysis of the Latin text, this first part of the poem, comprising twenty-three stanzas in all, constitutes a complete story in itself composed by one of the inmates of the abbey.[8] As adjunct to this basic recital, the second part of the narrative, written in a somewhat more lively style by another canon of Joyenval, purports to explain how the fleurs de lis happened to have been substituted for the crescents on the arms of Clovis who, no longer a petty chieftain, toward the end of the poem is finally restored to his rightful rank as a king.[9]

It seems that in the valley below the hill of the Montjoie, on the edge of a fountain, there resided a pious hermit whom Clotilda had nourished and befriended. Together they had often deplored her husband's worship of the pagan gods. One day an angel appeared to the hermit bearing an azure shield charged with golden fleurs de lis and instructed him to tell Clotilda that she must destroy the hateful crescents on her husband's arms and replace them with the golden flowers. Thus it was that in her husband's absence Clotilda carried out the angel's instructions that finally resulted in his conversion. In expiation of his earlier impieties, Clovis also took under his care the monks of a monastery he had founded. The writer then concludes this second part of the poem with the later history of the abbey, how it was founded by a certain Bartholomew near the site of the hermitage and how it was given the name of Joyenval *(Vallis Gaudii)* in honor of the Montjoie *(Mons Gaudii)* on the nearby hill. Bartholomew himself became one of the foremost personages of the realm and during the minority of Saint Louis wrought confusion among the king's enemies.

Such in brief outline is this famous story of the origin of the arms of France as set down in its pristine form by the canons of Joyenval, a composite work that nevertheless forms a single coherent narrative. No longer mere symbols of the triune Godhead, as in Geoffroy de Paris, the three mystic lilies are now the direct gift of the Holy Trinity itself, while the Christian monarchy is placed at its very inception under its divine protection. But in spite of its supernatural elements the legend was firmly anchored in identifiable features of the locality, some of which still survive (fig. E). The hermit's fountain still floods the sparse remains of the abbey church said to have been built on the site of the hermitage.[10] The neighboring village of Conflans, an ancient community at the confluence of the Seine and the Oise whose name obviously suggested that of the tyrant Conflat, later became known as Conflans-Ste-Honorine, now transformed into one of the "new towns" surrounding metropolitan Paris.[11] And on the hill near the abbey, an ancient tower still existed in the time of Charles V that could be identified as the dungeon of Clovis' stronghold of Montjoie.[12]

Nor can there be much doubt, as Robert Bossuat has concluded, that the heaven-sent shield of the angel was intended as a counterpart to the holy ampulla reputed to have been brought down by a dove at the baptism of Clovis and whose never-failing chrism was used for anointing the kings at their coronations at Reims.[13] But in case such an analogy might be thought presumptuous on the part of a minor monastic house such as that of Joyenval, toward the end of the poem we are advised that this story of the fleurs de lis should not be considered in any way prejudicial to the members of the Church of Reims where Clovis was baptized.[14] Thus it was tactfully implied that Joyenval intended no offense to the Reims clergy in claiming for itself the royal emblems that

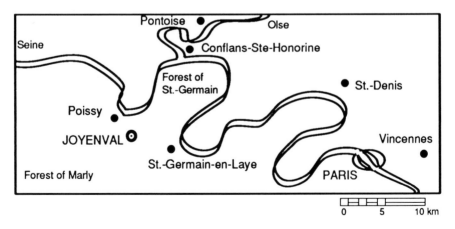

Fig. E. Environs of Joyenval

were also, like the holy ampulla, the gift of the Deity. Though the Bartholomew mentioned in the final stanzas can be none other than the renowned Barthelemi de Roie, the grand chamberlain of France who founded Joyenval in 1221,[15] the reference to an abbey built by Clovis may be taken as an attempt to credit its original foundation to a far more distant past.

As the abbey of the fleurs de lis, Joyenval had also on a few occasions enjoyed the patronage of the kings. Bossuat has even proposed that the poem may have been written on the occasion of a donation to the abbey of a prebend of the church of Poissy made in 1333 by Philip of Valois.[16] But there is no internal evidence that can supply even an approximate date for the work. However, in view of the three emblems on the arms of Clovis and their association with the Trinity, it would be most unlikely that the poem could have been composed before the *Dit des Alliés* of Geoffroy de Paris stemming from the end of 1316 or the very beginning of 1317, in the first year of the reign of Philip V. Nor could it have been undertaken after 1338 when another literary work on the royal lilies completed toward the end of that year evinces at least some knowledge of its content. A date in the early 1330s that Bossuat, as well as others, have suggested, though on quite different grounds, would thus seem to be appropriate for the completion of the poem.[17]

There is some reason to believe, moreover, that this story of Clovis and the fleurs de lis was by no means an entirely original creation of the canons of Joyenval. The idea of the divine origin of the arms of France seems already to have been in the air for some time if one can judge from the heading to the chapter on the symbolism of the petals in the French translation of Yves' *Life of Saint Denis* that reads: "Comment la foy (et) sapience et chevalerie sent segnefiées par les fleurs de lis qui furent de dieu envoiées au roy de France."[18] In this case, however, instead of referring to Clovis, the "roy de France" probably alludes to the emperor Charlemagne who was also generally considered a king of France and who is so referred to by Yves in the preceding chapters. At the very beginning of the Latin poem, moreover, the author of this first part of the legend states that what he is about to write down had formerly come to his ears—*olim ad aures meas quod venit.*[19] From this we may conclude that he was basing his work on an already established oral tradition. Although there is no way of ascertaining its exact nature, it may well be that behind the duel between Clovis and Conflat there existed a local tale of some mythical struggle between two barbarian chieftains that originally had nothing whatsoever to do with the Merovingian king, but that subsequently had become assimilated to the story of his conversion in the folklore of the forest people indigenous to this region of the Seine.

These speculations as to its sources, however, are of secondary importance in regard to other questions concerning the Latin poem. Although there is clear evidence that the abbot of the monastery himself had commissioned this joint literary undertaking,[20] one may well ask what prompted him to do so at this time and what was its immediate purpose. As had already been suggested by Bossuat in more general terms, in his analysis of the poem Chatillon has argued that it was written in response to the need for supporting Philip VI's authority in the face of the claims of Edward III.[21] In the absence, however, of any passsage that can be construed as specifically upholding the legitimacy of the Valois king or any references to related events, there may have been another more compelling reason for composing the work than that put forward by Chatillon. Since the author of the first part of the text confines the action of the narrative entirely to Conflans and the Mont-joie, totally ignoring the existence of the monastery, the abbot undoubt-edly felt the need of adding to this basic legend a second part that would not only explain the presence of the fleurs de lis on the arms of Clovis, but that would also place the site of the miraculous happenings unequiv-ocally at Joyenval. And to this addenda to the legend was then appended a eulogistic account of the achievements of Bartholemi de Roie who gave the name of Joyenval to the abbey. Thus the main thrust of the poem seems to have been directed toward insuring the rights of the abbey to the origin of the fleurs de lis and toward promoting its later reputation.

In proximity to the abbey of St-Denis, moreover, the inmates of Joyenval cannot have been unaware that the origin of the lilies of France was, in one form or another, being credited to the patron saint of their illustrious neighbor, since the Dionysian claims to the fleurs de lis must surely by now have become common knowledge. It was, after all, some four or five decades since Guillaume de Nangis had first launched the migration of the symbolic petals in the wake of Saint Denis, a theme that was later enunciated in the five verses posted on the tabernacle above the remains of the saint in the abbey church. And the canons of Joyenval must also have been aware that votive fleurs de lis were likewise being affixed to his shrine, including one from Philip the Fair himself. And should Philippe de Vitri have completed the *Chapel des trois fleurs de lis* prior to the Latin poem, the abbot of Joyenval might even have heard that the Dionysian claims were in the process of becoming a full-fledged legend before ever he had commissioned the canons to compose the work.

Thus the abbot may well have decided that it was time to set down in writing without further delay the story of Clovis and the fleurs de lis in order to quash once and for all these Dionysian pretensions. Compared to its august neighbor, whose reputed foundation dated only from the time of the later Merovingian ruler Dagobert, Joyenval could boast of a far more venerable past reaching back to the founding of a monastery by Clovis at the very beginning of the Christian monarchy. And if the possession of the oriflamme could not be disputed with St-Denis, it was duly recorded in the Latin poem that the battle cry of the king's army, "Montjoie-Saint Denis!," was derived, not from St-Denis, but from the hill of the Montjoie overlooking Joyenval.

The time would come, indeed, when the legend of Joyenval would be pitted against the Dionysian origin of the emblems of France in a lengthy literary contest. But long before the onset of these rivalries there appeared still another versified work dealing with the heraldic lilies, the *Roman de la fleur de lis* by Guillaume de Digulleville, that indisputably betrays some knowledge of the legend.[22] A monk of the Cistercian abbey of Châalis near Senlis, unlike the canons of Joyenval who had to adapt their Latin quatrains to a difficult rhyming scheme, Digulleville was a facile composer of vernacular poetry whose verses poured forth from his pen in an incessant stream.[23] Like the best known of his works, *Le pèlerinage de la vie humaine,* the *Roman* is couched in terms of an allegorical fantasy that purports to describe a dream that the author had between midnight and one o'clock on 1 November 1338. Whereas the legend of Joyenval tells how the three fleurs de lis came to be bestowed on Clovis from a celestial source, the *Roman* relates the manner in which they were first created in the heavenly sphere, not, however, as part of an armorial shield but affixed to a textile appropriate for a banner.

In his dream Digulleville is transported to the polar regions where he overhears a discussion between two celestial sisters named Grace Dieu and Sapience. They are trying to determine what should be done with two pieces of cloth, one golden, the other azure blue, that are remnants left over after Sapience had created the heavens. Grace Dieu, who is in possession of the two cloths, asks Sapience to fashion out of them a "parement" or "armoiment" for a dear friend she has encountered among the earthly mortals and who, it turns out, is none other than the king.

Acceding to the wishes of Grace Dieu, Sapience cuts out of the golden cloth a sign that gradually assumes the form of a fleur de lis, whereupon Raison, the daughter of Sapience, who has already joined the other two in their discussion, explains in detail the martial and monarchical significance of its petals.

Sapience then observes that the fleur de lis also possesses medicinal properties, at which Raison tells Grace Dieu that she should prepare a specially concocted ointment that will likewise be imbued with curative powers that is to be used for anointing her friend. Grace Dieu agrees but asks Sapience in the meantime to cut out two more flowers and to place them on the azure cloth, making three in all, in order that they may correspond to the three ladies who have created the "armoiment."

After grinding the ingredients of the special ointment with her mortar and pestle, Grace Dieu places the finished product in a round box that Raison has already fashioned. At this point a white bird appears. At the bidding of Grace Dieu it takes the box with the ointment in its beak and flies to "Remy" at Reims for the anointing of her friend. As her final act Grace Dieu descends to earth, and having entered the royal palace, tells her friend of the ointment she has specially made for him and shows him the three fleurs de lis on the azure cloth. These, she advises him, are the signs he is to place on his shield and on his banner, for they signify that it is through her, as the Grace of God, that he reigns as king.[24]

Such in very abbreviated form is the essential narrative content of this voluminous work. In spite of its originality, however, one can nevertheless discern in the names of the three ladies and in the symbolic treatment of the petals echoes of Philippe de Vitri and the Dionysian authors. But there can be little doubt that Digulleville must also have been acquainted with the legend of Joyenval.[25] The unmistakable allusion to the dove with the holy ampulla in the "blanc oisel" bidden by Grace Dieu to carry the ointment box to "Remy à Rains, pour oindre mon amy," has its counterpart in the legend when Clovis, now deemed ready for baptism, humbly presents himself to Saint Remi.[26]

Thus the *Roman*, like the legend of Joyenval, is linked to the conversion and baptism of Clovis. But the parallelism between the heaven-sent fleurs de lis and the chrism of the holy ampulla that was only implied in the legend, is now explicitly emphasized. In the *Roman* the curative qualities ascribed to the ointment can only be a direct reference to those thaumaturgic powers that the celestial chrism was thought to bestow on the kings of France at their sacring at Reims. In the poem these medicinal properties are even more emphatically attributed to the fleur de lis. As Sapience observes, "elle est medicinable / A maint mal dont on est malade," to which Grace Dieu replies that if her sister says the lily is medicinal, "Je veulz aussi que mon ami / Soit medicinable com li" (that is, like the lily).[27]

Thus the three fleurs de lis are raised to the status of the chrism brought down by the dove, both created at the same time in the celestial regions and both delivered simultaneously to the king in his palace and to Saint Remi at Reims. In the irrational manner of a dream, however, past and present are confounded. For unlike Clovis in the legend of Joyenval, there is good reason to assume that the friend of Grace Dieu can be regarded, not only as Clovis, but also as that contemporary sovereign of France, Philip VI, who had ushered in the new Valois dynasty and with it that seemingly endless and devastating struggle between England and France that has come to be known as the Hundred Years' War. As has been noted in connection with Philippe de Vitri's poem, by canceling the French king's ambitious crusade that was planned for 1335, the pope had hoped to avoid the impending conflict between Philip VI and Edward III. His efforts, however, proved to be in vain. With the confiscation of Edward's fief of the duchy of Aquitaine pronounced by Philip on 24 May 1337,[28] followed in October by Edward's fateful challenge to "Philip of Valois who calls himself King of France,"[29] the Hundred Years' War was officially begun.

Not only, as Edmond Faral has pointed out, was much of the *Roman de la fleur de lis* intended to uphold the right of Philip VI to the throne of France against the challenge put forward by Edward, but something of the apprehensive mood that was in the air before the actual outbreak of hostilities can also be detected in the poem. In explaining the symbolism of the petals of the fleur de lis, Raison indicates that the lower end of the central petal that points downward is "en signe que, se il estoit guerre, le royaume si garderoit," while the ends of the other two lateral petals represent the barons and knights "qui gardien sont des frontieres."[30]

Even before Edward had launched his challenge, the eastern frontier was already threatened by the preparations he was making for the encirclement of France. After having forged a coalition of Flemish allies, in August 1337 he concluded a pact against the French king with the German Emperor Ludwig of Bavaria. In a direct allusion to Edward's alliance with the emperor, Sapience lists among the king's enemies those who have the sign of the leopards and others the sign of the eagles who look in opposite directions since they have two heads. The passage not only recalls the reference to the leopards of the Plantagenets by Gerald of Wales over a century before but it is also equally directed at the treacherous Ludwig since the double-headed eagle was the recognized emblem of the resuscitated empire.[31]

The year 1338, the same year in which Guillaume de Digulleville claimed to have experienced his allegorical vision, saw the final achievement of Edward's grandiose design along the northern frontiers of France. Having been granted, at a price, from the impecunious Ludwig the title of Vicar-General of that portion of the Empire that lay west of the Rhine, the young Edward met the emperor amid splended festivities at Coblenz on 5 September 1338, on which occasion the German electors granted him full imperial prerogatives.[32] During the remainder of the year he traveled through the Low Countries to receive the homage of those who were now his liege men in his role as imperial deputy.

In contrast to the euphoric Edward jubilating over his new title and honors, in France prayers were ordered to be said in all the churches of the realm for the success of the king's armed forces, and sermons were directed to be preached, elucidating for the common people the legitimacy of the Valois cause.[33] In the meantime, as Guillaume de Digulleville may well have been aware of in his monastery at Châalis, rumors, however unfounded, of an imminent English invasion prompted the assemblage of a vast French army within the walls of Amiens, the great city of Picardy. As the moment of confrontation drew nearer, other convocations of men-at-arms began to assemble elsewhere as well.[34] And then on 26 January 1340, while holding court in the midst of his new Flemish subjects in the marketplace at Ghent, Edward at his own bidding was formally acknowledged King of France, in token of which he ordered the leopards on his coat of arms quartered with the fleurs de lis,[35] and the new escutcheon was later placed on his seal above the arrogant motto *Dieu et Mon Droit*.[36] What had started out as a feudal quarrel over Edward's French possessions was now to be transformed into a dynastic conflict.

# 4
# The Prologue
# to the *Cité de Dieu*

 he loss of the French fleet at Sluys, the slaughter at Crécy, and the Black Death when up to a third of the population perished, the defeat at Poitiers, and the capture of the French king John the Good, the son of Philip VI—who does not know the litany of those disasters that in the short span of some sixteen years, from 1340 to 1356, brought France to her knees and even threatened the very existence of the discredited monarchy? With the imprisonment of John the Good and his transfer to London, the prestige of French royalty appeared indeed to have suffered irreparable damage. The bitter reproaches directed toward the counselors of the king for their incompetency, the demands for drastic changes in the administrative structure of the government, and the revolt of the Jacquerie and Etienne Marcel against the nobility and the royal house had undermined the whole edifice on which rested the king's quasi-theocratic rule.

Astonishing as was the defeat of France by Edward III and the capture of the French king, equally remarkable was the recovery that followed under King John's astute son and successor, Charles V (1364–80). Although as a semi-invalid he was the only French monarch of the ancien régime, with the exception of Louis XVI, who never, even nominally, led his troops into battle, Charles nevertheless managed to outmaneuver the English militarily and to outwit them as well in legalistic tactics. And in order to repair the damage done to the institution of French kingship, the apologists for the Valois cause now assiduously collected those legends and beliefs that the earlier centuries had woven haphazardly around the monarchy and arranged them in a more or less orderly fashion. Couched in a succinct and unadorned prose, these collections, which formed what Marc Bloch has so appropriately named the monarchical cycle, furnished the credentials on which the kings of France could again lay claim to their religious and supernatural character.[1]

Among such works, three have survived in which the origin of the fleurs de lis now takes its place alongside the older monarchical themes. But there was no consensus as yet as to which was the authoritative account, the one attributed to Saint Denis or that contained in the legend of Joyenval. This state of indecision is graphically illustrated in the longest and most discursive of the three collections, a treatise on the French coronation ceremony by the Carmelite Jean Golein inserted in his translation of the *Rationale divinorum officiorum* of Durandus of Mende, which he undertook at the instigation of Charles V himself in the early 1370s.[2] After describing the royal coronation vestments, all "fleurde-lisées," the author observes that they were brought to the ceremony by the abbot of St-Denis, "car Monseigneur Saint Denis donna aux roys de France les armes de fleurs de lys."[3] But in a later passage on the benediction of the royal banner that was now also included in the coronation rite, he attributes to the hermit of Joyenval the three lilies that were painted on the banner.[4]

In contrast to these brief references by Jean Golein is the more expanded version of the Dionysian legend in a short Latin treatise on the monarchy composed sometime after 1380 in the early years of the reign of Charles VI by that learned bibliophile Etienne de Conty at the monastery of Corbie in Picardy.[5] Incorporating elements taken directly from the legend of Joyenval, the monk of Corbie tells how Saint Denis, while residing in the castle of Montjoie some seven leagues from Paris, was visited by an angel who showed him a shield with three golden lilies and informed him that these were the arms of the king of France and all his successors (appendix 5). In borrowing both the angel and the castle from the legend of Joyenval, however, Etienne de Conty was by no means attempting a mere compromise between the two conflicting accounts, nor was he solely intent on supplying thereby a much-needed local setting for the saga of Saint Denis. Rather, as he himself has clearly implied, this amendment to the Dionysian origin of the royal insignia also provided a fuller and more logical explanation for the war cry of the king's armies, "Montjoie-Saint Denis," than that given by the canons of Joyenval who failed to account for the inclusion of Saint Denis in the battle cry.[6]

With a score among the literati of two for Saint Denis and only one for Joyenval, the prestige of the royal abbey might have been expected to have carried the day for the patron saint of France were it not for another collection of the mystical cycle of the monarchy by one of the more dedicated literary servitors of Charles V, Raoul de Presles.

The illegitimate son of a Parisian lawyer who was also an adviser to the Parlement, Raoul de Presles came to the notice of Charles V in 1365 or 1366 with his moralistic Latin allegory *Musa,* which he dedicated to the king.[7] Always on the lookout for scholars capable of translating what were then considered the most notable writings of the Latin authors, Charles commissioned him to render into the vernacular one of the most prestigious works of the Church Fathers, Saint Augustine's *Civitas Dei.* In choosing him, moreover, the king may not only have been influenced by Raoul de Presles' scholarly qualifications. For in spite of the vast differences in their respective origins, Charles had also every reason to recognize in Raoul de Presles a kindred spirit who shared with him similar experiences and similar ideals. Both had known at first hand the horrors and miseries of the aftermath of the debacle at Poitiers,[8] and both had to contend against serious physical disabilities, Charles suffering from a lifelong chronic illness and Raoul de Presles from the infirmities of old age. Both shared the same ideal of the learned ruler as a lover of books and of the literature of the past—Raoul de Presles in the Prologue to his translation quotes the quaint adage "Roy sans lettre est un asne couronné"[9]—an ideal that was to find its expression in the surname *le roy sage* that was posthumously bestowed on Charles V himself, *sage* signifying erudite rather than wise.[10] And both were intent on restoring the sacrosanct character of French kingship that had been all but destroyed in the calamities of the war.

Already a counselor to the king, Raoul de Presles according to his own testimony began his formidable task on All Saints Day 1371 and finished it on 1 September 1375.[11] In his translation of the *Civitas Dei* he also added his own commentaries on Saint Augustine's text, including a spirited defense of the Salic law that debarred a woman from succeeding to the throne of France or from passing on the succession to her son, thus implicitly defending the Valois dynasty against the claims of Edward III.[12] His most enduring personal contribution, however, is his lengthy version of the monarchical cycle that he included toward the beginning of his Prologue (appendix 4). Addressing himself directly to his royal patron, to whom the Prologue itself is dedicated (plate 7), he first likens the king to an eagle since Charles can claim direct descent from the Roman emperors, whose emblem it was. He then reminds the king of that most sacred moment in his coronation ceremony when he was anointed with the chrism of the holy ampulla, by which he was endowed with the miraculous gift of the king's touch. In conclusion, he describes the solemn ritual when the king of France receives the oriflamme from the altar of the martyrs at St-Denis and the legendary episodes concerning Charlemagne and the sacred battle standard. But what above all sets the author's monarchical cycle apart from the others is the short summary of the legend of Joyenval that he has inserted immediately after the reference to the king's curative powers.

He begins by recalling that the three fleurs de lis on the king's arms are a sign of the blessed Trinity and that they were sent from God by an angel to Clovis for his combat against the pagan ruler from Conflans. The battle, says Raoul de Presles, began in the valley and ended in the mountain where now stands the tower of Montjoie, from which is derived the war cry "Montjoie-Saint Denis!" After the victory of Clovis over his more powerful adversary, Raoul de Presles, as in the poem by the canons of Joyenval, relates the previous events that accounted for the presence of the fleurs de lis on the arms of Clovis—the appearance of the angel to the hermit who resided next to a founain in the valley below and how the wife of Clovis substituted the three fleurs de lis for the three cresents on her husband's coat of arms. He concludes by observing that where the hermitage stood was founded a religious house that has been and is still called the abbey of Joyenval, whose coat of arms has for a long time commemorated these events (appendix 4.4–7).

In retelling the original story as related in the Latin poem by the canons of the abbey, however, Raoul de Presles also felt compelled to make certain emendations in order to bring his account more into line with the generally accepted historical record. Instead of a petty chieftain, Clovis is given the resounding title of "le premier roy crestien," the first of all Christian kings.[13] A major step was also taken in integrating the conversion of Clovis as described by the canons of Joyenval with the traditional account of his conversion during the battle against the Alemanni. No longer is it a question of a hand-to-hand combat between Clovis and the tyrant from Conflans. Raoul de Presles merely states that the battle began in the valley and ended at the tower of Montjoie. The tyrant, moreover, whose name has been changed from Conflat to Caudat, is now also referred to as a king. Before settling at Conflans he is said to have come from "l'Alemaigne" with "grant multitude de gens." Thus Caudat can be closely identified with the king of the Alemanni who in the *Grandes Chroniques de France* is called the "Roi d'Alemaigne," the King of Germany,[14] and the combat with the local tyrant is well on its way to being transformed into the battle against the Alemanni, who are now the "Alemanz."

Although the victory of Clovis over the South German tribe of the Alemanni was later conceded to have actually taken place, not near the banks of the Seine, but at Tolbiac near Cologne, [15] the fact that its exact location was at this time still unknown facilitated the transformation. More enigmatic is the etymology of the king's name. Marc Bloch has proposed that Caudat was derived from *caudatus,* meaning he who has a tail, a derisive French epithet that ever since the twelfth century had been applied to the English in both its Latin and vernacular forms.[16] Although this derivation has been questioned by Chatillon, since in Raoul de Presles' version of the legend the king came from beyond the frontiers of France, the adversary of Clovis could hardly have been given the name of the tyrant in the Latin poem, as the name "Conflat" would have undeniably implied that he was an indigenous native of Conflans.[17]

In spite of these several changes, however, there can be little doubt that Raoul de Presles' story of Clovis and the fleurs de lis was directly derived from the original Latin poem. In both versions the same inverted order in the sequence of the episodes has already been noted. As if in acknowledgement of the close connection between the two texts, in the mid-fifteenth-century manuscript that contains the only surviving copy of the poem, it has been placed immediately before a transcript of the legend as given in the Prologue.[18] It is quite possible, too, as Chatillon has proposed, that before writing the Prologue Raoul de Presles himself had actually visited the abbey of Joyenval[19] and there the inmates had not only pointed out to him the tower of the Montjoie and the hermit's fountain, but had also shown him the abbey's coat of arms charged with fleurs de lis in commemoration of the miraculous happenings.[20] Thus too he would have been able to vouch for the authenticity of the events described in the legend.

Inevitably, however, his version of the story, condensed into thirty-three short lines of prose from a poem of two-hundred verses, has left out certain not unimportant details that were included by the canons of Joyenval. So in the Prologue no mention whatsoever is made of the heraldic colors of the celestial arms, while Clotilda is referred to, not by name, but merely as the wife of Clovis, and nothing is said concerning her piety or her attempts to convert her husband prior to the appearance of the angel. And finally all references to the founding of a monastic community by Clovis have been omitted.

This somewhat drastic condensation is well to bear in mind, for it is only through hindsight that the story has come to be regarded as the Prologue's most memorable contribution to French monarchical lore. Far overshadowing not only the story of Clovis and the fleurs de lis, but most of the other items of the cycle as well, is the long final section that describes in detail the ritual of the raising of the oriflamme at St-Denis and how in time Charlemagne came to the abbey to receive it before embarking on his mythical crusade (appendix 4.8–16). And the monarchical cycle itself, it should be noted, is only one of the Prologue's four major themes. Preceded by a lengthy dissertation on the symbolism of the eagle, it is followed by a prolonged essay in praise of Charles V's studiousness and erudition. And finally in the fourth and concluding portion of the Prologue, Raoul de Presles writes at length about himself, and about both his relationship to his royal patron and the difficulties he has encountered in translating the Latin text of the *Civitas Dei*.[21] And in view of all this, the immediate impact of Raoul de Presles' version of the legend of Joyenval on those other literati engaged in collecting and reexamining the tenets of the monarchical cycle is all the more remarkable and can only be accounted for by the rapidity with which ideas were being exchanged among these independently minded and at times contentious scholars.

Even before Raoul de Presles' translation was finished in 1375, the content of the Prologue seems already to have been under discussion, since in the *Traité du Sacre* of his *Rationale des divins offices* presented to Charles V between 1372 and 1374, Jean Golein takes exception to a certain passage concerning the king's thaumaturgical powers by "mon maistre Maistre Raoul de Presles" in his "prologue du livre de *La Cité de Dieu*."[22] And from this one can only conclude that it must have been from the Prologue that Jean Golein came to know of the hermit of Joyenval. And since Etienne de Conty was also in Paris at this time, where he received his doctorate from the University in 1376 before returning to Corbie,[23] it was undoubtedly from the Prologue, too, that he borrowed those elements of the legend of Joyenval that he later incorporated into his expanded Dionysian account of the gift of the golden flowers. In another memorable work of this same period, a wide-ranging compilation of opinions on monarchical politics and beliefs known as the *Somnium Viridarii*, the author, who has not yet been fully identified among the scholars at Charles V's court, has nevertheless contributed an emendation to the legend that was eventually to become a permanent fixture in the story of Clovis and the origin of the fleurs de lis.[24]

As may be recalled, both in the Latin poem and in the Prologue to the *Cité de Dieu*, before they were replaced by the heraldic lilies, the emblems of the unconverted Clovis are said to have consisted of crescents. Just as the word *Saracen* had long been used as a general synonym for *pagan* (Raoul de Presles himself describes the "roy Caudat" of his Prologue as "Sarazin et adversair de la foy crestienne"),[25] so the crescents of the Turks, those latter-day enemies of Christendom, could also be employed as the insignia of any pagan ruler.[26] But according to the *Somnium Viridarii*, the heraldic emblems of the ancient kings of France before their conversion are said to have consisted of three toads *(tres buffones)* that were then miraculously changed into three fleurs de lis.[27]

Toadlike creatures had indeed long been known as the denizens of the infernal regions, who sometimes among the scenes of Hell in the sculptured reliefs of the Gothic cathedrals and churches cling to the cauldron of the damned or suckle at the breasts of Luxuria (plates 8a,b).[28] Similar amphibians can also be recognized in a miniature in that outstanding example of English thirteenth-century manuscript illumination, the Douce Apocalypse, composed between 1270 and 1274.[29] Here, in an illustration of verses seven and eight of the twentieth chapter of the Apocalypse, Satan at the extreme right leads a horde of warriors whom he has assembled for the final battle against the Lord (plate 9).[30] The heraldic display on their pennants acts as a prelude to Satan's shield and banner, both charged with three green amphibians. Although their silhouettes correspond closely to the toads on such representations of the boiling cauldron as that of the Bourges choir screen (plate 8b), they are not, however, toads but undoubtedly refer to the three unclean spirits who are likened unto frogs in the thirteenth verse of the sixteenth chapter of the Apocalypse.[31] And in the very next verse of this same chapter, as it is given in the Vulgate, in which the frogs are said to be the spirits of demons in the form of signs *(sunt enim spiritus daemoniorum, facientes signa),* the contemporary thirteenth-century interpretation of the word *signa* as meaning armorial devices provided further justification for employing the frogs as the emblems on Satan's coat of arms.[32]

In spite of the differences between the two related species of amphibians, however, the emblematic toads in the *Somnium Viridarii* might well have been derived from the frogs on Satan's coat of arms, since in the *Somnium* the word *buffones* has been modified by the adjective *marini* (here in the accusative form, *marinos*), and the two words together can then be translated as aquatic toads. Though the phrase *buffones marini* is a contradiction in terms in view of the preference of toads for dry land, it nevertheless assumes a positive meaning when regarded as a quasi-synonym for *ranae,* the water-loving frogs. And the three demonic frogs in the guise of aquatic toads would not, moreover, have been inappropriate as the emblems of the unconverted Clovis, who in certain early texts is said to have been a devotee of Satan.[33]

Although the author of the *Somnium* claims he is merely repeating what the histories have already stated were the emblems of the pagan kings, since no such description of their heraldic devices exists in any extant history or chronicle composed prior to his time, one might well question whether the author of the *Sommium* is indeed referring to some now lost sources for the *tres buffones marini* or whether he himself was responsible for transferring Satan's emblems onto the coat of arms of the pagan kings and had invented the vague *historiae* as the authorities, however fictitious, for his own observations in order to lend them additional weight.

One can only speculate, too, as to why he should have used the circumlocution *buffones marini* for the frogs of the pagan kings instead of the single word *ranae*. Since, however, toads not only appear on the choir screen of Bourges, but also cling to the cauldron of the damned among the magnificently carved Apocalyptic scenes on the Last Judgment portal of Notre-Dame (plate 8a), the author of the *Somnium Viridarii* may also have wished to acknowledge the existence of these other amphibians of the cathedral portal, ones that must have been familiar to many of the Parisians of his own day as the habitual fauna of the nether world.[34]

However that may be, the author's own personal contribution to the lore of the toads undeniably consists in having introduced them into the story of the celestial origin of the fleurs de lis in place of the crescents. And that he came to know of the miraculous story through Raoul de Presles' Prologue is strongly suggested by the fact that the *Somnium Viridarii* was completed in 1376, the very year in which Raoul de Presles presented his *Cité de Dieu* to Charles V. The debt to the Prologue, moreover, becomes immediately apparent when one is confronted with this same passage on the arms of the pagan kings in the French translation of the *Somnium,* known as the *Songe du Vergier,* which was undertaken by another unknown author at the request of the king in 1378.[35] And here the pagan emblems have at last been reduced to the single unqualified French word for toads, *crapauds*. The passage, quoted in full, reads as follows: "Ainsi comme aucunes Cronyques racontent, les roys de France soloient jadis, avant que ilz fusent convertis, en leurs armes porter troys crapaux, lezquel furent par miracle en troys f(l)our de lis, en l'oneur et remambrance de toute la Trenité, merveilleusement convertis."[36]

With its reference to the miraculous transformation of the three toads into three fleurs de lis and with the added invocation of the Trinity lacking in the earlier Latin text, this passage can also be seen as little more than an amplification of the opening sentence in Raoul de Presles' account of the legend of Joyenval: "Et si portez les armes de trois fleurs de lis en signe de la benoite Trinité" (appendix 4.4). And finally there can be no doubt either that it is due to this same passage in the French translation of the *Somnium* that henceforth in literature and art, with only one exception as far as I know, the emblems of the pagan Clovis are not the crescents of the original legend of Joyenval, but the "crapaux" of the *Songe du Vergier.*

# 5
# The Shield and the Crown

### The Charter of Limay

ith the completion of Raoul de Presles' monumental work, the impact of the legend of Joyenval in the Prologue also began to make itself felt in the art of the illuminators at Charles V's court. As might be expected, in the copy of the *Cité de Dieu* presented to the king in 1376, the royal escutcheon at the bottom of the first page of the Prologue displays three fleurs de lis (plate 7), while the two angels who support the shield were henceforth to become the preferred supporters of the arms of France.[1] A more impressive testimony, however, to the direct influence of the legend occurs in the historiated initial of a charter granted by the king in January 1377 for the founding of the abbey of the Celestines at Limay near Mantes.[2]

Since the abbey of Limay was under the invocation of the Trinity, in the preamble to the charter the analogy could be made between the patronal dedication of the monastery and the fleurs de lis on the king's coat of arms that, to borrow the phraseology of the Latin text, are not two, but three in number, so that they might produce the figure of the Trinity.[3] Though the reference to "not two" cannot be rationally accounted for, since two emblematic lilies do not appear on any known royal escutcheons,[4] like the reference to the transformation of the toads into fleurs de lis in the *Songe du Vergier* already quoted, this passage can also be aptly compared to the opening phrase of the legend of Joyenval in the Prologue to the *Cité de Dieu*, in which the king of France is said to bear "les armes de trois fleurs de lis en signe de la benoite Trinité."[5] But it is in the pen and ink drawing of the initial *K* of Karolus at the very beginning of the charter that the analogy with the Trinity is most vividly realized. In the upright stem of the initial Charles kneels in prayer toward the triune Deity that, in conformity with the text of the charter, is represented by God the Father, the Dove, and the crucified Christ (plate 10).[6] The kneeling king in turn is united to a group of the inmates of the abbey by a large scroll depicting the charter. Huddled together on their knees, the monks avidly grasp its other end. Above the king's head is his shield with the triple lilies surmounted by two angels holding a crown in token of the celestial origin of the royal arms and in recognition of the sovereign to whom they belong.

Crown-bearing angels had previously appeared in a miniature of the mystic coronation of a king of France placed at the head of a *Chanson de Geste* in a late thirteenth-century manuscript, now in the Bibliothèque de l'Arsenal (plate 11).[7] The earliest known instance of the arms of France surmounted by a crown also stems from this period. It occurs, however, neither on the royal seals nor on the coins of the realm, but on the seal of the city of Bordeaux. The matrix for the seal was presumably engraved between 1294 and 1297 during the few brief years when Bordeaux, freed from English domination, belonged to France.[8] The crowned shield was taken up again on the so-called secret seal of John the Good[9] and finally on Charles V's counterseal of 1364 where, as in the previous examples, the shield is charged with multiple lilies (plate 12).[10] In the most impressive of the historiated charters of Charles V, that declaring the inalienability of the royal residence of the Hotel St-Paul, drawn up in 1364, the two motifs of crown and fleur de lis form, as it were, the dual insignia of the monarchy in the large initial *C* in which the king is majestically enthroned (plate 13).[11] Here in the upper left corner of the initial the Deity, represented by the cross-nimbed bust of the Savior, bestows his benediction on a crown and a single heraldic lily proferred him by two angels, while below them, immediately to the left of the king, is the royal shield with triple emblems.

Both on the king's counterseal and in the Charter of the Hotel St-Paul, the way had thus already been prepared at the very beginning of the king's reign for the initial in the Charter of Limay (plate 10). The skill of the illuminator, moreover, in adapting the figures to the structure of the initial in the Charter of Limay must have been appreciated, since his design furnished the model for the historiated initials in two almost identical charters of 1379 establishing the foundation of the royal chapel of the Holy Trinity at Vincennes (plates 14, 15).[12] In these inferior copies, however, instead of kneeling, Charles stands in the tall stem of the letter, leaving no room for the shield, while his reverent attitude toward the

Trinity has perforce been abandoned. As a result of these changes, the angels now appear to be crowning the king. But instead of being properly seated in strict frontality, as is the king in the Arsenal miniature (plate 11), Charles is about to receive the crown incongruously standing upright, in one instance in profile (plate 14), in the other in three-quarter view (plate 15). A modified version of this same awkward scheme can be recognized in a third historiated initial in a charter granted by Charles V to the canons of Reims in 1380 at the very end of his reign.[13]

Speculation on the reasons for these disturbing incongruities must be reserved for a later occasion. They are incidental, however, to the larger implications that can be drawn from the Charter of Limay. For here at last, both pictorially and in the text, is what amounts to an official acknowledgment that the fleurs de lis on the king's coat of arms should be no more and no less than three. Although there is no direct evidence that Charles V was ever involved in this decision, as one who in his efforts to rehabilitate the prestige of the monarchy placed so much emphasis on the symbolic and ceremonial forms of kingship, it might be expected that he should also have turned his attention to the question of the proper number of lilies on the French coat of arms after the problem had been so flagrantly neglected by his predecessors for well over a century.

## Charles V and the Fleurs de Lis

As Max Prinet has demonstrated, beginning as early as 1228 the three fleurs de lis are ever more frequently encountered on the royal coat of arms displayed on the seals of the provincial cities and communes and on those of various local offices under the king's jurisdiction, as well as on the arms of some of the members belonging to the younger branches of the French royal house.[14] But on those other small monuments that can be regarded as of a truly official character, such as the king's counterseal and his so-called secret seal that were in the keeping of the chancellery and on the coins issued by the royal mints, the shield with the triple lilies is rare indeed.[15] Prior to the reign of Charles V, the number of heraldic lilies as officially represented is generally in excess of three,[16] while for some unaccountable reason the arms of France contin-ued to be entirely excluded from the most important of the royal seals, the *sceaux de majesté,* until the very end of the monarchy.[17]

As we have seen, however, in the very first year of Charles V's reign a certain predilection for the three fleurs de lis had already manifested itself in another creation of the chancellery, the Charter of the Hotel St-Paul (plate 13). As can be appreciated by their effectiveness on the escutcheon in the historiated initial of the charter, in contrast to the overall pattern of the smaller and more numerous emblems when scattered over the surface of a shield, the three heraldic lilies produced a greater clarity and unity, not only by their larger size, but also by admirably conforming to its triangular shape (plates 12, 13).[18] These were the years, moreover, when the art of heraldry was beginning to assume an ever greater importance in the hierarchical society of feudal Europe and when the office of the herald was being elevated by those in power to the position of a respected profession that included a comprehensive knowledge concerning the recognition and devising of armorial bearings.[19] Charles V's own participation in fostering the order of heraldry is attested to in a letter contained in a later treatise composed by a herald around 1400 that describes in lively fashion the crowning in Paris by Charles V of the herald Charlot as the Montjoie King of Arms of France.[20]

But there were more fundamental reasons why Charles should have been particularly concerned with his own coat of arms. In exchange for his direct sovereignty over the vast French territories ceded to him in 1360 at the Treaty of Brétigny, Edward III had renounced his title of *Rex Franciae* and had removed the French emblems from his escutcheon. But when in 1368, as a pretext for initiating the recovery of the lost provinces, Charles accused Edward on a technicality of having broken the terms of the treaty, Edward promptly reasserted his claim to the French crown and once again quartered the lilies with the leopards on his shield.[21]

Some idea of Charles' reaction to Edward's readoption of the fleurs de lis can be gained from a short discourse on heraldry that has been included in the *Songe du Vergier,* that famous allegorical dialogue that has been regarded as expressing many of Charles' own views on political and monarchical matters. Basing his discussion on a problem that had already been debated by the Italian jurist Bartolo di Sassoferrato in his oft-quoted *Tractatus de Insigniis et Armis* of circa 1354,[22] the anonymous writer of the *Songe* poses the question of whether or not two men can assume identical coats of arms without doing injury to each other. Like Bartolo, the author of the *Songe* decides that no possible harm can be done as long as they reside far apart, but when a neighbor assumes the armorial bearings of another, such an act can be prejudicial to him from whom he has borrowed them.[23]

"And when the adoption of another's coat of arms results in scandal and in the deception of the people," says the author, "it apertains to the sovereign to see to it that the people are not deceived. And if the wrong-doer ignores the rightful action of the sovereign, the latter can, as the injured party, initiate a just war against the wrong-doer until he lays down his weapons. For the right to declare war is also the prerogative of a prince."[24] He is then reminded of the King of England who has assumed the arms of the House of France and who calls himself King of France. "Not only has he thereby committed a serious offense against the French king," says the author, "but he is also in danger of deceiving the simple folk among his own subjects, as well as those others who harbor ill will toward the French crown and who wish to break their oath to the king and crown of France."[25]

All this, indeed, might well be construed as embodying Charles' own subsequent rationalization for reopening the war based, not on Edward's supposed violation of the Treaty of Brétigny but on his later reassumption of the fleurs de lis.[26] Although through the military exploits of his constable, Bertrand du Guesclin, Charles had managed to wrest from the English most of the French territories they occupied, including all of those they had recently acquired as victors in the war, there was of course no way by which Edward could have been compelled to renounce the French emblems, and their usurpation must have brought home to Charles, as nothing else could have, the vital function assumed by his own armorials as symbols of the king's authority and of his hereditary right to reign. And with this realization he must also have become aware that the number of the emblems on his escutcheon could no longer be left indefinitely to the vagaries of individual preferences. The time had come at long last to take some notice of what the poets and scholars had been proclaiming for over half a century were the only proper number of the lilies on the arms of France and the means by which they could be distinguished from the arms of all those others who also bore the fleurs de lis. Above all, the reduction of the lilies to three would decisively differentiate them from the multiple fleurs de lis that continued to be quartered with the three leopards on the English coat of arms (fig. F).

If the politics of heraldry may thus have prepared the way for the choice of the triple emblems, the decisive impetus nevertheless that was eventually to lead to their acceptance can only have stemmed from the legend of Joyenval in the Prologue to the *Cité de Dieu* whose contents, as we have seen from the evidence in Jean Golein's *Treatise on the Coronation Ceremony,* was probably already well known to the members of the court in the early 1370s. Soon afterwards the three fleurs de lis made one of their rare appearances on the escutcheon of a royal seal, in this case Charles' own secret seal (plate 16).[27] Though appended to a document of 1376, it may indeed already have been in use sometime prior to that date. And here, in a further elaboration of the motif of the crowned shield and as though in anticipation of the historiated initial on the charter of Limay, the crowned figure of the king himself surmounts his coat of

Fig. F. The English coat of arms, 1340–1360, 1368–1404/5

arms, while the two dolphins in the lobes of the circular frame are reminders that before his accession Charles had been the first Dauphin of France.[28]

One cannot claim, however, from the evidence at hand that there was any formal adoption of the three fleurs de lis in these last years of Charles V's reign, as has sometimes been suggested.[29] As Charles' secret seal already intimates and as the charter of Limay undeniably proclaims, a strong official bias in favor of the triple lilies seems to have existed at this time, but it does not appear to have extended beyond the confines of that perennial keeper of the seals and source of the charters, the royal chancellery. In Charles' own deluxe copy of the *Grandes Chroniques de France,* which was executed between 1375 and 1368 and whose abundant illustrations were in part remodeled by order of the king himself, the royal escutcheon on the opening page of the first book is charged with a quantity of fleurs de lis.[30] This reluctance to abandon older usages is even more strikingly illustrated in the presentation copy of Raoul de Presles' *Cité de Dieu* where one might rightly expect a consistent adherence to the triple emblems. Although the royal shield on the first page of the Prologue is represented twenty-one times in the following folios, in seven instances it is charged with multiple lilies.[31] And on the full-page illustration of the coronation of Charles VI that was added to his father's copy of the *Grandes Chroniques* after the death of Charles V in 1380, as well as on Charles VI's counterseal of that same year, the royal arms again follow the older precedent.[32] The general acceptance of the three fleurs de lis was not to be arrived at through the restricted category of the seals, nor for that matter through the historiated initials of the charters or through the illuminated manuscripts, but in the series of coins issued by the royal mints.

## The "Ecu à la Couronne"

No survey of the theme of the royal fleurs de lis during the thirteenth and fourteenth centuries can afford to omit an account, however cursory, of the developments that took place in the designs of the French coins.[33] Prior to 1266 the types of coins are of interest primarily to the specialist in the field of early Capetian numismatics. But in that year a new era begins marked by a superior quality in the silver species and by the introduction of gold into the currency.[34] Of the gold coinage known to have been minted during the reign of Louis IX, however, examples of only one emission survive, the "Ecu d'or" of 1266. Characterized by a technical precision and refinement in contrast to the perfunctory and even crude execution of the previous emissions, the "Ecu d'or" displays on its obverse side the earliest instance of the royal arms in French numismatics—a shield bearing six fleurs de lis within a polylobed circle (plate 17a).[35]

Another momentous change in the coinage took place under Philip the Fair with the introduction of the first full-length seated portraits of a king of France. Initially modeled on his *sceau de majesté* (plate 3e), in the third of the series of four portraits, the "Chaise d'or" of 1303,[36] the lion-headed curule chair borrowed from Philip's seal on the other three coins has here been replaced by a high-backed pinnacled throne that henceforth became standard in the designs of the currency (plate 17b). As on his seal, in all four of these numismatic portraits, the king continues to hold a single fleur de lis, not, however, in his right hand, in which has been placed a sceptre, but in his left.

Although none of Philip's three sons reigned long enough to allow any significant additions to the repertory of the designs, under Philip VI several of the gold coins can be cited as worthy examples of the so-called minor arts that dominated so much of the artistic activity of the fourteenth century. In the "Pavilion d'or" of 1339, in one of several exceptions to the usual type of ruler portrait, the king is framed by the graceful parted curtains of the royal pavilion in which he is seated (plate 17c).[37] Another coin, the "Angelot," issued in 1341 during the initial phase of the Hundred Years' War, with its aethereal quality and delicacy of line has sometimes been considered to be the masterpiece of the numismatic art of the later Middle Ages (plate 17d).[38] Crowned and standing on a dragon that he is about to pierce with his lance, the angel of the "Angelot" supports with his left hand a shield with the arms of France that for the first and, with one possible exception, the only time in French currency prior to the reign of Charles VI is charged with three fleurs de lis.[39] Although one might suspect that the angel with the triple lilies was the result of some connection with the legend of Joyenval, he is, however, no ordinary angel. Shield, crown, spear, and dragon all identify him as the warring Saint Michael who from his eminence in his sanctuary of Mont St-Michel has been called upon to slay the dragon that personifies the enemies of France.[40]

The series of remarkable coins created under Philip of Valois concludes with another dragon-slayer, a mounted Saint George (plate 17e).[41] The patron of warriors, he may well have been chosen, as Lafaurie has suggested, in order to demonstrate to the English that they had no monopoly on this Cappadocian saint and that he could also be propitiously invoked on behalf of the French. Issued in 1341 and again in 1346, the "Florins Georges" were especially struck in order to defray the expenses of two military campaigns, one in Brittany, the other in Languedoc.[42] But this second campaign was rudely interrupted by the incredible news from the north of an overwhelming defeat at Crécy inflicted by Edward's small army on the numerically superior French forces led by Philip VI.

With the debacle at Crécy this flourishing period of French numismatic art also suffered an eclipse. From 1351 to 1359 under King John the obverse of the gold coins is confined to variations of the pascal lamb and the seated and standing royal portraits, the models for which can be traced back to the time of Philip the Fair. In commemoration of the return of John the Good from his London imprisonment in 1360, a new type of the king's portrait, the "Franc à cheval," was borrowed from the equestrian images on the seals of the royal princes and feudatories.[43] Free (*franc*) at last, the king is portrayed as once again energetically leading the mounted nobility astride his caparisoned charger, both horse and rider liberally sprinkled with fleurs de lis (plate 17f). A second and final appearance of the "Franc à cheval" coincided with the advent of Charles V in 1364.[44]

Although Charles was mainly responsible for reestablishing the full monetary value of the currency after more than half a century of adulteration, the designs of the few gold emissions produced during his reign are still largely based on the formulas used under King John, while the coins minted under Charles VI until 1385 continue the types that had appeared toward the end of his father's reign. A dramatic turning point, however, was reached on 11 March of that year with the first appearance of the gold "Ecu à la couronne" in which a crown surmounts a shield with three fleurs de lis, precisely as it does on the Charter of Limay (plates 10, 17g).[45] But not only had the coinage caught up with the seals and the historiated initial of the charter. The "Ecu à la couronne" of 1385 also served as the prototype for the innumerable "Ecu d'or" that dominated French currency until the time of Louis XIV.[46] And in spite of the fact that multiple lilies are still encountered on a few royal monuments until as late as 1410,[47] the overwhelming success of this new form of the "Ecu d'or" can be said to have established once and for all the three fleurs de lis as the only proper number of the lilies on the arms of France. Nor was there any need of a formal proclamation or royal ordinance to enforce this choice. For what better way of establishing it could there have been than through the circulation of the currency whereby the triple emblems, spread far and wide, were officially sanctioned by the presence of the crown? The effects of this dissemination can already be perceived as early as 1389 in the decorations that greeted Charles VI at Bézier during his tour of the Midi. As on the "Ecu à la couronne," above each of the city gates was placed a crown surmounting the royal coat of arms. And on each of the shields were three heraldic lilies since, in the words of a contemporary writer describing the decorations, "las tres flors de li son las armas proprias de nostre senhor lo rey."[48]

# 6
# The Rival Claims to the Origin of the Fleurs de Lis

t might seem ironic that the "Ecu à la couronne" of 1385, which was so instrumental in establishing the universal acceptance of the three fleurs de lis on the arms of France, should have been created under Charles VI whose long reign has sometimes been described as the most disastrous in the history of the French monarchy, above all in its consequences, when it appeared for a time as though the Valois dynasty was again slated for extinction. Before the onset of the years of torment, however, a long reprieve was granted during which France seemed, outwardly at least, to have regained something of its stature as the leading European power. But in spite of the victories of Charles V, the reconquest of all the territories held by the English remained beyond the resources of a country ravaged by decades of warfare and pillage. With the death of the king on 16 September 1380, conditions at the Valois court would seem to have presented the English with a particularly favorable opportunity for launching a major offensive. Charles VI was less than twelve years old at his accession. His rapacious uncles, the regents, were more intent on furthering their own fortunes than in advancing the welfare of the crown and the state, and from 1380 to 1383, urban uprisings against the imposition of taxes recalled in their severity the revolt of Etienne Marcel and that of the Jacquerie after the defeat at Poitiers.[1]

It so happened, however, that a similar situation existed in England. Richard of Bordeaux was hardly ten when in 1377 he succeeded to the

49

throne at the death of his aged grandfather, Edward III. Like Charles VI he was soon confronted with a serious popular uprising that reached a climax in June 1381 when the rebellious peasants and artisans under Wat Tyler seized London in a brief paroxysm of arson, pillage, and massacre.[2] With the country financially unable to undertake a major military campaign, a series of peace negotiations ensued, culminating in a twenty-eight-year truce concluded on 9 March 1396 between Charles VI and the Francophile Richard II.[3] Although the truce was broken before its term expired, an interval of relative peace was granted during the years before and immediately after its conclusion. And it was within these few decades following the accession of Charles VI, when a final end to the interminable war seemed imminent, that there unfolded the last chapter in the long contest between the rival claims to the origin of the fleurs de lis.

## Charlemagne and the Angel

Still another mythical story concerning the genesis of the heraldic lilies was now added to those of Saint Denis and Joyenval. It is known, however, only from its inclusion in a somewhat later work, the *Tractatus de Armis,* composed by an insular author writing under the pseudonym of Johannes de Bado Aureo.[4] The third oldest surviving treatise on heraldry, it was undertaken at the behest of Anne of Bohemia, the first wife of Richard II, but was not completed until sometime after her death in June 1394.[5] Evan Jones has sought to identify the mysterious Johannes de Bado Aureo with the Welshman John Trevor who in 1394 was in Rome where he was consecrated bishop of the see of St-Asaph. After his return in October 1395 he became a close friend of Richard and took an active part in the momentous events that transpired in the last year of the king's reign.[6] Unfortunately no certainty exits concerning this identification that otherwise has much to commend it.[7] The author of the treatise, however, does tell us that his work was based in part on the teachings of a Frenchman, Franciscus de Foveis, who had been his master.[8] The French equivalent of his Latin name is assumed to have been François de Fossés.

The treatise begins by evaluating the heraldic colors. In Bartolo di Sassoferrato's early work on heraldry, as well as in the later *Songe du Vergier,* gold is extolled as the noblest of the colors, followed by *purpureus,* or the color of fire, then azure, and finally black.[9] But according to François, says Johannes de Bado Aureo, azure is the foremost of the colors, superior even to gold. And the reason this is so, says the author, is because this was the color that was sent from God by his angel to Charlemagne, the king of the French, to be the base and foundation of his arms. For the angel brought down an azure shield with three golden flowers. "And if you so desire," he adds, "you can say in French: 'Il porte d'azour treys floredelys d'ore.' "[10]

If mystery still surrounds the identity of Johannes de Bado Aureo, nothing but the fact that he was a Frenchman is known concerning François de Fossés from whom this little fable of Charlemagne and the arms of France was apparently derived. Nor have any of his writings been found. However, in view of the chapter heading in the French translation of Yves' early fourteenth-century *Life of Saint Denis,* which has already been quoted in reference to the possible sources of the Latin poem on the legend of Joyenval and in which the emperor is credited with having received the emblems of France from the Deity himself,[11] it would not have been surprising if this story of Charlemagne and the angel had already been known to Charles V.

The king's veneration for Charlemagne, however, is well attested to — a private cult, as Robert Folz has described it, largely confined to the royal chapel[12] in contrast to the widespread acclaim accorded the emperor in the decades following the death of Louis IX. Although Charlemagne was declared a saint at Aachen in 1165, his canonization was not recognized in France until the time of Charles V. The king's devotion to "Saint Charles" may even have preceded his accession to the throne, since the inscription on the base of the statuette of the emperor that surmounts the scepter ostensibly made for Charles' coronation in 1364 already refers to him as SAN(C)TUS KAROLUS.[13] According to Denis Foullechat and Jean Corbechon, moreover, both writing in 1372, Charles had commissioned the translation of Augustine's *Civitas Dei* precisely because it was said to have been Charlemagne's favorite reading matter,[14] a tradition concerning the emperor's literary preferences that was also cited by Raoul de Presles himself in his Prologue to the *Cité de Dieu,* as well as by Yves of St-Denis more than half a century before.[15]

If he was indeed acquainted with the story concerning Charlemagne and the angel that Johannes de Bado Aureo ascribed to François de Fossés, Charles must have been in a quandary as to which of the two versions of the origin of the royal arms to accept, the one that attributed the heavenly gift to his canonized ancestor or that other version of the story that ascribed their origin to the time of Clovis, the founder of the Christian monarchy, at whose baptism the chrism with which Charles himself had been anointed at his coronation was miraculously brought down from heaven. And was this state of indecision the reason why, after the Trinitarian symbolism of the royal emblems derived from Raoul de Presles' account of the legend of Joyenval was so clearly emphasized in the historiated initial of the Charter of Limay (plate 10), in the same initials in the two subsequent charters for the royal chapel of the chateau of Vincennes the standing figure of Charles was substituted for the earlier figure of the kneeling king, thereby blotting out the shield with the three lilies and repudiating their connection with the Trinity (plates 14, 15)?

Any answers to such questions of course can only be matters for speculation. But in view of the lack of any substantial evidence for the liturgical cult of the emperor during the reign of Charles VI,[16] such a crisis of indecision as might have occurred during Charles V's final years, pitting not only the legend of Joyenval against that of Charlemagne but Charlemagne himself against Clovis, "le premier roy crestien" of Raoul de Presles' Prologue would have been highly unlikely after the king's death in 1380. Nor did the story of the emperor and the arms of France appear to have had any residual attraction for the French literati. Only in Britain did the legend take root. Besides its appearance in the original redaction of the *Tractatus de Armis,* it is also included in two later versions of the same work on heraldry, both attributed by Evan Jones to John Trevor, one composed in Latin, the other in Welsh.[17] The text of the legend in the second Latin treatise was paraphrased in the *Libellus de Officio Militari,* a work on heraldry and the art of warfare composed around 1446 by the warrior-cleric Nicolas Upton and published in a printed edition in 1654 by Sir Edward Bysshe.[18]

## The Sermon for the Feast of Saint Louis

Although with the advent of Charles VI no partisans could presumably be found in France to uphold François de Fossés' account of the heavenly gift to Charlemagne, as if in homage to the scholarship of the historiographers of the abbey of St-Denis, those affiliated with the University of Paris continued to opt for the Dionysian origin of the fleurs de lis. So it was, as may be recalled, with Etienne de Conty in the first years of Charles' reign. A loyal graduate of the University, he thus followed in the wake of that earlier representative of that same illustrious institution, Thomas of Ireland, who had conscientiously copied down the verses on the migration of the petals posted on the shrine of Saint Denis. And although in his *Traité du sacre* Jean Golein had been lured by Raoul de Presles' Prologue into attributing to the hermit of Joyenval the emblems on the king's banner, nevertheless when it came to the coronation vestments seeded with fleurs de lis that were brought to the ceremony from the royal abbey, as a graduate of the university and one of its professors, who later was elected its spokesman,[19] Jean Golein stood by his commitment to Saint Denis as the donor of the royal lilies.

In a short Latin poem entitled "Carmen ut lilia crescant," a still more eminent exponent of the university, Jean Gerson, the famous Parisian theologian and reformer, whose long career extended into the age of Joan of Arc, also credits Saint Denis with having donated the *lilii flores* to the House of France.[20] Although the work is undated, Monsignor Glorieux has tentatively connected the poem with a sermon for the feast of Saint Louis composed by Gerson in 1393 when he was still "maître régent" at The University's theological faculty.[21] The relationship between the two works is further confirmed by comparing the text of the sermon with that of the poem.[22]

The well-known words of the Gospels, *Considerate lilia agri quomode crescunt,* from the sixth chapter of Matthew and the twelfth of Luke, that furnished the Biblical theme of the sermon, are echoed in the refrain *Lilia crescant* placed after each of the poem's nine unrimed triplets. In the last stanza of the poem, moreover, the author invokes not only Saint Remi of Reims, but also Saint Louis, that through their intercession the lilies may perpetually grow.[23] Other possible ties with the poem can be detected in a long passage on the fleurs de lis that is included in the sermon.

Should Saint Louis have been in the habit of contemplating the three golden lilies on his shield, says Gerson, he would have been reminded of the three theological virtues and of a series of other triple attributes that the author proceeds to enumerate, concluding with the three horticultural elements needed in order that the lilies may grow—*quae lilia ut crescant*—employing as in the refrain of the poem, the present subjunctive of *crescere*.[24] He then adds that he would like to acquaint his learned listeners with still more material derived from the chronicles of this famous king if he had the time.[25] And in what chronicles, may one ask, would Gerson have found a threefold symbolism of the heraldic lily associated with Saint Louis if not in the *Life of Louis IX* by Guillaume de Nangis and in his *Chronicon,* or *Chronique latine,* both ultimate sources for the Dionysian derivation of the royal emblems?[26]

If on the basis of these excerpts from his sermon the poem can be dated as early as around 1393, when Gerson was still a young man, it nevertheless remains the last instance, as far as I know, in which a major author was to ascribe the genesis of the fleurs de lis to Saint Denis. As the sermon itself demonstrates, however, Gerson was not unaware of those other beliefs stemming from the legend of Joyenval that attributed a Trinitarian source to the heraldic flowers. In contemplating the three lilies on his shield, described as both royal and divine, Saint Louis, says Gerson, would undoubtedly have remembered the blessed Trinity from whom they originated.[27]

*Le Roman de la belle Helaine*

The years following the accession of Charles VI witnessed the ever-growing dissemination of Raoul de Presles' version of the legend of Joyenval due to the increasing popularity of the *Cité de Dieu,* of which there still exist eleven copies made between 1380 and 1392.[28] But even before the advent of Charles VI the story of Clovis and the origin of the royal emblems had already been introduced in an abbreviated form into the fantastic adventures of the popular *Romans.* In the opening verses of the *Chanson de Charles le Chauve,* composed in Paris probably sometime after 1360,[29] the reader is reminded that in the time of the Merovingian rulers there was a king of France

> a qui diex envoia
> Le noble fleurdelis et fisse (?) baptisa
> Pour la sainte miracle que diex li demonstra.[30]

In spite of the ambiguity of the verses, the reference to a miracle at the baptism of the king clearly points to Clovis as the recipient of the celestial flower. In another of these late "chansons de geste," *Théseus de Cologne,* that was apparently composed in its present redaction in the latter part of the reign of Charles V, the author invokes the crown of France that stemmed from God himself,

> Qui les iii fleurs de lis envoia dignement
> Au noble Clovis qui regna loiaulment.[31]

Were these brief references to the Clovis story derived from Raoul de Presles, or did the verses in which they appear antedate the Prologue and can thus be considered as stemming from the original Latin poem of the canons of Joyenval? Although no categorical answers to these questions are possible due to the uncertainty as to exactly when these revisions of the *Romans* were undertaken, in the *Chanson de Charles le Chauve* the mention of the baptism of the king, an event featured in the Latin poem but not included in Raoul de Presles' version of the origin of the fleurs de lis, strongly suggests a derivation from the original legend, distant echoes of which may thus have entered into the repertory of the fabulous tales collected by these latter-day jongleurs.

By the 1380s similar abbreviated references to the legend appear in two separate passages in a work of a quite different character, a highly colored versified life of Charles V's celebrated constable Bertrand du Guesclin by the poet Cuvelier, which he finished in 1387.[32] In describing the freeing of Poitiers and La Rochelle from the English in 1372, the author has in each instance invented a similar rhapsodic outburst to express the joy of the citizens in greeting their French liberators when, to quote the passage from the freeing of La Rochelle, they exuberantly acclaim the fleur de lis "qui dignement fu transmise du ciel au roy Clovis."[33]

Sometime between 1378 and the last decade of the century, a fully developed if highly unusual version of the Clovis legend was included among the fantastic tales of *Le Roman de la belle Helaine*.[34] The battle against the "roy Caudat" of Raoul de Presles' Prologue has here been metamorphosed into the siege of the town of Chartres that is occupied by a horde of Turks and other pagan miscreants under the leadership of the wicked Admiral Hertaut.[35] When his besieging army fails to make any headway, Clovis declares his faith in the true God of his Christian wife Clotilda and calls upon him for assistance,[36] whereupon Jesus sends down his angel, who promptly replaces the three golden toads on the king's shield with "troix fleurs de lis d'or fin en champaigne azurée."[37] After rendering thanks for the celestial miracle, Clovis promises the Lord that he and all his people shall be converted and, exhorting his men to advance, calls their attention to his new coat of arms, the gift of the Christian God who has now come to their aid.[38] Thus inspired, they proceed to vanquish Hertaut's rabble army.

Inserted into an account of the adventures of Clovis and the boy Joseran with which it otherwise has no connection whatsoever, this version of the origin of the arms of France appears to be indebted to several different sources, not all of which can be determined with any degree of accuracy. Whereas the choice of Chartres as the site of the siege may possibly have been suggested by the fact that the abbey of Joyenval was in the diocese of Chartres, the appeal of Clovis to the true God of Clotilda during the siege is certainly reminiscent of his similar entreaties to Clotilda's God and his subsequent conversion in the traditional account of his victory over the Alemanni. And finally, of major importance in setting a precedent for the story of Clovis and the fleurs de lis is the fact that prior to their transformation his heraldic ensigns are not the crescents of the legend of Joyenval but the toads of the *Songe du Vergier*.

Although one could hardly expect any mention of Clovis and the origin of the fleurs de lis in the *Grandes Chroniques de France*, since the history of the Merovingian dynasty in these famous annals of the French kings was composed over half a century before the first appearance of the legend in the Latin poem, in a copy of the *Grandes Chroniques* illuminated in Paris toward the very end of the fourteenth century the angel of the *Roman de la belle Helaine* can nevertheless be recognized in a miniature illustrating Clovis' celebrated encounter with the Alemanni (plate 18).[39] As at the siege of Chartres, above the clashing armies he bears the familiar shield with the three golden lilies that he is about to substitute for the king's pagan emblems. Whereas in later representations of the battle they are usually black on a light ground, here in conformity with the verses of *La Belle Helaine* the toads on the shield and banner of Clovis are, like the heraldic lilies, rendered in gold on an azure field, while two of the emblems on his banner are seemingly in the process of being transmuted into fleurs de lis.[40]

There was some justification, moreover, for introducing the angel of the *Roman* into the illustration of the battle. As has been noted, the appeal of Clovis to the God of Clotilda during the seige of Chartres undoubtedly stemmed from the traditional account of his conversion during his encounter with the Alemanni. And this tradition has likewise been faithfully preserved in the text of *Grandes Chroniques,* which was most likely the one consulted by the author of this redaction of *La belle Helaine*.[41] But the miniature can also be associated with Raoul de Presles' version of the legend of Joyenval. As has already been seen, the tyrant from Conflans who challenged Clovis to a duel in the Latin poem was transformed by Raoul de Presles into the "roy Caudat" who came from "l'Alemaigne" and who thus can be identified with the "roy d'Alemaigne" who is the king of the "Alemanz" in the *Grandes Chroniques*. And with this illustration of the battle against the Alemanni, to which has been added the shield-bearing angel from the *Roman de la belle Helaine,* the story of Clovis and the origin of the fleurs de lis, in however distorted a form, can now be said to have entered into the main stream of French monarchical lore.

And so, as the outcome of this contest demonstrates, the victor among the contending legends was not the one derived from the literary conceits of the scholars of the abbey of St-Denis and endorsed by the academicians of the university, but was that other mythical story that in its basic form had first come to the ears of a canon of Joyenval from the oral folklore of an unlettered people and hence from that same collective mentality that was most conducive for initiating the legends that endure.

In these same final years of the fourteenth century, when in France the three heraldic lilies were gaining universal acceptance as the only recognized number of the fleurs de lis on the royal coat of arms and the Clovis version of their origin had finally won out over its several competitors, across the Channel unexpectedly disparaging remarks concerning the French emblems were being made by that man of mystery, Johannes de Bado Aureo.

# 7

# The Leopards and
# the Fleurs de Lis

"Portare Flores est Signum Instabilitatis"

he *Tractatus de Armis* of Johannes de Bado Aureo that he completed shortly after the death in 1394 of Anne of Bohemia, the wife of Richard II, has not only preserved the story of Charlemagne and the gift of the arms of France that was derived from his French master François de Fossés; in a later passage in the treatise the author presents what appear to be his own views on floral emblems in general and on their particular significance within the context of the Charlemagne legend. "To bear flowers such as roses," he says, "is a sign of instability since they are impermanent and are not destined to last through the year. Therefore," he concludes, "when through the agency of his angel God bestowed the arms with the triple flowers on the king of France (i.e., Charlemagne), he quite justifiably demonstrated that inconstancy and lack of steadfastness existed in France at that time," adding that François himself has said these things concerning his native land.[1] Whether or not these conclusions concerning the significance of floral emblems were indeed those of his master or of Johannes de Bado Aureo himself, one may well ask what prompted him to include in his treatise these derogatory remarks concerning the inconstancy of France symbolized by the *flores* on the royal escutcheon.

In the first decade of the reign of Charles VI, the leopards of the Plantagenets could still evoke expressions of scorn from the French literati. In describing the liberation of Poitiers from English domination in 1372, the poet Cuvelier scoffs at "le liepart felon" and advises him, now that he has been chased out of the city, to make his nest elsewhere.[2] No such animosities, however, could reasonably be projected onto the fleurs de lis by the English. Not only were the lilies of France joined to the English leopards on the royal coat of arms, where they occupied the places of honor in the first and fourth quarterings;[3] even before the death of Queen Anne in 1394 John of Gaunt, Richard II's uncle and Europe's most renowned feudal dignitary, was undertaking negotiations on Richard's behalf that were finally to lead to the truce of 1396 and the king's second marriage to Charles VI's daughter Isabel. To have openly cast aspersions on the significance of the fleurs de lis under these circumstances would have been highly impolitic on the part of the author of the treatise, especially in a work that was commissioned by Richard's much-beloved first wife and that after her untimely death may well have come to the notice of the king himself. Johannes de Bado Aureo seems indeed to have been particularly sensitive on this point.

Not ony has he omitted any mention of the "flordelys" in these later comments, referring to them simply as *flores;* but in order to make doubly sure that in describing flowers as symbols of instability he could not be accused of alluding to the heraldic lilies, he cites roses as examples of floral emblems, as though these were the only flowers he had in mind.[4] And he has furthermore been careful to attribute the inconstancy and lack of steadfastness represented by the arms of France not to his own era but to the time of Charlemagne. From all this one can only conclude that in these gratuitous and unflattering comments concerning the significance of floral emblems, without specifically disparaging the fleurs de lis that also appeared on the escutcheon of the English king, the author of the treatise was nevertheless issuing a veiled warning concerning the pitfalls that the Francophile Richard should be aware of in dealing with an erstwhile enemy whose coat of arms proclaimed his fickleness and unreliability—a warning he may well have felt was all the more necessary at a time when the peace negotiations with Charles VI were approaching a critical stage.[5]

### L'Epistre au roi Richard II

In the spring of 1395 Richard II received two missives that contained French proposals for achieving a lasting peace through joint undertakings of a far-reaching and decidedly Utopian nature. One of the missives was a letter from Charles VI himself addressed to his "very beloved cousin and brother" outlining two of the projects.[6] In the first of these the end of hostilities between England and France was contingent upon their unified efforts in healing the Great Schism of the Church that at that time not only divided Christendom but had also been an added source of dissension between the two countries.[7] And secondly, just as the Roman curia had once attempted a reconciliation between Edward III and Philip VI by encouraging them to cooperate in the preparations for the aborted crusade of 1335, so now Charles VI invited Edward's grandson to join with him in another and far more extensive crusade that was not only designed to free the Holy Land but also "by virtue of the Cross" was to "spread the Holy Catholic Faith throughout all parts of the East."[8]

These ambitious proposals, however, did not originate with Charles VI but had been developed over a long period of time by that renowned political idealist Philippe de Mézières, who was also Charles' mentor. As revealed in his extensive writings, a crusade that was to unite all of Christendom had been a major goal of Philippe de Mézières long before 1373, at which time he entered the service of Charles V and became not only counselor to the king but also tutor to his son and heir. Although with the accession of Charles VI in 1380 he retired to the Convent of the Celestines in Paris, he nevertheless continued to advise the young king who ardently espoused his former tutor's ideas.[9]

It is not surprising therefore that the agenda for peace outlined in Charles' letter is but a brief summary of the more expanded program enunciated in the second missive sent to Richard in the spring of 1395, Philippe de Mézière's *Epistre au roi Richard II*. Addressed to Richard on Charles' behalf, the *Epistre* is a lengthy and at times rambling essay rather than a letter; but neither the overloaded metaphors nor the often obtuse allegorical and Biblical allusions are able to obscure the magnitude of the grandiose design envisioned by the author.[10] To the joint undertaking of the crusade that, together with the settlement of the Great Schism, is to confirm the peace, de Mézières adds a plea for another cause to which he had long been devoted, the establishment of the Militant Order of the Passion of Christ. In a passage reminiscent of Philippe de Vitri's poem on the preparations for the crusade of over half a century before in which the fleurs de lis are to lead the crusaders in retaking Palestine, the new Order that de Mézières offers Richard is to precede the two kings on their voyage to the Holy Land.[11] In conclusion de Mézières presents himself as the ardent advocate of the proposed marriage between Richard and the infant daughter of Charles VI, a union that is to serve as a bond between the two rulers, both descendants of Saint Louis and who as brothers shall embark on the reconquest of the East and on the final journey to Jerusalem.[12]

The crusade, the Order of the Passion, and the reconciliation they are to bring about between the erstwhile adversaries are symbolically repre-

sented in two large miniatures inserted at the beginning of the presentation copy of the *Epistre* now in the British Library.[13] On the second folio
Philippe de Mézières kneels to proffer his work to Richard (plate 19).[14] In
his left hand he holds aloft the banner of the *Militia Passionis Jhesu
Christi*. In the center of a red cross on a white field the banner displays
the *Agnus Dei* on a dark quarterfoil ground,[15] an image that recalls a
passage in the letter of Charles VI in which the Holy Land is said to have
been "won for us by the precious blood of the Lamb."[16] Facing the
presentation scene is an impressive full-page allegorical picture (plate
20).[17] The main area of the miniature is occupied by a parti-colored field
of blue seeded with fleurs de lis and red seeded with leopards. Superimposed on both halves of the field is a large *YHS,* the monogram of the
Savior who is to reconcile the emblems of the two opposing dynasties. In
the center of the three compartments at the top of the frontispiece is the
Crown of Thorns, not only one of the most sacred relics of the Passion but
also, as indicated in the rubric below, the Crown of Christ, "le roy de
paix." Flanking the pinnacle of the gabled canopy above are the words
*Pax vobis.* From the Crown of Thorns golden rays that are to unite the two
kings in the bonds of peace emanate toward the crown of Charles, King
of France, which surmounts the fleurs de lis at the left and at the right
toward the crown of Richard of England placed above the leopards.[18]

Several references to the insignia of the two kings in his writings
strongly suggest that Philippe de Mézières himself may have had a hand
in deciding on the layout of the frontispiece. In the *Epistre* the transformation of the leopards from ferocious animals to benign beings prepares
them for their inclusion with the fleurs de lis in the allegorical picture.
Addressing Richard as "la royale majesté des iii lupars doré," de Mézières
takes note of their change from rigor, animosity, and cruelty to gentle-
ness and love of Mont Joye.[19] Whereas no mention is made of the heraldic
lilies in the *Epistre,* the reconciliation between the emblems of England
and France that in the frontispiece was represented by their juxtaposition on the parti-colored ground beneath the monogram of the Savior
had already been envisaged by de Mézières in his *Oratio Tragedica*
written between 1389 and 1390.[20] Although he sees in the youthful and
energetic Charles VI the liberator of Jerusalem, this role cannot be
fulfilled, says de Mézières, unless God dispels the long drawn-out
conflict between the lilies and the *animalia ferocia*.[21] With the establishment of an enduring peace, however, the lamb and the lion, the leopard
and the lily can then together receive proper care and nourishment.[22]

Although Philippe de Mézières' symbolic reconciliation between the
leopards and the fleurs de lis was, in part at least, realized in the
amicable relations that were established between the two kings and their

courts, a final peace treaty eluded their best efforts, and with the news of the disastrous defeat of the Christian armies by the Turks at Nicopolis in September 1396 the project of a joint crusade, at one time enthusiastically endorsed by Richard, quickly faded into oblivion.[23] On the other hand, Johannes de Bado Aureo's veiled warning concerning the pitfalls Richard might encounter in dealing with the French turned out not to have been necessary. From the very start of the serious negotiations between the two countries through the final truce of 9 March 1396 Richard, as it has now been established, proved to be a realistic and statesmanlike negotiator.[24] And the inconstancy and fickleness attributed to the French in the *Tractatus de Armis* could with better reason have been imputed to those who in 1399 turned against the king.

Heading the list of those in rebellion against Richard was his cousin and arch-rival Henry Duke of Lancaster, the son of John of Gaunt who had once been Richard's strongest supporter. And among the first to desert his sovereign for Henry of Lancaster upon the latter's return from exile on 4 July 1399 was Richard's close friend, John Trevor,[25] that same bishop of St-Asaph whom Evan Jones, not without some justification, has proposed as the author of the *Tractatus de Armis*. And finally, after the king was ignominiously imprisoned, on 30 September 1399 in the great hall of the Palace of Westminster and in the presence of Henry of Lancaster, who was waiting to assume his seat on the vacant throne, Bishop Trevor, in spite of the fact that he had previously been opposed to the king's abdication, read the sentence that formally deposed his erstwhile friend Richard of Bordeaux.[26]

## The Dual Monarchy

With the deposition of Richard II and the advent of Henry IV all hopes of a final settlement of the interminable struggle between France and England vanished, and France began that swift decline, ushered in by civil strife, that inexorably led to Agincourt, the ultimate disaster of the war. Although Henry V, the son of the Lancastrian usurper, is remembered primarily as the victor of that famous battle, his most momentous achievement was the Treaty of Troyes of 1420 that consolidated his conquests. Now at last, so it seemed, the ambitious dreams of Edward III were to be fully realized. Declared *heres Franciae* by Charles VI whose youngest daughter Catherine he was soon to wed, Henry according to the provisions of the treaty was to succeed Charles as King of France. The disinherited Dauphin, already repudiated by his father in 1418, was now also brazenly pronounced a bastard by his own mother, the sensual Isabeau de Bavière. The terms of the treaty itself, however, were far from being those imposed by a conqueror on a vanquished enemy. England and France were to remain two separate kingdoms under two separate crowns. Each country was to retain its own distinct administration, laws, and customs. But after the death of Charles VI the two crowns were now to be worn by the same sovereign, Charles' newly adopted son, the Lancastrian king. Thus the idea of the dual monarchy came into being.[27]

An eventuality not foreseen in the treaty, however, was the premature death of Henry V at Vincennes on 31 August 1422, less than two months before that of Charles VI whom he had been destined to succeed.[28] Immediately following the prayers at Charles' internment at St-Denis on 11 November Henry's infant son, who as Henry VI had already succeeded his father on the English throne, was proclaimed both King of France and King of England in the abbey church by order of the regent, his uncle the Duke of Bedford.[29] With all of the provinces of central and southern France except Gascony loyal to the Dauphin Charles and much of northern France controlled by England's great if mercurial ally, the Duke of Burgundy, the area in the north under direct English administration did not comprise much more than Normandy, the ancient patrimony of the Anglo-Norman kings, and that region centered around Paris that in the time of Philip Augustus had been the royal domain.[30] Faced with the overwhelming difficulties of imposing the Lancastrian dynasty on a divided France, the Duke of Bedford promptly took measures to coerce, on the one hand, a largely hostile population into denying the claims of the Dauphin to the succession and, on the other, to persuade them of Henry's rights to the French crown.[31] And to that end early in 1423 he commissioned the notary Laurent Calot to compose verses extolling Henry's descent from the royal houses of England and France and demonstrating that through both lines he was "Filz Saint Loys" and therefore "Roy de France à bon droit."[32] The poem in turn was intended to elucidate a genealogical chart of Henry's royal ancestry that was likewise the work of Laurent Calot. Both the chart and the poem were hung side by side in Notre-Dame, while copies were probably also distributed elsewhere.[33]

What has long been considered a reproduction of Calot's chart in Notre-Dame occupies an entire page in a book of poems and romances offered by the Earl of Shrewsbury to Margaret of Anjou on the occasion of her marriage to Henry VI in 1445 (plate 21).[34] As rendered in the illuminated copy, the chart is divided vertically into three separate sections. The portrait medallions in the narrow strip at the left represent the members of the Valois line, those on the right, Henry's English lineage beginning with Edward I.[35] In accordance with Calot's poem, at the apex of the central lozenge-shaped area is the portrait of Saint Louis, the progenitor of all the members of both royal houses with the exception of the first two Edwards of the English line. Saint Louis is followed in the central section by his immediate successors Philip III and Philip IV and by a horizontal arrangement of four medallions representing the children of Philip IV. Three of them are the last three Capetian kings of direct descent, the fourth being Isabel who is placed at the extreme right next to Edward II to whom she was wed. Hence she was not only the mother of Edward III but also the ancestor of all his later descendants, including the Lancastrians. At the bottom of the chart, the two ancestral lines bend in toward the portrait of Henry VI, which is centered directly below that of Saint Louis at the top. His mother Catherine, the daughter of Charles VI, is at the end of the Valois line at the left, while his father Henry V terminates his English lineage at the right. Two angels descend toward the head of the little boy king, each bearing a small gold crown.[36]

With some justification Henry's genealogical chart has sometimes been regarded as a visual statement of the Treaty of Troyes that offered, in theory at least, a sweeping solution to all the dynastic problems involved in the Hundred Years' War.[37] But as a pictorial creation the chart can also be fittingly regarded as an answer to that quest for a reconciliation between France and England pursued by Philippe de Mézières and that was illustrated in the allegorical picture in the presentation copy of his *Epistre au roi Richard II*. Although no direct connection between Calot's work and the frontispiece of the *Epistre* has been established, similar images and phrases nevertheless inform both Calot's chart and poem on the one hand and the allegorical picture on the other. In the first verse of the poem, "Le doulx Jhesus . . . Prince de paix" who has been grieved by the discord between the kings of France and England[38] finds his counterpart in Christ "le roy de paix" whose Crown of Thorns is placed in the central compartment at the top of the picture between the crowns of Charles VI and Richard II (plate 20). Through the sanctity of his holy life that in the text of the *Epistre* was held up by Philippe de Mézières as a model to be followed by these same two kings,[39] Saint Louis can also be said to assume a role in Henry's genealogical chart comparable to that of the Crown of Thorns in the allegorical picture[40] and becomes the source of that reconciliation that is consummated at the bottom of the chart in the person of Henry VI, in whom were finally united the two contending dynasties; and the two crowns of France and England in the lateral compartments of the picture have now become those of the dual monarchy that the two angels are about to place on the head of the little king (plate 21).

One significant difference between the chart and the allegorical picture, however, remains to be noted. Whereas in the latter the fleurs de lis and the leopards are evenly divided on the parti-colored field, in the illuminated page of the genealogy the golden lilies completely occupy the azure field in both the left and central sections, relegating the leopards entirely to the right strip. And beginning with the third medallion from the top, the emblems of France even share the ground with the leopards to form the arms of England as established by Edward III in 1340. Should this same asymmetrical pattern of fleurs de lis and leopards have occurred in Calot's original poster, it would undoubtedly have further enhanced Henry's rights to the French crown in the eyes of many who saw the chart in Notre-Dame. On the other hand, for those who were still attached to the French monarchical tradition embodied in the Salic law that prohibited a woman from succeeding to the throne or from passing on the succession to her son, the genealogy would have unequivocally debarred Henry VI from the French succession, since his descent from Louis IX is clearly shown to be derived only through the female line, that is, through Isabel, the wife of Edward II, and through his own mother Catherine.

Because of their wide circulation, of potentially greater effectiveness than Calot's work at Notre-Dame in attempting to win over the civilian population to an acceptance of Henry VI's claims was the Anglo-Gallic coinage issued by the Bedford regency immediately after the proclamation at St-Denis in 1422. The coins of Henry V struck in Normandy between 1417 and 1422 followed closely the types and denominations of those minted under Charles VI.[41] An entirely new element foreign to the earlier French currency, however, was introduced into the coinage of Henry VI. As heraldic counterparts of the two crowns and as a vivid expression of the dual monarchy, twin shields displaying the arms of France and England were used on the obverse of all the gold and silver denominations. Presumably as part of a concerted effort by the Bedford administration to strengthen the bonds with England's wavering Burgundian ally, most of these coins, as John McKenna has demonstrated, were modeled on those struck in 1387 to celebrate the union of Flanders and Burgundy under Philip the Bold.[42] But just as Henry's great seal for French affairs was adapted from the impressive *sceau de majesté* of Charles VI, though with the incongruous addition of the twin shields (plates 22, 23),[43] so the most elaborate of these Anglo-Gallic coins was inspired by Charles' "Salut d'or" commissioned in August 1421, a year before the king's death, and was thus, like Henry's seal, undoubtedly intended to emphasize the continuity of the succession between Henry VI and his Valois grandfather.

Although the phenomenal success of the "Ecu à la couronne" of 1385 had all but eliminated human and animal figures from the French coinage, an exception occurred in Charles' "Salut d'or" in which the angelic salutaton is represented by Gabriel and the Virgin Mary placed on either side of the crowned arms of France (plate 24a).[44] Far from being an irreverant intrusion, however, the shield with the three fleurs de lis, symbols of the Trinity, could be considered an acceptable substitute for the vase bearing the natural lily that in art is sometimes placed between Gabriel and the Annunciate.[45] And the fact that the plant in the vase occasionally blossoms with three separate flowers may well have provided an additional justification for replacing the vase with the arms of France on the "Salut d'or" (plate 25).[46]

In adapting Charles VI's "Salut d'or" to the requirements of Henry VI's Anglo-Gallic version, however, in order to combine the two quite different shields of the dual monarchy with Gabriel and the Annunciate, the designer of the coin was compelled to resort to an awkward overlapping and has placed the Virgin Mary, the principal figure of the Annunciation, behind and above the arms of France that were, of course, the dominant armorials in the Anglo-Gallic coinage, while Gabriel as the less important of the two personages has been relegated to a comparable position behind the leopards and the lilies of the English escutcheon (plate 24b).[47] And since, as on all the other Anglo-Gallic coins minted between 1422 and 1423, the arms of France are on the heraldic right, that is, on the viewer's left, the preferred position, the Virgin was also transferred to the place of honor on the viewer's left.

Although in Late Medieval and Renaissance art the positions of Gabriel and the Virgin are generally, as on the "Salut d'or" of Charles VI, reversed, the Annunciation from the right on Henry VI's coin was far from being unique, as has sometimes been thought.[48] One example of Parisian origin in the style of Pucelle can be cited as early as around 1340 on the embroidered mitre from the church at Sixt (plate 25).[49] On the other hand, in spite of the fact that between 1404 and 1405 the fleurs de lis on the English escutcheon had finally been permanently reduced to three,[50] the presence of the heraldic leopards nevertheless precluded any symbolic analogies that might be drawn between the triple lilies and the Trinity on Henry VI's "Salut d'or." And the ungainly juxtaposition of the figures and the shields could well have been regarded as an omen of the difficulties to be expected in attempting to impose the alien English king of the dual monarchy on a dismembered France that was also in the throes of a foreign invasion and a chaotic civil war.

# 8
# The Fleurs de Lis
# and the Holy Ampulla

### The Mumming at Windsor

ust as the two shields on Henry VI's Anglo-Gallic coinage signified two separate kingdoms united under one sovereign, so the two crowns of the dual monarchy also required two separate coronations of the same king in his dual role as sole monarch of each of the two realms. Less than nine months old at his father's death, the litle Henry, reared at Windsor where he was born, was not yet eight years old when on 6 November 1429 he was compelled to undergo the day-long ordeal of his English coronation in Westminster Abbey and the other festivities that were customary on that occasion.[1] On the following Christmas in preparation for his second crowning at Reims as king of France a theatrical divertisement commonly known as a mumming was given at Windsor in his presence. Acted out in silent pantomime, the performance was preceded by a spoken prologue that explained the events to be portrayed. The verses of the recitation were composed, not in the Parisian French or in the Norman vernacular of Edward III's time, but in the language and idiom of Chaucer and were the products of that prolific, if at times uninspired, rhymester John Lydgate, the peripatetic monk of Bury St. Edmunds and the poet laureate of his age.[2] Seemingly responsible for having been the first to elevate the usual boisterous dumb show and masquerade of a mumming to the status of a dignified literary event by the addition of an explanatory prologue, he was probably also the speaker on this occasion.[3]

As the conclusion of the poem indicates, one important purpose of the recitation was to acquaint the boy king with the sanctity of the holy ampulla that was preserved at Reims in order

> To anoint of custom kings which in France
> Justly succeed . . .
> Of which Sixth Henry, just now sitteth here,
> Right soon shall, with God's holy grace,
> As he is born by succession,
> Be well received in the same place . . .
> Receive his crown, he and his successors
> By title of right like his progenitors.[4]

The introductory verses of the recitation are followed by an extended eulogy of Saint Clotilda who had brought the true faith to France:

> When that an angel was from heaven sent
> Unto a hermit, of perfect life indeed,
> Presented it, whoso can take heed;
> A shield of azure, most sovereign by device,
> And in the field of gold three fleurs de lys.
> At Joyenval, without more obstacle,
> Fell all this case.[5]

Thereupon the pagan Clovis, at the instigation of "Saynte Cloote," embraces Christianity and exchanges the three "crepaudes" on his shield for the golden lilies. His conversion is immediately followed by a detailed account of the miraculous appearance of the dove with the ampulla during his baptism by Saint Remi. The poem concludes with the verses that have already been quoted and that anticipate the young Henry's anointing and crowning at Reims.

The more immediate purpose of this shortened version of the legend of Joyenval (the battle between Clovis and his pagan adversary is omitted) was undoubtedly to acquaint the young Henry with the divine origin and peculiarly sacred character of his French coat of arms that were included on the Anglo-Gallic coinage minted in his name as well as on his seal for French affairs. Of more basic significance, however, was the fact that the story of Clovis and the hermit of Joyenval was now deemed just as essential in initiating Henry into the mysteries of the French monarchy as the account of the appearance of the ampulla at the baptism of Clovis. And this latest additon to the wonders that made up the French monarchical cycle was at last raised to that same exalted rank that had been occupied by the legend of the holy ampulla, the oldest and for a time the only supernatural saga upon which rested the mystique of the monarchy. And the arms of France with the three fleurs de lis were now accorded the same sanctity as had for so long been bestowed on the little crystal vial containing the celestial chrism used for anointing the kings at the coronations at Reims.

The pairing of the Reims ampulla and the French royal arms as the two most important manifestations of the quasi-divine character of French kingship can be traced back in allegorical form to Guillaume de Digulleville's poem on the fleur de lis when Grace Dieu first sends the "blanc oisel" with the ointment box to Saint Remi "pour oindre mon amy" and then takes the azure cloth with three golden lilies to the king's palace.[6] Only later, however, in the popular Parisian *Romans* was the miracle of the ampulla incorporated into the various versions of the legend of Clovis and the fleurs de lis. Whereas in the reference to the baptism in the Latin poem, the canons of Joyenval refrained from any mention of the miracle, both of them, as we have seen, are briefly recalled in the *Chanson de Charles le Chauve,* while in the *Roman de la belle Helaine,* following the conversion of Clovis, the "ampolle" is delivered to Saint Remi at the baptismal rite at Reims for the sacring of the king.[7] Moreover, the union of the two legends into a continuous narrative, as it is given in the Mumming at Windsor of 1429, had already been well established in Paris, as is attested to by an illustrated poem composed in Paris in the late 1420s that was destined to introduce the young Henry once again into the mysteries of his French heritage.

## The Bedford Hours

On 23 April 1430, as a preliminary step in the preparations for his French coronation, Henry VI was brought from England to Calais and on 11 July was ensconced in Rouen, the chief city of Normandy and the main bastion of the English occupation in France.[8] And there on Christmas Eve, exactly one year after the Mumming at Windsor, Anne of Burgundy, the Duke of Bedford's wife and Henry's aunt by marriage, presented her nephew with a magnificently decorated Book of Hours, now in the British Library. The product of a Parisian atelier, the book had apparently been given to her by Bedford on the occasion of their wedding at Troyes in April 1423 or shortly before.[9] Besides numerous fully illuminated pages, the manuscript also includes on both sides of one of the two folios that were later added at the end of the book a short poem of thirty lines on the origin of the fleurs de lis and on the miracle of the ampulla (appendix 6).

A more fully developed account, in spite of its brevity, than that given by Lydgate at the Mumming at Windsor, the story of Clovis and the hermit of Joyenval in the Bedford Hours appears to be indebted both to the original legend by the canons of Joyenval and to Raoul de Presles' later abbreviated version in his Prologue to the *Cité de Dieu*. In certain details, however, the poem differs from its two prototypes, notably in the new identification that is given the adversary of Clovis. Though he is a king, as in Raoul de Presles, he is not "le roi Caudat" from "l'Alemaigne" but is named Candar or Cander and is the "roy des Gothoys," a designation probably suggested by Alaric the King of the Goths whom Clovis also defeated in the account of his battles in Gregory of Tours.[10] Of greater consequence are the changes which have been made in the general structure of the story. Instead of surreptitiously placing the fleurs de lis on her husband's arms as in the original legend, Clotilda herself now openly presents him with the azure shield bearing the golden lilies.[11] And now too, in contrast to the inverted sequence of the events in the two earlier accounts of the legend, the whole story, as in Lydgate's prologue to the Mumming at Windsor, is told in chronological order, beginning with the visit of the angel to the hermit. And finally, as in Lydgate's recitation, this latest variant of the legend of Joyenval leads immediately to the miraculous appearance of the Reims ampulla during the "regeneracion" of Clovis at the hands of Saint Remi.[12]

Benedicta Rowe, moreover, has called attention to certain phrases in Lydgate's recitation that are reminiscent of some of the verses in the Bedford Hours.[13] In view of all this, a common source can be proposed for both of these texts. And this too can only lead to the conclusion that Lydgate undoubtedly derived the material for his recitation when he was in Paris, where he is known to have been during the early months of 1426.[14] There is good reason to believe too that much of this source material stemmed from the Latin poem by the canons of Joyenval, independently of Raoul de Presles. Whereas in the Prologue to the *Cité de Dieu* the queen is mentioned only briefly and then not by name, but merely as the wife of Clovis, Lydgate's prolonged and effusive eulogy of Saint Clotilda seems to be an amplified echo of the long passages devoted to the pious deeds of this Burgundian princess in the Latin poem.[15] In the Bedford Hours other traces of the original legend can be detected in three of the small roundels that decorate the borders of the two pages on which the verses are inscribed. Subtitles at the bottom of each of the pages further identify the subject matter of these miniscule scenes (appendix 6).

Confined to illustrating only the latter portion of the poem, the series begins with the roundel in the right border of the first page (plate 26). His armor covered by a surcoat strewn with fleurs de lis and surrounded by his mounted henchmen, Clovis proceeds on a white charger toward his encounter with Candar. In the combat itself, depicted in the second roundel on the lower border, Clovis is about to slay the cowering "roy des Gothoys"; still other fighting warriors can be fleetingly glimpsed in the background. All of the contestants, however, are now on foot. Thus both of these roundels, in spite of the fact that the enemy of Clovis is a king, are also suggestive of the original Latin poem in which Clovis goes forth to keep his engagement with the local tyrant Conflat and then vaquishes him in a hand-to-hand duel. On the second page the Baptism of Clovis and the appearance of the dove with the ampulla in the left roundel is followed by the final scene in the lower border (plate 27). As the subtitle makes clear, Clovis, clothed in a royal mantle of state, is supervising the building of the abbey of Joyenval that he founded, a subject whose ultimate source can only have been the Latin poem.[16]

These little scenes, however, are incidental to the magnificent full-page miniature that faces the first page of the poem and that illustrates the opening events of the story (plate 28).[17] At the top, in the center of a star-studded sky and surrounded by a blazing aureole of cherubim and golden rays, God the Father hands over to the angel a celestial banner that bears "sur champ d'azur, ces trois fleurs de lis d'or."[18] Like those other keepers of their flocks on the night of the Nativity, the tiny figure of a shepherd on the hillside below looks up at the sky while shielding his gaze against the glory of the Lord. On the other side of the central aureole, the angel, having delivered the banner to the hermit, benignly gazes down at the aged recluse as he reveals the sacred coat of arms to Clotilda. Behind her trainbearer, a lady-in-waiting holds the prayer book and rosary of the pious queen. The sequence of the scenes culminates below in the close-up of the interior of the hall in the king's castle. Towering over his attendant squires in his resplendent suit of plate armor, the youthful, bareheaded and as yet unconverted Clovis is all but ready to depart for his encounter with Candar.[19] In accordance with the new version of the transformation of the arms of Clovis as given in the text of the poem, Clotilda herself, kneeling before her lord and accompanied by her ladies, presents him with a large shield on which she has had copied the celestial arms. Too heavy a burden for her to bear, the shield is hung from its straps by a courtier who stands in the background between Clovis and the queen. As a member of her retinue, he wears the colors of Burgundy—green, white, and black—displayed on his parti-colored headdress since, like the Duchess Anne for whom the Book of Hours was made, Clotilda was also a Burgundian princess before her marriage to the Frankish king.[20]

Much admired and often reproduced, this first surviving illustration of the divine origin of the fleurs de lis was created at a time when the emerging realism of northern painting was still bound to older conventions of medieval art. But it is precisely through this commingling of the new and the old that the artist has succeeded in fusing the reality of the courtly events portrayed with the supernatural character of the legend. Although there is no way of determining how dependent the artist of the miniature may have been for his composition on earlier pictorial representations of the same theme, of which at least one is known to have existed, he nevertheless seems to have been directly indebted for the illusionistic landscape and for the treatment of the cloud-streaked starry sky to the scene of the Visitation in one of the outstanding achievements of Parisian illumination in the first decade of the fifteenth century, the Hours of the Maréchal de Boucicaut (plate 29).[21] Among the smaller details shared by both miniatures are the diminutive trees on the lower borders and the shepherd and his flock that appear again on a distant hill in the Visitation, while Clotilda's trainbearer finds her couterparts in the two angels who are lifting up the cloak of the Virgin Mary.

Along with other aspects of the Bedford Hours, however, conflicting views have also been expressed concerning the approximate date of the additional folios containing the poem and the full-page illustration and the reason for their inclusion in the manuscript. But since the Clovis miniature as well as four others that were later inserted toward the beginning of the book that deal with the story of Noah and other Old Testament themes differ markedly in style and treatment from the rest of the decoration, it is reasonable to assume that all of these later additions were commissioned between 1429 and 1430, shortly before the presentation of the Book of Hours, in order to enhance its value in the eyes of the young king.[22] Whereas the precise reason for including the story of Noah and the other Biblical episodes remains obscure,[23] the house carpenters building the ark and the many exotic animals emerging from it after the deluge cannot have failed to have exerted a fascination for the eight-year-old Henry (plates 30, 31), while the legend of Joyenval followed by the miracle of the ampulla in both the pictures and the poem would have vividly reminded him of the Mumming at Windsor of the year before.

Just as Lydgate's recitation was intended to explain the meaning of the pantomime that followed, so the poem serves primarily as an explanatory text for the large illustration that precedes it, as is pointedly emphasized in its very wording—"cest angle," "cest hermite," "ces armes," and "ces trois fleurs de li d'or." In one important respect, however, the folios added at the end of the book differ from Lydgate's recitation. Instead of preparing the young Henry for his anointing with the celestial chrism at his coronation at Reims, in the Bedford Hours, as has been seen, both the poem and the illustrations are chiefly concerned with the legend of Joyenval.

A certain predilection for the story of Clovis and the origin of the fleurs de lis seems indeed to have existed in the family of the Duchess of Bedford. Among the many tapestries acquired by the Valois dukes of Burgundy was one depicting "L'Histoire du roi Clovis" that was ordered by Anne's grandfather Philip the Bold at Arras and given to John of Gaunt in 1376. Since it may have subsequently entered the English royal collection (it was bequeathed by John of Gaunt to Richard II), this tapestry is possibly the one referred to in a Windsor inventory of the time of Henry VIII as "an olde Cloth of State of rich Arras of King Clovis with the flower de luce."[24] Although there is no sure way of knowing if this "Cloth of State" was indeed the same as that given to John of Gaunt or exactly what specific subject matter was meant by "flower de luce," there are no such doubts concerning another tapestry. As a present for the duc de Guienne in 1412, Anne's father John the Fearless bought from André Rousseau in Paris a "drap fait de tapisserie d'or de l'Hystoire comment Dieu envoya les fleurs de lis en France qui Bailliées furent au roy Clovis."[25] Whereas neither of these works is extant, a remaining fragment still exists of the legend of Joyenval from the set of tapestries of the History of Clovis that was later acquired by Anne's brother Philip the Good.

In conclusion, since Anne herself seems to have shared with her husband a fondness for richly illuminated books, it is quite possible that before presenting the Book of Hours to her nephew she herself had commissioned the composition of the poem as an explanatory text for a set of pictures and had furthermore instructed the head of the Parisian workshop in charge of executing the illustrations to include, along with the small roundels, a full-page illustration of the story of Clovis receiving the fleurs de lis, a subject that may already have attracted her grandfather and for which her father had certainly shown an interest when he acquired the tapestry in Paris in 1412. And it may well have been Anne too who had stipulated that the colors of Burgundy be included in the costume of Clotilda's courtier, thus establishing a historical link between Anne and the queen, both of whom, as has been noted, were Burgundian princesses.

Besides these more personal reasons for the emphasis on the origin of the fleurs de lis in the Bedford Hours, it would seem indeed as though the partisans of the dual monarchy, whether Burgundian or Parisian, had made the legend of Joyenval their own at the expense of the miracle of the ampulla that in the Bedford Hours was relegated to little more than a footnote at the end of the poem. As subsequent events were to make plain, moreover, the reduced importance given the Reims ampulla in the Bedford Hours was not without relevance in preparing the young Henry for his forthcoming coronation.

## The French Coronation of Henry VI

The French coronation, which should have been the culminating act in the formal recognition of Henry VI as the only lawful king of France, turned out to be a rather hastily conceived and ill-planned attempt to bolster the waning fortunes of the Lancastrian cause. Bedford's initial military efforts had brought Brittany under English control and seemed about to result in the conquest of all of Maine, Anjou, Poitou, and Saintonge.[26] But the victories of Joan of Arc had turned the tide. In view of the worsening situation, long before Henry's arrival in France the date scheduled for the French coronation had been set forward to 16 December 1431. And since Reims was now beyond the reach of the English forces, it was decided to hold the ceremony in Notre-Dame, thereby of course renouncing all hopes of a consecration with the Reims ampulla that was the jealously guarded possession of the abbey of St-Remi. Even so, a prolonged, intricate, and expensive military maneuver was required to insure the safe conduct of the king from Rouen to Paris.[27]

The coronation festivities began auspiciously enough. At Henry's solemn entry into the city on 2 December the civic authorities, most of whom were faithful adherents of the Anglo-Burgundian party and supporters of the Treaty of Troyes that had been endorsed by the Parlement and the University, provided Henry with the most elaborate series of dramatic spectacles and religious tableaux that up to that time had ever been presented to a French king.[28] But Paris itself was in a deplorable condition. The supply routes for provisioning the city had been disrupted and some of the inhabitants had already left Paris in despair. Among those who remained many were starving.[29] And the cries of "Noël! Noël!" that rang out as the little king was escorted along the rue St-Denis were probably prompted more by hopes of a bountiful largesse than by any enthusiasm for the sovereign of the dual monarchy. The arrangements for the coronation ceremony itself had been unwisely left entirely in the hands of Bedford's uncle, Cardinal Beaufort.[30] Instead of the customary Gallic rite, the ritual chosen was that derived from the English Sarum usage, though with some revisions based on the coronation ordo of Charles V. To make matters worse, the cardinal himself officiated, much to the indignation of the bishop of Paris in whose cathedral the proceedings took place.[31] And then, adding insult to injury, after it was all over the English officers of the king made off with the large silver gilt chalice the canons of Notre-Dame had brought out from their treasury for the communion.

At the coronation banquet that followed, chaos reigned below the marble table reserved for the king. No special seating arrangements had been provided for the representatives of the Parlement and the university and for the other Parisian dignitaries who had been invited. Hence they were compelled to take their place amidst a raucous mob who had earlier invaded the hall, some of whom were guzzling up all the food they could lay their hands on, while thieves and purse-slitters roamed through the hall at will. Shortly afterwards, on Saint Stephen's day, 1432, in the bitter cold of a particularly severe winter, Henry left the stricken city without having freed the prisoners or rescinded the illegal taxes as would otherwise have been customary, while grumblings were being voiced concerning the meagerness of the bounty.[32] "At his departure," says the anonymous Bourgeois de Paris, "no one was heard to praise him, he who had been honored at his coming as no king had ever been before him."[33] Toward the end of January Henry was taken back across the Channel, never to set foot again on French soil.[34]

If the debacle of Henry's visit to Paris marked the twilight of the dual monarchy, his formal entry into the city nevertheless introduced one memorable feature that was later to become an indispensable element in the popular veneration of the kings of France. For the first time an azure cloth seeded with golden fleurs de lis completely covered the canopy that was borne by four aldermen over the head of the little king.[35] Modeled on those used during the Corpus Christi processions to shelter the sacrament, these state canopies had once before briefly appeared during Charles VI's visit to the cities of the Midi in 1389.[36] When covered with an azure cloth and fleurs de lis, as on the occasion of Henry's entry into Paris, they were particularly fitting to be known by their usual Parisian name of "ciel" from their resemblance to a star-studded sky, and they henceforth became the standard type for all those later canopies provided by the municipalities for the civic reception of French royalty.

Whereas this new use of the heraldic lilies and the azure cloth pointed toward the future of a prosperous and united France and away from the miseries that had engulfed the city, during the lavish and triumphant welcome with which Henry was received into London on 21 February 1432 and which was undoubtedly intended in part to compensate for the fiasco of his stay in Paris, he was confronted with a monumental reminder of the past that recalled Calot's genealogical chart stemming from the early years of his reign. Besides the numerous allegorical and Biblical figures stationed along his route, he was greeted with, not one, but two genealogical trees celebrating his double lineage from Saint Louis and Saint Edward.[37] In the branches of the trees, as described in the verses of the indefatigable Lydgate, were "kyngis off grete pryse; / Some bare leopardes, and some bare fleurdelys."[38] Understandably enough, however, in none of the royal imagery with which Henry was surrounded in Paris and London nor in the verses that continued to pour forth from the bard of Bury was any reference made to the holy ampulla that had been so conspicuous by its absence at Notre-Dame.[39] But there was another more compelling reason for this omission. Some five months prior to the Mumming at Windsor, the Maid of Orleans had led the Dauphin to Reims where his coronation as Charles VII took place in her presence on 17 July 1429.[40] What did it matter that the regalia was sequestered at St-Denis or that all but three of the twelve peers of France did not attend? It was the anointing with the miraculous chrism of the ampulla that counted and that in the minds of so many effectively annulled the Treaty of Troyes by which Charles VI had bequeathed his kingdom to the Lancastrians. His disinherited son, the ineffectual Dauphin, now stood forth as the only legitimate sovereign of France, a priest-king of the order of Melchisedek, imbued by his anointing with the supernatural powers of a thaumaturge.

# 9

# The Burgundian
# Illustrations of the
# Legend of Joyenval

he departure of Henry VI from France in 1432 not only foreshadowed the demise of the dual monarchy but also marked a turning point in the fortunes of the royal fleurs de lis. As has been seen in the previous chapters of this study, ever since the first half of the fourteenth century, activated by the tensions arising from the events that immediately preceded the outbreak of the Hundred Years' War, the numinous powers of the mystic lilies had repeatedly been invoked—at first by Geoffroy de Paris on behalf of Philip V's claim to the crown, then by Philippe de Vitri in support of the crusade that was initially intended to avert the impending conflict, and lastly by Guillaume de Digulleville in defense of the new Valois dynasty against a threatened encirclement of the eastern frontiers by Edward III. Later still, after half a century of devastating warfare, in a symbolic act of reconciliation with the leopards of England, the emblems of France had been called upon by Philippe de Mézières to assist in the quest for an enduring peace. And finally the French royal escutcheon, embodying the sacred symbolism of the three heraldic lilies, had been appropriated by the Lancastrians as part of their propagandistic efforts to establish the dual monarchy over a divided France.

As though propelled by the same underlying currents, the Clovis version of the origin of the arms of France had won out over its several competitors in those very same years in which the three armorial lilies had finally under Charles VI been universally recognized as the only proper number of the fleurs de lis on the royal coat of arms. The Clovis story itself, as recounted by the canons of Joyenval, had emerged from the obscurity of an isolated Premonstratensian abbey to take its place under Charles V as an intrinsic element of Raoul de Presles' monarchical cycle, and then, under the partisans of the dual monarchy, it had been raised to that same exalted position occupied by the oldest and most revered of the sagas of the royal mythology, the miracle of the holy ampulla.

This climactic moment in the fortunes of the legend, however, also coincided with the final literary phase of its evolution, when the bonds that had for so long linked the history of the fleurs de lis to the course of the Hundred Years' War were also about to be permanently severed. Although after the departure of Henry VI from France the struggle between the two warring countries continued intermittently for several more decades, with the defection of the Duke of Burgundy to Charles VII at the conclusion of the Treaty of Arras in September 1435 and the entry into Paris of Charles' royal troops in April of the following year, few doubts could have remained as to the eventual outcome of the conflict. And with the prospects of a reunited France and the lessening of the tensions that had activated the poets and the propagandists concerned with the fleurs de lis, the later changes that took place in their evolution were no longer brought about by the legend makers and the literati but by the creators of the works of art. And since the arms of France had now ceased to be effective instruments of English propaganda and the fleurs de lis on the English escutcheon no longer presented a serious challenge to the Valois monarchy but became in time as innocuous as the vain title of King of France that the English kings also continued to retain, those later manifestations of the fleurs de lis that merit our particular attention are restricted to the pictorial illustrations of their celestial origin as related in the legend of Joyenval.

## The Pictographic Illustrations

The illustrations of the legend of Joyenval with which we shall now be concerned can be divided into two main categories: the narrative scenes, examples of which have already been encountered in the four small roundels and the full-page miniature in the Bedford Hours, and those abbreviated references to the legend that are included in what may be called the pictographic representations illustrating the monarchical cycle in Raoul de Presles' Prologue to the *Cité de Dieu*. Paradoxically as it might seem, the four illuminated copies of the *Cité de Dieu* containing the frontispieces that constitute this second series and that were chiefly designed to glorify the mystique of French kingship did not originate in

Paris, where after 1436 the administrative departments of the legitimate government were gradually being reestablished, but were exclusively the products of those Flemish ateliers that flourished under those inveterate adversaries of the kings of France, the Valois dukes of Burgundy. And since two of the manuscripts containing the pictographic illustrations were commissioned by trusted advisers of Philip the Good the third of the Valois dukes, and since another copy belonged to that dedicated champion of the ducal house, Antoine de Bourgogne known as the Grand Bâtard, the most famous of Philip's many illegitimate offspring, it can readily be assumed that the sentiments they harbored toward the French monarchy reflected the attitude of the master they served. For in spite of the disputes that marred his relationships with his Valois cousins and the bitter hatred engendered by the murder of his father John the Fearless at the hands of the partisans of the Dauphin, Philip was only too glad as a Prince of France and the First Peer of the realm to assist at the coronation of Louis XI in 1461 (see genealogical chart).[1]

As Huizinga has pointed out, moreover, the Burgundian chroniclers were unanimous in declaring that the dukes never ceased to be "bon et entier Franchois."[2] And even though the most important of the territories acquired by Philip the Good were those in the Low Countries that formed an integral part of the Empire, in his *Mémoires* composed in the latter part of the fifteenth century, Olivier de la Marche, who for many years had served at the Burgundian court, could say of Philip, "il vesquit et mourut noble et entier Francois de cueur et de voulonté."[3] In still another passage in his *Mémoires* he relates how the duke's grandfather, Philip the Bold, at the very beginning of the founding of the new Burgundian state, showed his reverence for the French crown by quartering the ancient arms of Burgundy with the multiple lilies of France since, according to La Marche, the three fleurs de lis should be reserved only for the king of France and his heir apparent.[4] Although the story is palpably apocryphal and ignores the fact that the fleurs de lis on the new Burgundian arms were also on rare occasions reduced to three,[5] it nevertheless demonstrates how those who served at the ducal court attempted to explain the sometimes inexplicable attachment of the Valois dukes to the dynasty from which they sprang and with which they were so often in conflict. And in spite of the fact that he became Louis XI's inveterate enemy, one can safely assume that the Grand Bâtard, who likewise bore the new arms of Burgundy quartered with the fleurs de lis and crossed with a bar sinister,[6] saw no inconsistency in commissioning a manuscript whose frontispiece extolled the celestial origins of the emblems of France and the supernatural powers of its kings, whom he could also number among his most illustrious ancestors.

The earliest of the pictographic illustrations and the model for the other three occurs on the frontispiece of a copy of the *Cité de Dieu* commissioned sometime in the 1430s by Philip the Good's esteemed treasurer, Gui Guilbaut, whose shield supported by two angels is contained in the historiated initial at the beginning of the text (plate 32).[7] Combined with an author portrait of Saint Augustine himself and set within a rocky outdoor landscape, a novel form of pictorial shorthand has been used by the artist to illustrate the major items of the Prologue's monarchical cycle (plate 33).[8] In an age that delighted in the riddles posed by cryptic mottoes and arcane emblems of all sorts, the prospective reader of the Prologue, intrigued by these enigmatic images, would discover that the crowned eagle, the king of the birds, has been placed directly above the author's head because, according to Raoul de Presles, Saint Augustine can be called the king of the Early Church Fathers and like the eagle soars above them all. At the top of the picture, emerging from a cloud, is the sun that the eagle is able to look at directly, without flinching, just as Augustine can look directly at the other sun that is the Trinity and that he has come to know more profoundly than all the other doctors of the primitive church, whose books in the frontispiece lie scattered about him at his feet.[9]

Immediately below the sun in the middle distance is the fiery red banner of the oriflamme on its gilded staff (hence its name). Just as it is the subject of the lengthiest and most discursive of the Prologue's monarchical themes, so the oriflamme is likewise the most prominent of the objects in the frontispiece. With the exception of its narrow border, which has been added by the artist, it also appears to be a particularly faithful reproduction of the original, if one compares it with one of the earliest representations of this famous battle standard and probably the most authentic, contained in a clerestory window of the cathedral of Chartres, of around 1225 to 1230, depicting Saint Denis himself bestowing the oriflamme on the constable Jean Clément (plate 34).[10] Although in both instances the battle standard is shown fully extended, it was not, like the king's banner with the fleurs de lis, attached to a rigid frame, but it was a free-floating gonfalon whose streamers unfurled as it was carried forward in the vanguard of the army. Unlike the royal banner, too, which could be reproduced at will, the oriflamme was a unique object, the very one reputed to have been given to St-Denis by the Merovingian king Dagobert, and when not in use, according to Raoul de Presles, it was kept like a relic on the altar of the martyrs in the abbey church.[11]

In the frontispiece, beyond the oriflamme, the dove bearing the miraculous ampulla flies over the crowned figure of Clovis who, however, turns his head, not toward the dove, but in the direction of the angel who is proferring him the celestial shield (plate 33). And finally, for the sake of symmetry, the artist has included another angel, not mentioned by Raoul de Presles, who descends precipitously toward Augustine at the left. The legend of Joyenval is further illustrated topographically by a steep jagged hill labeled "Mont Joie" at the extreme right and by a stream of water representing the Fontaine des Lys that flows beneath the slablike rocks, while the small building in the background, too large nevertheless for the hermitage, was probably also intended to represent the abbey church itself.

Although the exact date of Gui Guilbaut's copy of the *Cité de Dieu* remains unknown, there can be little doubt that it was made and illuminated at Lille. Whereas Guilbaut's services to the duke of Burgundy took him elsewhere, other duties must have periodically required his presence at Lille since in 1419 he was appointed director of the accounting office at Lille, and in 1436 he was made head of the fiscal court in the same city,[12] while both his son-in-law and his grandson were governors of Lille under Philip the Good.[13] The anonymous artist responsible for the frontispiece as well as for most of the other illustrations in Guilbaut's manuscript, moreover, has been identified with the so-called Master of Guillebert de Mets, a prolific if somewhat retardataire illuminator who at this period is known to have been active in Lille and probably also in the neighboring city of Tournai.[14]

As in other works by the Master of Guillebert de Mets, the frontispiece combines the stodgy, somewhat ponderous manner of contemporary illumination in the southern Netherlands with the more antiquated features of Parisian manuscript painting represented by the tessellated background and by those diminutive trees that have already been encountered in the Clovis miniature of the Bedford Hours and in the Visitation of the Boucicaut Master (plates 28, 29, 33).[15] In startling contrast to this old-fashioned idiom is the new interpretation of the visual world that was perfected by Jan van Eyck and that is so unmistakably proclaimed by one of his followers in the second of the pictographic illustrations contained in a *Cité de Dieu* that was also calligraphed at Lille and finished in 1445 for another of Philip the Good's administrative advisors, Jean Chevrot, Bishop of Tournai (plate 35).[16] Substituting a radiant cloud-flecked sky and an extended vista of gently rolling hills for the mosaic backdrop and the cutout slabs of the rocky terrain in the earlier miniature, the artist of this second frontispiece has clarified the images and stabilized the composition by placing the oriflamme in the foreground near the center of the picture (plate 36).

Since Jean Chevrot's interest in theological matters can be inferred from the verses derived from Scripture and the patristic writers that are included in the magnificent triptych of the Seven Sacraments that he commissioned in the 1450s for his private chapel,[17] the emphasis in this frontispiece centers around Saint Augustine at the expense of the legend of Joyenval. Dispensing with any indications of the Fontaine des Lys and reducing the hill of the Montjoie to a small pile of boulders at the outer edge of the picture, the artist has prominently displayed the author enshrined in a lofty episcopal throne conspicuously placed at the further end of a large checkerboard platform. Seated on the platform are those lesser Church Fathers who have now materialized from their books that in the earlier illustration were scattered at the author's feet. Their smaller scale indicative of their inferior status, these erudite doctors appear too absorbed in their own discussions to notice the tall elegant bishop who towers above them at his writing desk.

As a complement to the figure of the author, the title of the work in which he is engaged is visualized in the middle distance, where the abbey church of Joyenval has been replaced by the City of God represented by a walled medieval town dominated by the soaring spire of a large cathedral (plate 37). The same spire and church and the same cityscape appear again in a painting of *The Virgin and Child with Two Saints and a Carthusian Monk* in the Frick Collection (plate 38), an eclectic work in which a background adapted from the distant view of a river valley in Jan van Eyck's *Madonna of the Chancellor Rolin* has been combined with an inanimate figure style alien to Eyckian art.[18] Both renderings of the cathedral, however, presumably stem from a common source, possibly a drawing, concerning whose authorship one can only speculate. But there can be little doubt that the cathedral is London's Old St. Paul's, whose central tower and spire with their supporting flying buttresses have in each instance been studiously reproduced (plates 39, 40).[19] And in spite of an occasional Flemish stepped gable, may one not also recognize in these cityscapes a portrait of fifteenth-century London itself, studded with the towers and spires of its parish churches (plates 37, 38)?

Whatever one's response may be to this latter proposal, as Frederic Lyna has successfully demonstrated by means of several Morellian comparisons, the artist of this second frontispiece can certainly be closely identified with that continuator of Eyckian traditions who was responsible for the series of miniatures ascribed to "Hand G" in the celebrated Turin-Milan Hours.[20] And since several of these miniatures are known only from the photographs made shortly before their destruction in the fire of the Turin Library in 1904, the frontispiece is all the more valuable as a surviving example of this atelier's work.[21]

Around 1445 Philip the Good began assiduously adding to his own collection of books, many of them lavishly illustrated, and that by the time of his death in 1467, numbered in the neighborhood of a thousand.[22] Fostered by his extensive patronage, a new pictorial mode of illumination evolved in the southern Netherlands that, unlike the high art of panel painting reflected in the frontispiece of Jean Chevrot's manuscript, was exclusively restricted to the lesser art of the miniaturists. And to this new naturalistic style of illumination, often surcharged with a plethora of picturesque details and anecdotal digressions, belong the last two pictographic illustrations of Raoul de Presles' Prologue.

The earlier of these two frontispieces occurs in a *Cité de Dieu*, now in the library at Turin, that was made in 1466 for the Grand Bâtard, who was not only a formidable warrior but also something of a bibliophile,[23] and his copy of the *Cité de Dieu*, composed at Lille like Guilbaut's manuscript, can thus be counted among the forty-odd volumes that have survived from his collection of books in his chateau of La Roche in the Ardennes (plate 41).[24] Uncertainty, however, still surrounds the identity of the patron of the last of the copies of the *Cité de Dieu* containing the pictographic illustrations (plate 42).[25] Warner and Gilson have indeed proposed that the arms in the lower border beneath the beginning of the Prologue might be those of the house of Saulx de Tavannes.[26] But this gives us no clue as to which member of this ancient Burgundian family might possibly have commissioned the manuscript. Nor is there any internal documentary evidence on which to base its date and provenance.

The style of the frontispiece, however, and of the nine grisaille miniatures done by another hand that illustrate the main text indicate that the manuscript was most likely illuminated in the 1470s at Bruges, since certain features of the frontispiece can be associated with the workshop of Loyset Liédet, a prolific illuminator who was active in Bruges from the mid-1460s until his death in 1478.[27] In the grisaille illustrations, the marked elongation of the figures, ultimately derived from Hugo van der Goes, is characteristic of the style of certain other miniaturists working at Bruges in the late fifteenth century (plates 43a,b).[28] The presence of this copy of the *Cité de Dieu* in the old Royal Collection of the British Library, moreover, argues for the probability of its having been among the books owned by Edward IV who is known to have acquired another manuscript of the *Cité de Dieu*, now also in the Royal Collection, that has been dated between 1473 and 1478 and that is likewise thought to have been made in Bruges.[29]

In spite of the many differences between these last two pictographic illustrations, both of them adhere somewhat more closely to the model provided by Guilbaut's copy in their inclusion of recognizable features of the Joyenval landscape. In the earlier of the two, the Fontaine des Lys can be seen flowing in a serpentine rivulet from the hill of the Montjoie (plate 41), while in the last of the illustrations, a large bright blue roof studded with golden lilies surely identifies the buildings in the background as those of the abbey of the fleurs de lis (plate 42). The similarities in pose and costume between the figure of Clovis in the frontispiece of the Bruges *Cité de Dieu* and his counterpart in the corresponding miniature in the Grand Bâtard's Lille copy also suggest some connection between the two manuscripts, in spite of their separate origins. In conclusion, it should also be noted that in all four pictographic illustrations the debonair Clovis is almost as dominant a component of the picture as is the studious Saint Augustine. Nor was this solely the result of artistic license, for it is also indicative of the importance that came to be attached to this Frankish ruler as one of the heroes of the Burgundian Pantheon along with such other notables as Hercules, Alexander the Great, and the half-mythical Carolingian worthy, Girart de Rousillion.[30]

### The Clovis Tapestries of Philip the Good

The high esteem in which the first Christian king of France was held at the Burgundian court is reflected in a grand set of tapestries of the "Histoire du fort roy Clovis" that was acquired by Philip the Good either at Arras or, as has been recently proposed, at Tournai sometime in the middle years of the century.[31] Although only two of the original set of six tapestries survive, now preserved in the museum at Reims,[32] three of those that are missing are known from the more extensive remains that still existed at Reims in the early nineteenth century and that are described and illustrated by Louis Paris and Casimir Leberthais in their monograph on the tapestries published in 1843.[33] Important additional information is provided by the Sire de Haynin in his description of five of the original set of six hangings that he saw in the ducal palace at Bruges in 1468.[34] And to judge from these indications, they not only must have constituted the largest and most extensive pictorial record of the exploits of this Merovingian ruler, but they also included what was probably the most monumental of the narrative illustrations of the legend of Joyenval, a subject that, it may be recalled, had attracted Philip's father, John the Fearless, when he acquired the tapestry for the duc de Guienne in 1412 and that his sister Anne had chosen for two of the folios that were added to the Bedford Hours between 1429 and 1430.[35]

Based mainly on the *Grandes Chroniques de France*,[36] the set begins chronologically with the coronation of Clovis, the first event of his reign, followed by the taking of the city of Soissons, both episodes represented on one of the extant tapestries at Reims (plate 44a). The "Histoire" continued on the next two tapestries with the courtship of Clotilda by an emissary of Clovis at the court of her uncle Gondebaud, the King of Burgundy, followed by the marriage ceremony itself and concluding with the conversion of Clovis during the battle with the Alemanni and the miracle of the ampulla at his baptism. The other extant tapestry, which was the fourth of the original set, depicts the founding of a church in Paris by Clovis and Clotilda (plate 44b), his victory over the evil Gondebaud and the miracle of the stag who led his Frankish army across the river Vienne in pursuit of Alaric the Goth.[37]

No trace of the fifth tapestry is recorded at Reims by Louis Paris nor does it seem to have been among those seen by the Sire de Haynin at Bruges.[38] By the 1840s only a tattered fragment remained of the sixth tapestry that featured the legend of Joyenval and on which Louis Paris claimed one could still distinguished the hermit standing on the thresh-old of his church and raising his eyes heavenwards as the angel de-scended towards him bearing an azure banner with the golden lilies. Nearby were Clovis and Clotilda and the warriors of the king's army with his ensign of the "trois crapauds."[39] All that now survives are the bearded head and shoulders of the ancient anchorite gazing, not heaven-wards, but towards the ground and beyond him the head of the queen, both still visible, along with the azure banner, among the small rem-nants from various tapestries that have been used as fillers for a large square gap in the second of the two extant tapestries at Reims (plate 44c).

As can be gathered from the "ensigne des trois crapauds" mentioned by Louis Paris in his description of the sixth tapestry, since the gift of the celestial arms occurred at the very end of the "Histoire," throughout the set the king's banners continued to display his original emblems of three black toads on a light golden field. Nor could this Burgundian variant of the legend of Joyenval have had any connection with the conversion of Clovis that chronologically had taken place long before. But as the culminating wonder in the whole preceding series of events, the heavenly gift of the fleurs de lis also assumed a new significance in placing the seal of divine approval on the king's earlier conquests. Thereby, too, in the words of the last lines of the accompanying inscription, he was assured of still further triumphs in his future career and an enduring fame.[40]

In spite of the preponderance of the battle scenes, however, the tapestries also contained another message that must have had a special appeal for Philip the Good. In the numerous instances throughout the set in which Clotilda appears with Clovis—in their marriage ceremony and at his baptism and again in supervising the construction of the new Parisian church of St-Peter and St-Paul (plate 44b) that, later rededicated to Sainte Geneviève, the patroness of Paris, was to become the site of their final resting place, and lastly in the legend of Joyenval—the queen is revealed, not only as the one who was instrumental in the conversion of her husband, but also as the cofounder with him of the Christian monarchy. Moreover, according to the Burgundian chroniclers, she was likewise the daughter of the rightful king of Burgundy who had been murdered by his treacherous brother Gondebaud.[41] For if Philip the Good could be proud of his Merovingian lineage and could be hailed by Jean Waukelin in his preface to the *Chroniques de Hainaut* as descended from the high noble blood of the Trojans,[42] the fabled forebears of the Merovingian line, he could also regard himself as the heir to the ancient kings of Burgundy who had embraced the faith long before Clovis, when one of their number was converted by Mary Magdalene and whose godfather at his baptism was none other than Saint Trophime of Arles, the reputed nephew of the apostle Paul.[43] And the claim put forward by the French literati, from Raoul de Presles and Eustache Deschamps to Jouvenel des Ursins and other still later writers, that Clovis was "le premier roy crestien," the first of all Christian kings,[44] was effectively refuted by the Burgundians who simply added a short qualifying phrase to this resounding title and repeatedly referred to the Frankish rule as "le premier roy crestien de France."[45] And even after the death in 1477 of Charles the Bold, the last of the Valois dukes, and the dissolution of their empire, the die-hard Burgundian patriot Philippe Barton in his *Chroniques de Bourgogne,* composed shortly before 1486, could still proudly say, "et estoit xpistiens les roix de Bourgogne longtemps avant qu'il y eust roy crestien en France."[46]

# 10
# The Frontispiece
# of the Mâcon *Cité de Dieu*

lthough little is known concerning the narrative illustration of the legend of Joyenval that figured in Philip the Good's Clovis tapestries, the Parisian traditions that evolved from the full-page miniature of the origins of the fleurs de lis in the Bedford Hours are brilliantly represented in a magnificently illuminated frontispiece illustrating the monarchical cycle of Raoul de Presles' Prologue in a copy of the *Cité de Dieu* now in the library at Mâcon (plate 45).[1] Whereas no clue exists as to the identity of the patron of the manuscript, Alexandre Delaborde has nevertheless assumed that he was someone close to Charles de Gaucourt, who was counselor and chamberlain to Louis XI, since another *Cité de Dieu* made in 1473 for de Gaucourt apparently served as the general model for the Mâcon copy, which can thus be dated shortly after 1473.[2]

Created during that last flowering of French manuscript painting initiated by its foremost fifteenth-century practitioner, the celebrated Jean Fouquet, the Mâcon illustration of Raoul de Presles' monarchical cycle has recently been ascribed by Nicole Reynaud to a prolific and talented artist to whom Paul Durrieu originally gave the name of the Master of Coëtivy and whom he later tentatively identified as Henri de Vulcop, painter and illuminator to Charles of France, the younger brother of Louis XI.[3] Some of the hallmarks of this artist's style can indeed be recognized in the frontispiece, such as the rustic features of the bearded figures with drawn-in mouths and jutting beards, as well as the delicate vernal color scheme and the general Flemish character of his work.[4] His fondness, moreover, for cryptic inscriptions, which prompted him to include in the frontispiece the apparently meaningless lettering below the traceried parapet of the Gothic church in which the baptism of Clovis is being enacted (plate 48), has also been noted by Durrieu in other miniatures by the Master of Coëtivy.[5] Similar arcane inscriptions occur again on several of the architectural elements in a series of preliminary cartoons made for a set of Trojan War tapestries that has likewise been attributed by Nicole Reynaud to this same artist.[6] The same talent for marshalling the myriad figures into a coherent series of separate events in the cartoons is also evident in the even more successful organization of the ten separate scenes, including four for the legend of Joyenval, that make up the subject matter of the frontispiece.

Although the identification of the Master of Coëtivy with Henri de Vulcop, first put forward by Durrieu and reinforced by Reynaud, has much that is commendable, it remains, nevertheless, only in the realm of an unproven hypothesis. And even if the artist's activities may indeed have centered at Bourges, where Henri de Vulcop appears to have settled after 1463, considering the relationship of the Mâcon *Cité de Dieu* to the copy made for Charles de Gaucourt, who in 1472 was appointed governor of Paris, and considering the Parisian sources that the artist has used in illustrating the Prologue, as well as the firsthand knowledge he shows of one important monument in the immediate vicinity of Paris, the frontispiece can be regarded, in the treatment of its subject matter at least, as stemming primarily from a Parisian milieu.

In line with a growing tendency in manuscript illumination during the second half of the fifteenth century to integrate the painted picture with the accompanying text by means of various illusionistic devices, the beginning of the Prologue in the frontispiece is conceived as having been written on two rectangular placards suspended in front of the lower portion of the painting, but at the same time slightly behind the frontal plane occupied by the foreground figures at the bottom of the illustration, so that the tops of some of their heads can be seen protruding over the lower edge of the unpainted vellum (plate 45). And here, in the portion of the miniature that is visible between the two parts of the text and that continues below in the horizontal space at the left, is the first of the series of subjects inspired by the Prologue. But instead of Saint Augustine at his writing desk, as in the Burgundian pictographic illustrations, the artist has depicted Raoul de Presles himself who kneels to offer his work to Charles V (plate 46), a theme which can be directly associated with the opening words of the dedication that is inscribed above: "A vous, tres excellent Prince, Charles le quint, roy de France . . ."

And in place of the crowned eagle in the pictographic illustrations that was likened by Raoul de Presles to Saint Augustine, above the head of Charles is the Roman eagle that in the Prologue is associated with Charles V because, says Raoul de Presles, as the most powerful Christian king he can consider himself heir to the Roman emperors (appendix 4.1).

The choice of the presentation scene rather than the portrait of Saint Augustine follows a Parisian precedent that was first established in Charles' own dedication copy of the *Cité de Dieu* where in the small vignette at the top of the opening page the seated king likewise receives the manuscript at the hands of Raoul de Presles (plate 7). Closer to the composition in the Mâcon frontispiece, however, with its rectangular format and numerous subordinate figures, including those of two small youths, is the presentation scene in another manuscript owned by Charles V, that of the *Songe du Vergier* of 1378, where another little boy stands behind the throne (plate 47).[7] A clue to his identity is provided by the two ermine bands on the shoulders of his cloak that according to contemporary usage are the distinguishing marks of a member of the royal house and thus probably identify him as the future Charles VI.[8] In a related presentation scene in a later Parisian copy of the *Cité de Dieu* of around 1410, where the figures have been somewhat rearranged to conform to the square format of the miniature, the young Charles wears an even more elaborate court costume topped by a feathered hat.[9]

It should be added, however, that if the two small youths in the Mâcon frontispiece were indeed ultimately derived from the boy in Charles V's copy of the *Songe du Vergier*, nothing indicates that either of them could have been intended to represent the heir to the throne. The manuscript of the *Songe,* moreover, could hardly have been available to the artist of the Mâcon frontispiece since it was one of the books in Charles V's library that was purchased in 1425 by the Duke of Bedford and that was subsequently acquired by his brother Humphrey Duke of Gloucester.[10] One must therefore assume that the artist of the frontispiece was acquainted with a later version of the miniature or with a sketch preserved in a collection of drawings in a Parisian workshop.

Guided by the sequence of the items in the Prologue, which are not always arranged in chronological order, our circuitous journey through the main area of the painting begins inside the spacious entrance to the Late Gothic church, where is being enacted the familiar appearance of the ampulla at the baptism of Clovis (plate 48). In spite of the fact that, with the inclusion of the dove, there are only three principals in this little drama as compared to the more numerous participants in the other scenes, the energetic gesture of Saint Remi as he reaches up for the ampulla and the silhouette of the white dove against the dark interior immediately arrest our attention, so that the miracle at the baptism, on which was founded the whole supernatural character of the monarchy, becomes in the painting the focal center of the entire composition. And to this central theme the artist has added two separate episodes that are connected with the baptism but that Raoul de Presles has not included in his Prologue.

According to the *Grandes Chroniques* and its earlier sources, prior to the baptismal rite, Saint Remi, at the urging of Clotilda, instructed Clovis in her presence on matters concerning the faith,[11] an incident that is illustrated in the sanctuary of the little church where the bishop of Reims is indoctrinating the king, who raises both hands in a gesture of receptivity (plate 48). Nearby, in watchful attendance, stands the queen herself in a dark blue gown with a white ermine bodice and a red outer skirt, on the edge of whose train there nestles a little dog. Of greater significance, however, than this introductory episode is the epilogue to the miracle that adds a new element to the traditional tenets of the monarchical cycle.

Although in the Prologue he reminds Charles V that through his anointing with the holy chrism at his coronation at Reims he, as well as his predecessors, were all endowed with the power of curing that "tres horrible maladie" known as the "escroelles" or scrofula, Raoul de Presles fails to address himself to the crucial question as to whether or not Clovis was similarly endowed as a result of his baptismal unction. According to Marc Bloch in his study of the thaumaturgical powers of the kings, evidence for the belief that Clovis also possessed the ability to cure scrofula does not appear until 1579, when it was incorporated into a little anecdote concerning Clovis and his equerry Lanicet by Etienne Forcatel of Béziers, who included it in a treatise published in that year.[12] As P. S. Lewis has pointed out, however, the scene that forms the epilogue to the miracle of the "sainte ampoule" in the Mâcon frontispiece provides conclusive evidence that this belief was already current a full century before the appearance of Forcatel's little legend.[13]

Preceded by a group of courtiers who are emerging from the interior of the church where the baptism is taking place, Clovis can again be recognized, crowned and clothed in the same dark blue mantle lined with ermine and long tunic spangled with fleurs de lis that he was previously wearing in the introductory scene (plate 48). In front of him kneels a youth whose neck the king is lightly touching with his left hand. Two other youths are kneeling in the foreground, one of whom is pointing to his neck, the usual region of the scrofulitic sores.[14]

Graphic as is this illustration of the king's curative touch, is it indeed the earliest testimony to Clovis' thaumaturgical powers, as Lewis has claimed? In stating that he had been unable to find any evidence prior to 1579 for such a belief, Marc Bloch has nevertheless called attention to a passage in an address to Pope Pius II delivered at Mantua by the ambassadors of Charles VII in 1459 in which they expressed themselves, to quote Marc Bloch, "comme s'ils pensaient que Clovis avait déjà guéri les écrouelles." But, says Bloch, "ils semblent bien avoir été tout simplement entraînés par un mouvement d'eloquence, plutot qu'ils ne font allusion à un trait légendaire précis."[15] However, in spite of the convoluted Latin in which the representatives expressed themselves and the lacunae in the text itself, as reproduced in Luc d'Achéry's *Spicilegium*,[16] in view of the scene in the Mâcon frontispiece this passage of the discourse, rather than mere rhetoric, can now be taken as indicative that by the late 1450s Clovis was indeed thought to have possessed the ability to cure scrofula, and the contention of P. S. Lewis that the scene in the frontispiece is the very earliest witness to this belief can now also be amended.

However important in adding to the contemporary repertory of the monarchical cycle, the epilogue to the baptism is nevertheless incidental to the panoramic illustration of the legend of Joyenval that occupies most of the right-hand section of the frontispiece (plate 45) and whose composition is modeled on the same general scheme used in the full-page illustration of Clovis and the Origin of the Fleurs de Lis in the Bedford Hours (plate 28). Moreover, unlike the presentation copy of the *Songe du Vergier* that was taken across the Channel, the artist of the Mâcon *Cité de Dieu* may well have had access to the original illustration, since the Bedford Hours apparently remained in Rouen after the departure of the English and from there eventually found its way into the French royal library.[17]

As in the Bedford miniature, the series of events in the frontispiece begins in the more distant upper regions of the landscape with the story of the hermit, here illustrated in three separate scenes, each of which features the little hermitage and the bright waters of the Fontaine des Lys (plate 49). At the left, Clotilda, as was her wont, brings the ancient recluse his daily sustenance of bread and water; in the center, veiled in darkness, the hermit kneels to receive the shield from the angel and at the right he hands it over to the queen. The larger portion of the four-part illustration depicts various stages in the battle between the army of Clovis and that of the "roy Caudat" of the Prologue. Like Clotilda in the interior of the castle in the Bedford miniature, beyond the lower edge of the massed warriors the queen herself presents the shield with the fleurs de lis directly to her husband, who is already mounted on his war-horse (plate 48). Above and behind him the banners suspended from the trumpets of his two heralds display the king's pagan emblems that are not, however, the usual toads of the *Songe du Vergier,* but the original crescents of the Prologue. Overhead, in token of his conversion, his red and gold banner is inscribed "le roi Clovis premier roi cretien" (plate 49).

In the middle distance, amidst the melee of the battle, Clovis raises his weapon as he is about to deliver the death blow to the "roy Caudat" who is reeling backwards on his white charger. Beyond them, in conformity with the topography of the battle as described by Raoul de Presles, "combien que la bataille commencast en la valée, toutevoies fu elle achevée en la monteinge (appendix 4, 5)," the warriors of the enemy can be seen fleeing through a deep gorge toward the distant mountain of the Montjoie.

Together with the story of the origin of the fleurs de lis Raoul de Presles was the first to integrate into the monarchical cycle an account of the ritualistic reception of the oriflamme at St-Denis (appendix 4.8–10), a theme that proclaimed the age-old attachment of the monarchy to the abbey and that likewise introduced into the Prologue that most revered of Charles V's ancestors, the emperor Charlemagne, who was also said to have obtained the oriflamme at St-Denis before embarking on his legendary crusade (appendix 4.11).

Near the lower right-hand corner of the frontispiece, the figure of the emperor can be recognized by his imperial crown and by his emblems of the eagle and the fleurs de lis displayed on his parti-colored surcoat (plate 50).[18] Reverently kneeling before him, the abbot of St-Denis hands him the red battle standard, whose streamers are hidden behind one of the superimposed placards of the text. Behind the abbot a procession of the inmates of the monastery are emerging from an outer doorway of the abbey's precinct. As can be appreciated by comparing this "portrait" of St-Denis with the cavalier view of the monastery in Michel Germain's seventeenth-century *Monasticon Gallicanum* (plate 51), the artist has correctly indicated the curving boundary of the abbey precinct and the great Rayonnant rose of the south transept of the abbey church. Although otherwise he has made no attempt to give an accurate rendering of the main body of the church, like the central tower of London's Old St. Paul's in the frontispiece to Jean Chevrot's *Cité de Dieu* he has nevertheless faithfully reproduced the south tower of Suger's twelfth-century facade and the thirteenth-century spire that surmounts its northern neighbor (plate 45). The scene terminates at the bottom of the painting with a lively group of the emperor's equerries (plate 50). In their midst is Charlemagne's white horse already saddled for the long journey to the East and the retaking of Jerusalem, a blue cloth with three golden fleurs de lis hanging from its side.

With Charlemagne receiving the battle standard our own journey through the multifaceted incidents and legendary wonders of the miniature has come full circle. But this is not the end. One final episode has been reserved for the historiated initial at the beginning of the text that explains why the emperor embarked on his crusade and how he learned of the oriflamme. As related in the *Grandes Chroniques,* the emperor Constantine of Constantinople had written to Charlemagne, entreating him to liberate his Christian subjects from their bondage to the Saracens. His letter, he says, was prompted by a nocturnal vision in which he saw at the foot of his bed a mounted knight accoutred in full armor and holding the gilded shaft of a lance, from whose top there issued a flame.[19] "Et comme il feust en grant perplexité de savoir quele signification c'estoit," says Raoul de Presles in describing the vision, "un angre (ange) s'apparut a luy, qui dist que celui qu'il avoit veu, c'estoit celui qui deliveroit le pays de Sarrasins." Whereupon Constantine immediately knew that the mounted knight was "le roy Charlemaigne" (appendix 4.13–14). And it is this nocturnal vision, painted as a night scene in grisaille with sharp linear highlights against a dark background, that has been chosen for the historiated initial (plate 46) and that as the last of the items in Raoul de Presles' monarchical cycle fittingly introduces the reader to the text of the Prologue.

Ingenious as is the intricate compositional structure of the frontispiece, it should not be overlooked that a full century separates the painting from the Prologue. Although the artist has in many instances adhered closely to the details in Raoul de Presles' text, by adding the two supplementary scenes to the miracle at the baptism he has not only enhanced the role of Clovis as the dominant figure of the entire painting, but has also introduced a new pictorial concept of the Merovingian ruler, not that of the conquering hero of Philip the Good's tapestries, decked out in fantastic armor (plate 44a), nor yet that of the youthful romantic figure of the pictographic illustrations (plates 33, 36, 41, 42), but a benign patriarch whose crown and dark blue robes spangled with fleurs de lis are echoed in the presentation scene below (plates 46, 48).

In certain texts of the French literati this revised image of Clovis had already begun to emerge with some clarity in the late 1420s, when he is described as a paragon of the Christian virtues and even in some instances is referred to as a saint;[20] while references to Saint Clovis continue to occur throughout the fifteenth century, even in a few official documents.[21] By the 1450s, as the ideal type of French king and as the territorial founder of the nation, he could now be regarded as the model and counterpart of Charles VII, who with divine assistance had reestablished the new France that almost miraculously, as it must have seemed, was reconstituted from its dismembered fragments.[22] In this same decade of the 1450s, when peace and tranquility had descended upon a reunited, if still war-ravaged, realm,[23] the Merovingian ruler became the recipient of the full set of sacred objects and attributes pertaining to the religion of the monarchy. Not only was he given the celestial arms and was anointed with the miraculous chrism by which he was endowed with healing powers; the oriflamme, once claimed to have been donated to the abbey of St-Denis by Dagobert, was now also said to have been bestowed upon Clovis as a heavenly gift.[24]

Changes, however, had occurred in the status of this famous *vexillum.* Although the war cry "Montejoie-Saint Denis!" was still occassionally heard on the battlefields, the oriflamme itself had long since been permanently retired as a museum piece among the other relics of the royal abbey.[25] And the old feudal levies, headed by the mounted nobility, which it had once led to ignominious defeat at Poitiers and Agincourt, had finally been replaced by a standing army whose insignia was a white cross worn by the troops as a badge on their clothing.[26]

In other ways, too, the new age was announcing itself. In 1462 the first examples of a printed book, Fust's folio Bible, were seen in Paris,[27] and in the summer of 1470 appeared the very first book printed in France, a Parisian copy of the collection of the letters of Gasparin of Bergamo, in elegant Latin. Printing presses were also being established in the provinces. The earliest printed book in French, an edition of *La Légende dorée,* was published in Lyons in 1476.[28] With few exceptions, moreover, the illustrations in these early printed books were supplied, not by hand-painted miniatures, each a unique creation, but by easily reproduced black-and-white woodcuts whose sharp angular strokes harmonized with the angularity of the contemporary Gothic script imitated by the type cutters.

Among the most notable of these illustrated incunables can be counted an edition of the *Cité de Dieu* printed at Abbeville in northern France in 1486.[29] As was the custom with other provincial publications, the woodblocks with which it is embellished were executed in Paris, in this case in the atelier of Jean du Pré, who also happened to be a close associate of the Abbeville printer, Pierre Gérard. The compositions themselves, however, appear to have been inspired by the miniatures of the Turin copy of the *Cité de Dieu* that was illuminated at Lille in 1466 for the Grand Bâtard who, coincidentally, had enthusiastically entered into the service of his erstwhile enemy, Louis XI, less than a decade earlier as a result of his capture at the battle of Nancy in 1477.[30]

This union, if we can so call it, of Paris and what had formerly been Burgundian Flanders in the creation of the Abbeville illustrations is strikingly represented in the frontispiece (plate 52). Whereas the portrait of Saint Augustine and the pictographic images in the frontal plane of the picture were ostensibly borrowed from the Grand Bâtard's Turin copy (plate 41), the presentation scene in the middle ground, rendered lengthwise in profile view, and, in the farther distance, the reception of the celestial arms by the kneeling hermit hark back to the Parisian traditions incorporated in the miniature of the Mâcon *Cité de Dieu* (plate 45). In the Abbeville woodcut, a curious stereometric effect has been created by the two almost identical arms-bearing angels who, one behind the other, seem to be defining the exact distance that separates the background from the frontal plane and its Burgundian-Flemish pictographs (plate 52). In the far distance, beyond the conventual buildings of the abbey of Joyenval, appears the pyramidal hill of the Montjoie, while at the extreme right, behind the figure of Clovis, Raoul de Presles himself can be seen in a small writing booth at work on his translation.

With this merger of the two contrasting modes of illustrating the monarchical cycle, which up to this time had led independent existences, the Abbeville frontispiece can be said to have closed the portal, as it were, on a segment of the past. In a later woodcut by this same engraver the now all too familiar themes of the baptism of Clovis and the celestial origin of the fleurs de lis have been drastically reinterpreted in terms of the changing attitudes of the new age and its expanding world.

# 11
# Pierre le Rouge's Double Illustration in *La Mer des Histoires*

ecause of their high quality the woodcuts of the Abbeville *Cité de Dieu* of 1486 have generally been credited to the outstanding Parisian engraver of the period, Pierre le Rouge. This attribution is further confirmed by several details in the Abbeville frontispiece that are found again in Pierre le Rouge's best-known work, a double illustration of the baptism of Clovis and the legend of Joyenval that first appeared several years later in an edition of *La Mer des Histoires* of 1488.[1] As can be seen in the upper right-hand section of this more ambitious composition (plate 53), the angel and the kneeling hermit, as well as the tall tower behind him, are but enlarged duplicates of the same subjects in the earlier engraving (plate 52).

Although the general layout of Pierre le Rouge's woodcut, as was pointed out long ago by Alexandre de Laborde, is undeniably reminiscent of the Mâcon frontispiece (plates 45, 53),[2] the marked division between the two halves of the double illustration separates it conclusively from the tapestrylike work of the earlier miniature, and the scene of the baptism, which is interior, static, and ritualistic, has been effectively contrasted with the legend of Joyenval, which is suffused with an explosive energy. This juxtaposition of the opposites is further enunciated in the two contrasting figures of Clovis who in the lower section of the baptism humbly presents himself to the circle of attendant bishops and, in the legend of Joyenval, threateningly brandishes his sword over his head while astride his charging war-horse.

These visual contrasts are accompanied by new and opposing inter-
pretations of the content. On the one hand, both the holy ampulla and
the celestial arms are now being delivered simultaneously to the kneeling hermit (plate 53), a concurrency that, however much a distortion of
the legends, is nevertheless symptomatic of the inseparable ties with
which these two monarchical themes were now bound together in the
popular imagination until they had become for most pictorial purposes
well-nigh interchangeable.[3] On the other hand, the resultant omission
of the miraculous appearance of the dove in the scene of the baptism and
its replacement by the rite of the baptism by water has not only brought
into clear visual focus the claim that Clovis was the first of the Christian
kings, but the omission of the ampulla in the baptism can also be seen as
indicative of the reduced importance that was by this time attributed to
its role in the coronation ceremony. As Marc Bloch has shown, ever since
the coronation of Charles VIII in 1484, the members of his court had
attributed his healing powers, not to the anointing with the celestial
chrism, but to the intercession of an obscure Merovingian holy man,
Saint Marcoul, to whose shrine in the immediate vicinity of Reims the
kings were wont to repair immediately after their crowning.[4]

Other drastic changes have been made in Pierre le Rouge's reduced
rendering of the legend of Joyenval. Now all but eliminated from the
story, Clotilda is relegated to a single episode in the first of the three
scenes at the top of the illustration, where she is vigorously pointing out
a crucifix to her unbelieving husband,[5] while below them the hermit
hands over the banner with the three fleurs de lis, not to the queen, but
to Clovis himself who stands before him, his tabard adorned with three
"crapauds."

The most startling innovations, however, have been reserved for the
battle scene which has been completely transformed from the encounter
with the "roy Caudat" of Raoul de Presles' Prologue into an illustration of
the victory of Clovis over the Alemanni mentioned briefly in the text
(nothing whatsoever is said in the Mer des Histoires concerning the
origins of the fleurs de lis). Although in the woodcut a precedent for the
double-headed eagle of the Empire on the banner of the fleeing Alemanni had long ago been established in the grisaille illustration of the battle
in Yves' Life of Saint Denis where it appears in its earlier unicephalic form
(plate 6), unprecedented, as far as I know, is the elevation of the "roy
d'Alemaigne," mentioned as the leader of the "Alemanz" in both the
Grandes Chroniques and the Mer des Histoires, to the prestigious rank of a
Holy Roman Emperor (plate 53). Wearing a large imperial crown and a
short tunic adorned with still more eagles, he can be seen in the middle
distance, fleeing from the advancing enemy with no more signs of injury

than an arrow stuck in the right buttock of his horse. Nor could he, as is the leader of the Alemanni in other representations of the battle, have been depicted on the verge of imminent death at the hands of Clovis, since there is every reason to believe that the aged ruler in the engraving was also intended to represent the contemporary Hapsburg emperor Frederick III who, in spite of his advanced years, continued to reign until 1493.[6]

The allusion to the emperor, moreover, is underlined by the prominent figure of the youth riding next to him who is made still more conspicuous by the three tall plumes in his hat, for he can be none other than Frederick's better-known son Maximilian who had been elected King of the Romans and future emperor in 1486.[7] Hence his own banner in the woodcut bears the appropriate monogram S. P. Q. R., already familiar to Jean Golein in the time of Charles V as the initials for *Senatus Populusque Romanus*.[8] And the whole scene, more rout than battle, now assumes the aspects of a contemporary military encounter in which, under the aegis of the fleurs de lis, the spearmen of the French army are tumultuously rushing forward in pursuit of the German lancers who flank the emperor and his son, not one of whom turns to defy the enemy. The same theme of France overcoming the forces of the Empire is illustrated in the foreground by the prominent figure of the "roy Clovis," beneath whose war-horse lies the imperial banner with the double-headed eagle, now attached to a mere fragment of its broken staff. Another fragment of the staff has pierced the breast of the banner bearer himself, who expires while still astride his prostrate steed.

These topical allusions were particularly timely in the late 1480s in view of the hostilities that had already existed for over a decade between France and the Empire. At the death of Charles the Bold without male issue in January 1477, Louis XI had immediately undertaken a swift military campaign that resulted in the annexation to the royal domain of most of the lands that the Valois dukes had held in France. This aggressive act in turn soon brought him into direct conflict with Maximilian of Austria who in April of that same year married Charles' only child, Mary. Thus she brought to her husband the whole of the Burgundian inheritance, which he now felt obliged to defend. Although he attempted to take the offensive, the young Maximilian soon found himself in a hopeless military situation and in December 1482 he was compelled to accede to the Treaty of Arras, which legalized all of the French king's conquests.[9]

In the unsettled conditions that prevailed during the regency of Louis XI's son Charles VIII, who succeeded to the throne in 1483 at the age of thirteen, Maximilian saw what he thought was a golden opportunity to recapture the lost provinces and to rid himself once and for all of the French threat to the Burgundian inheritance.[10] Again the headstrong young Duke of Austria took the offensive, only to be again confronted with the superior power and effectiveness of the French forces who were attacking the Low Countries by land and by sea. To confound his misfortunes Maximilian, who had vowed to wipe France off the face of the map, was now obliged to allow his Swiss troops to return to their homeland, since they were not permitted by the Swiss authorities to fight against the French, while soon afterwards his German "Landsknechte" began leaving him in droves for want of pay; whereupon the impecunious young duke retired to Antwerp and then to Brussels, where he bade farewell to his father, who was occupying himself with the "Ostpolitik" of the Empire while his son attempted to deal with the West.

In July 1487 this on-again, off-again warfare suddenly turned into a catastrophic defeat for Maximilian's imperial army when at Béthune in the Artois they were overwhelmed by the French forces from both sides and suffered by far the severest casualties of the entire war.

Similar opposing aspects of the conflict can be detected in the woodcut, where the comic situation inherent in the flight of the imperial pair, who have nothing more belligerent to present to the enemy than the rumps of their horses, is contrasted in the foreground with the agony of the dying banner bearer and the gruesome details of the dismembered body that lies on the ground before him (plate 53). Although there is no evidence by which to conclude that these grim reminders of the carnage of the battlefield might have been intended to commemorate the defeat of the imperial army at Béthune, Pierre le Rouge would have had every reason to be interested in the progress of the war since he himself originally stemmed from Chablis in the old French province of Burgundy, where he had set up a printing press before migrating to Paris.[11] Granted the title of "imprimeur du roi" in 1488, he must also have realized that these allusions to the victory over the Empire would have been especially appreciated by the young Charles VIII, who was presented with a deluxe copy on vellum of this edition of *La Mer des Histoires*.[12] The appearance in February 1489 (1488 Old Style) of the second volume with the woodcut came, moreover, at a particularly opportune moment for its presentation to the king, at a time when the Flemish cities, in revolt against Maximilian, were declaring their allegiance to the crown of France, and the luckless king of Rome and future emperor was experiencing the ultimate indignity of the war as a prisoner of the citizens of Bruges.[13]

The allusions to the war over the Burgundian inheritance, however, cannot have been solely responsible for the phenomenal success of

Pierre le Rouge's woodcut. Reprinted again and again, it was also copied in a wide variety of versions (plate 54) which, however inferior or distorted they may be, nevertheless attest to the continued popularity of Pierre le Rouge's double illustration far into the first half of the sixteenth century, long after the conflict with Maximilian had been resolved in October 1492.[14] Above all, the mounted figure of Clovis in the legend of Joyenval must have continued to exert a fascination throughout these years (plate 53). Cast in the same mold as is the conquering hero of the Burgundian tapestries (plate 44c), this is, however, no fantastically conceived figure appropriate for a court pageant, but an image of the fervent militancy of a resurgent nation that was the legacy of Louis XI, the unloved king who had, nevertheless, restored the prestige of France until it had once again become the most powerful realm in Christendom and now also the most feared.[15]

The use of the legend of Joyenval, however, as a mere vehicle for the expression of a more militant patriotism, like the omission of the ampulla in the baptism of Clovis, can also be seen as symptomatic of the reduced importance accorded the monarchical beliefs in the more so-phisticated and skeptical society of the new age. Although a miniature in a manuscript copy of Noël de Fribois' *Abrégée des croniques et hystoires de France* dating from the early sixteenth century includes a series of episodes illustrating the legend (plate 55), from these little framed scenes that are but quaint variations of those in the Mâcon *Cité de Dieu*, one can only conclude that the creative phase of this pictorial theme had already come to a close.[16]

The legend of Joyenval was not the only monarchical theme of the medieval past dealing with the fleurs de lis that was revived for illustra-tive or patriotic purposes during this era of artistic renewal. The idea of the white lily as the model for the heraldic emblem of the House of France, first sounded in the early years of the fourteenth century, is given an amplified representation in a miniature at the head of an illuminated copy of Guillaume de Nangis' *Chronique Abrégée*. Now in the Walters Art Gallery in Baltimore, the manuscript stems from the 1470s and is thus approximately contemporary with the Mâcon *Cité de Dieu*.[17]

In the miniature (plate 56), in an allusion to the dead kings buried at St-Denis mentioned directly below in the opening sentence of the text, eight departed kings of France are enjoying eternal bliss while seated in a semicircle in the Garden of Paradise.[18] In their midst a giant lily plant with three white blossoms is framed by the parted curtains descending from a canopy inscribed REX FRANCORUM. As in certain representa-tions of the three lilies in the vase of the Annunciation, one of the flowers is still in bud, another is half open, while the third is in full bloom. But instead of the petals alternating with the sepals in the fully opened flower, as in the actual lily, they have been divided into two clearly separated groups of three each, thus vividly recalling the similar division of the floral leaves of the lily in the late thirteenth-century *Vitis mystica*, in which the mystic meaning of the triangular head of the pistil in the center of the flower was eventually to lead, in Geoffroy de Paris' *Dit des Alliés,* to the Trinitarian symbolism of the three fleurs de lis.[19] And finally, in front of the stem of the plant and as a fitting tableau for the conclusion of this study, two angels support the crowned arms of France, whose triple emblems have been so amply foreshadowed by the three gigantic flowers.

Plate 1. Seal of Louis of France, 1211 (Photo: Archives nationales).

Plate 2. Louis of France with royal banner and shield. Clerestory rose, Cathedral, Chartres, before 1223 (Photo: author).

a. Seal of Robert I, the Pious, c. 997

b. Seal of Henry I, 1035, Cast

c. Seal of Philip I, 1082

d. Seal of Louis IX, 1240

e. Seal of Philip IV, the Fair, 1286

Plate 3. The evolution of the fleur de lis on the seals of the Kings of France (Photos: a,c,d Archives nationales; b,e by permission of the British Library).

Plate 4. Counterseal of Louis IX, 1240 (Photo: Archives nationales).

Plate 5. Jean Fouquet, Inhumation of Philip IV in St-Denis. *Grandes Chroniques de France,* after 1461. Bibliothèque nationale, ms. fr. 6465, fol. 323 (Phot. Bibl. Nat. Paris).

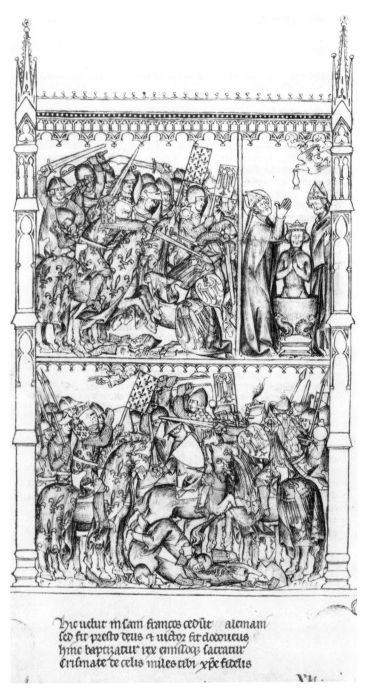

Plate 6. Battle Against the Alemanni, Baptism of Clovis. Yves, *Life of Saint Denis,* book 3. Paris, Bibliothèque nationale, ms. lat. 5286, fol. 131 (Phot. Bibl. Nat. Paris).

Plate 7. First page. Raoul de Presles' Prologue to the *Cité de Dieu*. Presentation Manuscript, Paris, 1376. Paris, Bibliothèque nationale, ms. fr. 22.912 fol. 3 (Phot. Bibl. Nat. Paris).

8b. Relief from the choir screen. Cathedral, Bourges, c. 1260. Bourges, Musée du Berry, on deposit in the Musée du Louvre (Photo: Hirmer Verlag, Munich).

Plate 8. Toads clinging to the boiling cauldron. a. Lowest inner right voussoir, Last Judgment Portal, Nötre-Dame, Paris, 1220–30 (Photo: Arch. Phot. Paris / S.P.A.D.E.M.).

Plate 9. Satan released from prison and leading the host of Gog and Magog. Apocalypse, 1270–74. Oxford, Bodleian Library, MS Douce 180, fol. 86 (p. 87) (Photo: Bodleian Library, Oxford).

Plate 10. Initial *K*, Charter of the foundation of the Celestine Abbey of Limay, January 1377. Archives des Yvelines et de l'ancien département de Seine-et-Oise, 41 H 48 (Photo: Archives départementales des Yvelines).

Plate 11. Crowning of a King of France. *Chanson de Guitelclin de Sassoigne,* end of the thirteenth century. Paris, Bibliothèque de l'Arsenal, ms. 3142, fol. 229 (Photo: author).

Plate 12. Counterseal of Charles V, 1364 (Photo: Archives nationales).

faisons a tous présens et avenir qu ue nous qui auons tous jours désire et désirons de tout uir auer laceor

Plate 13. Initial *C*, Charter of the Inalienability of the Hotel St-Paul, Paris, July 1364 (Photo: Archives nationales).

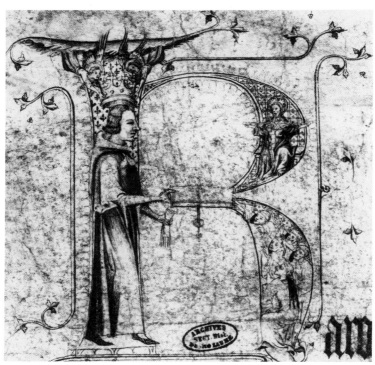

Plate 14. Initial *K*, First charter of the foundation of the Chapel of the Holy Trinity, Vincennes, 1379 (Photo: Archives nationales).

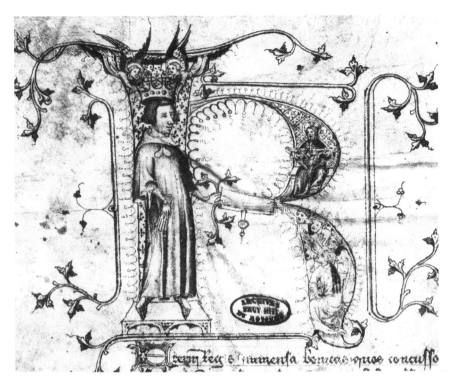

Plate 15. Initial *K*. Second charter of the foundation of the Chapel of the Holy Trinity, Vincennes, November 1379 (Photo: Archives nationales).

Plate 16. Secret seal of Charles V, 1376 (Photo: Archives nationales).

a. "Ecu d'or" of Louis IX, 1266        b. "Chaise d'or" of Philip IV, 1303

c. "Pavilion d'or" of Philip VI, 1339      d. "Angelot" of Philip VI, 1341

e. "Florin Georges" of Philip VI, 1341      f. "Franc à cheval" of John II, 1360

g. "Ecu à la Couronne" of Charles VI, 1385

Plate 17. Highlights of French gold coinage, 1266–1385 (Photos: a,b,c,d,g Bibl. Nat. Paris; e,f courtesy of the American Numismatic Society, New York).

Plate 18. Battle Against the Alemanni. *Grandes Chroniques de France*, Paris, end of the fourteenth century. Paris, Bibliothèque nationale, ms. fr. 2600, fol. 2 (Phot. Bibl. Nat. Paris).

Plate 19. Philippe de Mézières presents his work to Richard II. *L'Epistre au roi Richard II*, Paris, May 1395. London, British Library, Roy. MS 20 B. VI, fol. 2 (Photo: by permission of the British Library).

Plate 20. Allegorical picture. Frontispiece, *L'Epistre au roi Richard II*. London, British Library, Roy. MS 20 B. VI, fol. 1 (Photo: by permission of the British Library).

Plate 21. Genealogical chart of the claims of Henry VI to the crowns of England and France. *Miscellanea*, c. 1444. London, British Library, Roy. MS 15 E. VI, fol. 3 (Photo: by permission of the British Library).

Plate 22. *Sceau de majesté* of Charles VI, 1385–86. Paris, Bibliothèque nationale, Cabinet des Médailles (Phot. Bibl. Nat. Paris).

Plate 23. Henry VI's great seal tor French affairs, 1430 (Photo: Archives nationales).

a.  Charles VI's "Salut d'or," 1421

b.  Henry VI's "Salut d'or," 1423

Plate 24.  The "Saluts d'or" (Phot. Bibl. Nat. Paris).

Plate 25. The Annunciation from the right. Embroidered mitre, c. 1340. Church Treasury, Sixt (Haute Savoie) (Photo: © Arch. Phot. Paris / S.P.A.D.E.M.).

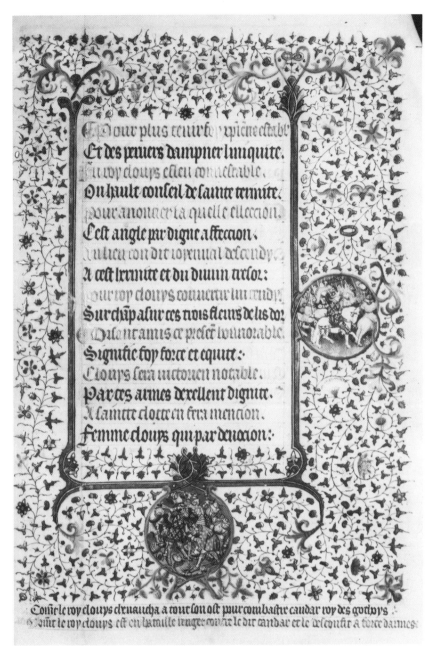

Plate 26. First page. Poem on the fleurs de lis and the holy ampulla, Paris 1429–30, Bedford Hours. London, British Library, Add. MS 18.850, fol. 289 (Photo: by permission of the British Library).

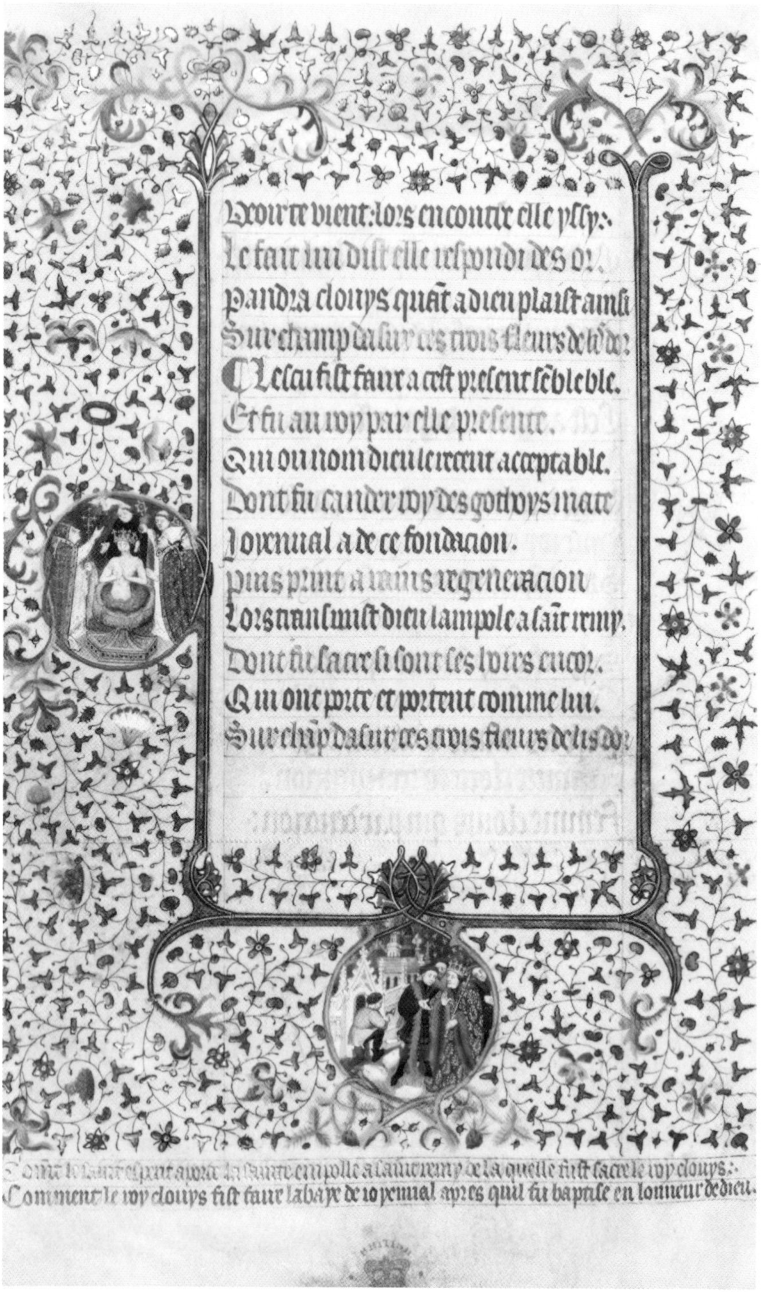

Plate 27. Second page. Poem on the fleurs de lis and the holy ampulla, Bedford Hours. London, British Library, Add. MS 18.850, fol. 289v (Photo: by permission of the British Library).

Plate 28. Clovis and the origin of the fleurs de lis. Bedford Hours. British Library, Add. MS 18.850, fol. 288v (Photo: by permission of the British Library).

Plate 29. The Visitation. The Hours of the Maréchal de Boucicaut, Paris, 1405–8. Paris, Musée Jacquemart-André, ms. 2, fol. 65v (Photo: Bulloz).

Coment leag comenda a noel faur une airlr et y mecter une pair de tout lestes pour le deup

Plate 30. Building the ark. Bedford Hours. London, British Library Add. MS 18.850, fol. 15v (Photo: Conway Library, Courtauld Institute of Art).

Còmè noel ap̃s le deluge auriua a terre et mist hors le bestail et fist sacrifice et planta la uigne.

Plate 31. The animals leaving the ark, Noah sacrificing and tending vines, Drunkenness of Noah. Bedford Hours, London, British Library, Add. MS 18.850, fol. 16v (Photo: Conway Library, Courtauld Institute of Art).

Plate 32.  Frontispiece. Gui Guilbaut's copy of the *Cité de Dieu*, vol. 1, Lille, 1430–40. Brussels, Bibliothèque royale Albert Ier, ms. 9005, fol. 3 (Copyright, Bibliothèque royale Albert Ier, Bruxelles).

Plate 33. Miniature. Frontispiece, Gui Guilbaut's copy of the *Cité de Dieu*. Brussels, Bibliothèque royale Albert Ier, ms. 9005, fol. 3 (Copyright, Bibliothèque royale Albert Ier, Bruxelles).

Plate 34. Saint Denis gives the oriflamme to the constable Jean Clément. Cleres-tory window, Cathedral, Chartres, c. 1225–30 (after Y. Delaporte and E. Houvet, *Vitraux de la cathédrale de Chartres* [1926], 3:pl. CCVIII) (From the Avery Architec-tural and Fine Arts Library. Columbia University, New York).

Plate 35. Frontispiece. Jean Chevrot's copy of the *Cité de Dieu*, vol. 1, Lille, c. 1445. Brussels, Bibliothèque royale Albert Ier, ms. 9015, fol. 1 (Copyright, Bibliothèque royale Albert Ier, Bruxelles).

Plate 36. Miniature. Frontispiece, Jean Chevrot's copy of the *Cité de Dieu*. Brussels, Bibliothèque royale Albert Ier, ms. 9015, fol. 1 (Copyright, Bibliothèque royale Albert Ier, Bruxelles).

Plate 37. The City of God. Detail, frontispiece, Jean Chevrot's copy of the *Cité de Dieu* (Copyright, Bibliothèque royale Albert Ier, Bruxelles).

Plate 38. View of a walled city. Detail, *The Virgin and Child with Two Saints and a Carthusian Donor*, c. 1453. The Frick Collection (Copyright, The Frick Collection, New York).

Plate 39. Old St Paul's, before 1561. Detail, Van den Wyngaerde's *Panoramic View of London*, Ashmolean Museum, Oxford (after W. Benham and C. Welch, *Mediaeval London* [1901], fig. 3) (From the Avery Architectural and Fine Arts Library. Columbia University, New York).

Plate 40. Old St Paul's and medieval London. Engraving partly based on Wyngaerde (after G. H. Cook, *Old St. Paul's Cathedral* [London: 1955], fig. 19) (From the Avery Architectural and Fine Arts Library. Columbia University, New York).

Plate 41. Miniature. Frontispiece, Antoine de Bourgogne's copy of the *Cité de Dieu*, vol. 1, Lille, 1466. Turin. Biblieteca Nazionale, MS L.I.6, fol. 1 (Photo: Biblieteca Nazionale Universitaria di Torino).

Plate 42. Frontispiece. *Cité de Dieu*, probably Bruges, c. 1470–80. London, British Library, Roy. MS 14. D. I, fol. 1 (Photo: Conway Library, Courtauld Institute of Art).

a. Saint Augustine Teaching Two Clerics, fol. 399

b. Janus and Other Pagan Deities, fol. 299v

Plate 43. Grisaille illustrations. *Cité de Dieu*. London, British Library, Roy. MS 14 D. I (Photos: by permission of the British Library).

Plate 44a. Clovis at the siege of Soissons. Detail of first tapestry.

Plates a, b, and c. "L'Histoire du Fort Roi Clovis," Arras, c. 1450. Musée des Beaux-Arts, Reims (Photos: Giraudon/Art Resource).

Plate 44b. The founding of the Church of St Peter-and-St Paul. Detail of fourth tapestry.

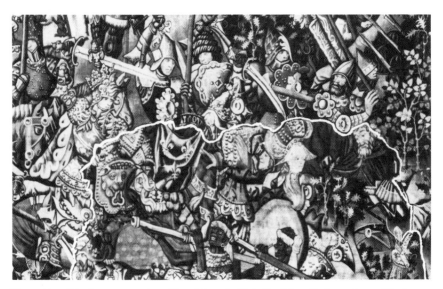

Plate 44c. Clovis overcoming Gondebaud. Detail of fourth tapestry with fragments of other tapestries.

Plate 45. Frontispiece. *Cité de Dieu*, vol. 1, Paris(?), after 1473. Mâcon, Bibliothè-que municipale, ms. 1, fol. 2 (Photo: Mâcon, Bibliothèque municipale).

Plate 46. Historiated initial and presentation scene. Frontispiece, *Cité de Dieu.* Mâcon, Bibliothèque municipale, ms. 1, fol. 2 (Photo: Mâcon, Bibliothèque municipale).

Plate 47. Presentation scene. *Le Songe du Vergier,* Paris, 1378. London, British Library, Roy. MS 19 C. IV, fol. 2 (Photo: by permission of the British Library).

Plate 48. Saint Remi instructs Clovis, Baptism of Clovis, Clovis touches for scrofula, Clotilda presents Clovis with the fleurs de lis shield, Clovis slays the Roy Caudat. Frontispiece, *Cité de Dieu,* Mâcon, Bibliothèque municipale, ms. 1, fol. 2 (Photo: Mâcon, Bibliothèque municipale).

Plate 49. The Hermit of Joyenval and Queen Clotilda, Clovis slays the Roy Caudat, the retreat of the Alemanni. Frontispiece, *Cité de Dieu.* Mâcon, Bibliothèque municipale, ms. 1, fol. 2 (Photo: Mâcon, Bibliothèque municipale).

Plate 50. Charlemagne receives the oriflamme from the abbot of St-Denis. *Cité de Dieu*. Mâcon, Bibliothèque municipale, ms. 1, fol. 2 (Photo: Mâcon, Bibliothèque municipale).

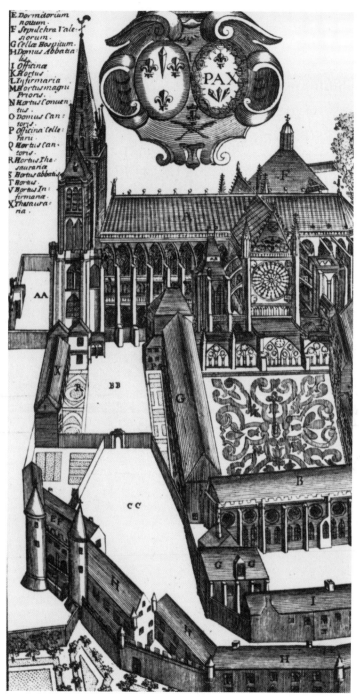

Plate 51. Cavalier view of the Abbey of St-Denis. Detail from Engraving in Dom Michel Germain's *Monasticon Gallicanum* (From the Avery Architectural and Fine Arts Library. Columbia University, New York).

Plate 52. Frontispiece. *Cité de Dieu*, vol. 1, Abbeville edition of 1486 (Phot. Bibl. Nat. Paris).

Plate 53. Pierre le Rouge's double illustration. *La Mer des Histoires,* vol. 1, fol. 137, Paris edition of 1488 (Photo: The Pierpont Morgan Library, New York. PML 17593).

Plate 54. Frontispiece. Robert Gaguin, *La mer des chroniques et mirouer historial de France,* Paris edition, Nicolle de la Barre, 1518 (Photo: Rare Book and Manuscript Library, Columbia University).

Plate 55. Frontispiece. Noël de Fribois, *Abrégé des croniques de France*, Paris, early sixteenth century. *From top left,* The Hermit and the Angel, The Hermit and Clotilda, Clotilda gives the shield to Clovis, Baptism of Clovis; *At right,* Clovis touches for scrofula; *Below,* Clovis kills the Roy Caudat. Paris, Bibliothèque de l'Arsenal, ms. 3430, I, fol. 1 (Phot. Bibl. Nat. Paris).

Plate 56. Frontispiece. Guillaume de Nangis, *Chronique abrégée*, Paris, 1470s. Baltimore, Walters Art Gallery, MS W 306, fol. 1 (Photo: Walters Art Gallery, Baltimore).

Abbreviations
Appendixes
Notes
Selected Bibliography
Index

# ℋbbreviations

| | |
|---|---|
| BL | London, British Library. |
| Bloch | Marc Bloch. *Les rois thaumaturges.* Strasbourg and Paris: 1924. |
| BM | Bibliothèque municipale. |
| BN | Paris, Bibliothèque nationale. |
| Bossuat, 1940 | Robert Bossuat. "Poème latine sur l'origine des fleurs de lis." *Bibliothèque de l'école des chartes*" 101 (1940): 80–101. |
| BRA | Brussels, Bibliothèque royale Albert Ier. |
| Chatillon, 1955 | François Chatillon. "Lilia crescunt." *Revue du moyen age latin* 11 (1955): 87–200. |
| Contamine, 1973 | Philippe Contamine. "L'oriflamme de Saint-Denis aux XIVe et XVe siècles." *Annales de l'Est,* 5e série, 25e année, no. 3, 1973, 179–244. |
| Dennys | Rodney Dennys. *The Heraldic Imagination.* New York: 1975. |
| Douët d'Arcq | Louis Douët d'Arcq. *Archives de l'Empire . . . Collection de sceaux.* 3 vols. Paris: 1863–68. |
| Faral, 1949 | Edmond Faral. "Le roman de la fleur de lis de Guillaume de Digulleville." *Mélanges offerts à E. Hoepffner.* Paris: 1949. 327–38. |
| Faral, 1962 | Edmond Faral. "Guillaume de Digulleville, moine de Châalis." *Histoire littéraire de la France* 39 (1962): 1–132. |
| FG | *Les Fastes du Gothique: Le siècle de Charles V.* Exh. Cat., Grand Palais. Paris: 1981. |
| Griffiths | Ralph A. Griffiths. *The Reign of King Henry VI.* Berkeley and Los Angeles: 1981. |
| Guenée and Lehoux | Bernard Guenée and Françoise Lehoux. *Les entrées royales françaises de 1328 à 1515.* Paris: 1968. |
| Hindman and Spiegel | Sandra Hindman and Gabrielle M. Spiegel. "The Fleur-de-Lis Frontispieces to Guillaume de Nangis' *Chronique Abrégée*." *Viator* 12 (1981): 381–407. |
| HLF | *Histoire littéraire de la France.* |
| Jackson | Jean Golein. "The 'Traité du Sacre' " (ed. Richard A. Jackson. *Proceedings of the American Philosophical Society:* 113: (1969): 305–24. |

151

| | |
|---|---|
| Jones | Evan John Jones. *Medieval Heraldry: Some Fourteenth Century Heraldic Works.* Cardiff: 1943. |
| *JWCI* | *Journal of the Warburg and Courtauld Institutes.* |
| Laborde | Alexandre de Laborde, *Les manuscrits à peinture de la "Cité de Dieu" de Saint Augustin.* 2 vols. Paris: 1909. |
| Lafaurie | Jean Lafaurie. *Les monnaies des rois de France: Hugues Capet à Louis XII.* Paris and Basle: 1951. |
| Palmer, 1972 | John J. N. Palmer. *England, France and Christendom, 1377–99.* Chapel Hill and London: 1972. |
| Pastoureau, 1978 | Michel Pastoureau. "La fleur de lis: emblème royal, symbole marial ou thème graphique?" In *La monnaie, miroir des rois.* Exh. Cat., Hotel de la Monnaie. Paris: 1978. 251–71. |
| Pastoureau, 1979 | Michel Pastoureau. *Traité d'heraldique.* Paris: 1979. |
| Perroy, 1945 | Edouard Perroy. *La guerre de cent ans.* Paris: 1945. |
| Piaget, 1898 | Arthur Piaget. " 'Le chapel des fleurs de lis' par Philippe de Vitri." *Romania* 27 (1898): 55–92. |
| Piaget, 1936 | Arthur Piaget. "Un poème inédit de Guillaume de Digulleville, 'Le roman de la fleur de lis.' " *Romania* 62 (1936): 317–58. |
| Pinoteau, 1979 | Hervé Pinoteau. *Héraldique Capétienne.* Paris: 1979. |
| *RHGF* | *Recueil des historiens des Gaules et de la France.* |
| Roman | Jules Roman. *Manuel de sigillographie française.* Paris: 1912. |
| Spiegel, 1978 | Gabrielle M. Spiegel. *The Chronicle Tradition of Saint-Denis: A Survey.* Brookline, Mass. and Leyden: 1978. |
| SV | *Le Songe du Vergier* (ed. Marion Schnerb-Lièvre). 2 vols. Paris: 1982. |
| Viard | Jules Viard, ed. *Les Grandes Chroniques de France.* 10 vols. Paris: 1920–53. |
| Wagner, 1956 | Arthur Richard Wagner. *Heralds and Heraldry in the Middle Ages.* 2d ed. Oxford: 1956. |
| Warner and Gilson | George F. Warner and Julius P. Gilson. *British Museum: Catalogue of the Western Manuscripts in the Old Royal and King's Collections.* 4 vols. London: 1921. |
| Wolffe | Bertram Wolffe. *Henry VI.* London: 1981. |

# Appendix 1:
# The University Riots and the Symbolism of the Petals of the Fleur de Lis, from the *Life of Louis IX* by Guillaume de Nangis

The Latin text and the appended French translation are from *RHGF* 20: 318–21. For convenient reference the Latin text has been divided into seven numbered sections, each section followed by the English translation.

1. "Anno 1230: Eodem anno magno dissensio Parisius inter clericos et burgenses fuit orta. Nam burgenses quosdam de clericis occiderunt, et ideo clerici a Parisius recedentes per diversas mundi provincias dispersi sunt."

(In the year 1230: In this year a major disturbance broke out between the students and the townsmen. For the citizens killed a certain number of the students, in consequence of which the students fled from Paris and then were dispersed throughout various parts of the world.)

2. "Videns autem rex Franciae Ludovicus, quod studium literarum et philosophiae, per quod thesaurus scientiae, qui cunctis aliis praeeminent et praevalet, acquiritur, recessisset Parisius, quod primo venerat ab Athenis Romam, et a Roma cum militiae titulo in Galliam, graviter coepit dolere."

(And when King Louis of France saw that the study of letters and philosophy, through which is acquired that inestimable treasure of knowledge that surpasses and outvalues everything else and that had first come from Athens to Rome and then, together with chivalry, had arrived in Gaul, was now, alas, leaving Paris, he was filled with sorrow and grief.)

3. "Metuens que rex piissimus ne tantus et talis thesaurus a regno suo elongaretur, eo quod divinae salutis sapientia et scientia, et ne ipsi aliquando a Domino diceretur: *Quia repulsit scientiam, repellam te,* supra dictos jam clericos mandans Parisius redire, redeuntes clementissime recepit, et ab ipsis burgensibus quicquid antea clericis forefecerant, fecit ipsis celeriter emendari."

(Fearing that his kingdom was about to be permanently deprived of this great treasure of divinely inspired learning and knowledge and lest the Lord should say of him, "You have rejected learning, therefore I reject you," he ordered the said students to return immediately to Paris and received those who did return with the utmost indulgence. And he furthermore required the citizens to make immediate amends for what they had done.)

4. "Si enim tam pretiosissimus thesaurus sapientiae salutaris, quod olim de Graecia sequendo Dionysium Areopagitam Parisius ad partes Gallicanas devenerat, cum fides et militiae titulo, de regno Franciae tolleretur, maneret utique liliatum signum regis Franciae, quod trini floris folio depictum est, in una parte sui mirabiliter deformatum."

(For should this most precious treasure of salutory learning that, together with faith and chivalry, had formerly followed Dionysius the Areopagite from Greece to parts of Gaul and then to Paris, be banished from the kingdom of France, the lily, which is depicted with three floral petals and which is the sign of the King of France, would in some part or other suffer major disfigurement.)

5. "Nam ex quo Deus et Dominus noster Jesus Christus voluit tribus praedictis gratiis, scilicet fide, sapientia et militia, specialius caetera regna, regnum Franciae sua gratia illustrare, consueverunt regis in suo armis et vexillis florem lilii depictum cum tribus foliis comportare. Quasi dicerent toti mundo: fides, sapientia et militiae titulum abundantius quam regnis ceteris sunt regno nostro, Dei provisione et gratia servientes."

(But since our Lord Jesus Christ wishes above all other kingdoms to illuminate the kingdom of France with the three aforementioned attributes, that is, faith, learning, and chivalry, it has become customary for the king to bear on his coat of arms and on his banner the flower of the lily with three petals, as if the three petals said to the whole world: faith, learning, and chivalry thrive more abundantly in our kingdom than in any other kingdom, serving us through the care and grace of God.)

6. "Duplex enim par flos lilii sapientiam et militiam significat, quae duo sequentes de Graecia in Galliam Dionysium Areopagitam cum fide, quam ibidem Dei gratia seminavit, tertium florem lilii facientem custodiunt et defendunt. Nam fides gubernatur et regitur sapientia, ac demum militia defensatur."

(For the double petals of the lily represent learning and chivalry; having, moreover, followed Dionysius the Areopagite from Greece into Gaul, they guard and defend the third petal, which is faith and which through the grace of God he has been able to propagate. For faith is governed and ruled by knowledge and is defended by chivalry.)

7. "Quandiu enim praedicta tria fuerint in regno Franciae pariter et ordinate sibi invicem cohaerentia, stabit regnu n. Si autem de eodem separata fuerint, vel avulsa, omne illud in seipsum desolabitur atque cadet."

(And furthermore, as long as the aforesaid three are together in the kingdom of France and are firmly united to each other, the kingdom will also remain firm. If however they should be separated from each other or be torn asunder, everything will be reduced to desolation and will fall into ruin.)

*French Translation.* "En cel an . . . grant dissentions mut a Paris entre les clercs et les bourgois, et ocirent li bourgois aucuns des clercs; parquai li universités se departi et issi hors de Paris et alerent en diverses provinces. Quant li roys vit que lestude des lettres et de philosofie cessoit parmi Paris, par quoi li tresors de sens et de sapience est aquis, qui vaut et seurmonte tous autres tresors, sestoit ainsi parti de Paris, qui estoit venu de Grece à Roume et de Roume en France avec le titre de chevalerie: si se douta mout et ot päour grant li roys dous et debonnaires, que si grans et si riches tresors ne se eslongat de son royaume, pource que il ne li peut estre dit ne reprouchie de Nostre Seigneur: Pource que tu as geté et eslongie science de ton royaume, saches que je te eslongere de moy; ne demoura mie grammente apres que il manda les clers et les bourgois, et fit tant que li bourgeois amenderent aus clers ce quil leur avoient mefait. Et pour ce especialement le fit li roys; car si precieus joiaus come est sapience, et lestude des lettres et de philosofie qui vint primierement de Grece a Roume et de Grece en France avec le titre de chevalerie, ensuivant saint Denis qui prescha la foy en France; la baniere le roy de France et les armes qui sont paintes de la fleur de liz par troys fuelles (feuilles), fusent mervellieusement enlaidies; quar puisque Nostre Sires Jhesu Crist vout especialement suz tous autres royaumes enluminer le royaume de France, de foy, de sapience et de chevalerie, li roy de France acoustumerent en leur armes à porter la fleur de liz paintes par trois fuellies, aussi comme se il deissent à tout le monde: foys, sapience et chevalerie sont, par la provision et par la grace de Dieu, plus habundamment en nostre royaume quen ces autres. Les 11. fuellies de la fleur de liz qui sont oeles (ailes), senefient sens et chevalerie, qui gardent et deffendent la tierce fuellie qui est ou milieu de elles, plus longue et plus haute, par laquele foys est entendue et senefié; quar elle est et doit estre gouvernée par sapience et deffendue par chevalerie. Tant comme ces troys graces seront fermement et ordenement jointes ensemble ou royaume de France, li royaumes sera fors et fermes; et se il avient que eles en soient ostées our desseurées, li royaume charra en desolacion et en destruiement."

# Appendix 2:
# The Symbolism of the Petals of the Fleur de Lis and the Poem on Their Migration, from the *Life of Saint Denis* by the Monk Yves

The Latin text is from book 3, chapter 99, BN, ms. lat. 5286, fols. 175–175v. As in appendix 1, the text is divided into numbered sections, each section followed by the English translation.

1. Chapter heading: "Quomodo fides, sapiencia, milicia per signum regis Francie, scilicet per lilium designatur."

"Prefatorum autem trium, fidei videlicet et sapientie et militie grata connexio videtur esse triplex, ille funiculus qui iuxta Salomonem difficile rumpitur. Quandiu videlicet tria hec adinvicem fuerint pacis et amoris federe sociata. Quod si quando separata fuerint aut divisa, dissolutionis malum imminere poterit ac timeri."

(Chapter heading: How faith, learning, and chivalry are represented by the sign of the king of France, that is, by the lily.

These three attributes that are mentioned above, that is, faith, learning, and chivalry, can indeed be seen to have a triple and meaningful connection, forming the cord that, according to Solomon, it is difficult to break as long as the three attributes are in mutual harmony in peace and love. If, however, they become separated or divided, the woes of dissolution can follow and this is indeed something to be feared.)

2. "Trina nichilominus prefatorum trium, fidei videlicet sophos et milicie, prerogativa dignitas per beati Areopagitis meritis, pre ceteris mundi regnis Francorum regno concessa triplicis folii lilio, quod in signo suo defert Rex Francorum christianissimus non incongrue designatur; de quo et dictorum egregius ita dicit:"

(But the superior dignity of the above-mentioned three, that is, faith, learning, and chivalry, through the merits of the blessed Areopagite has nevertheless been conferred upon the kingdom of France, to the exclusion of the kingdoms of the rest of the world, by means of the lily with its triple petals; and because it has become his emblem, the lily not inappropriately also represents the most Christian king of France, concerning which an eminent poet has this to say:)

> 3. "Flos duplex Achaie, sophis et milicie,
> Sequens Dionysis, servit regno Francie.
> Fides summa specie florem facit tertium.
> Trini floris folium effigiat lilium,
> Signum regis Francie."

("The two petals of the flower of Achaia, learning and chivalry, following Dionysius, watch over the kingdom of France. The third petal, which is taller in appearance and which represents faith, completes the flower. The triple petals of the flower form the lily, the sign of the King of France.")

4. "Siquidem lilii folio superiori convenienter designatur fidei christiane virtus nos illuminando dirigens ac superna, in duobus vero aliis floribus quasi sub tercio humiliter inclinatis denotantur salutaris sapientia militarisque potencia, que fidei subesse debent obsequio. Hec quidem scilicet sapientia per dextrum, illa vero scilicet militaris potencia per sinistrum. Siquidem fidei sapientiam militiciaque sociari convenit."

(Because the virtue of the Christian faith, which guides us with its celestial enlightenment, is appropriately designated by the taller petal of the lily, as if assuming a more humble position in regard to this third petal, the other two petals represent salutory learning and military prowess, both of which should be subservient to faith, with learning on the right and military prowess on the left since, after all, it is only to be expected that learning and chivalry should be associated with faith.)

In the foregoing sections, Yves' dependency on Guillaume de Nangis is graphically illustrated in section 1, which bears close comparison with appendix 1.7, while section 2 can be compared to appendix 1.5. In Yves' section 4, the specific assignment of each of the three attributes to a particular petal of the lily not only conforms to de Nangis' later *Chronicon* (see chap. 1, n. 32) but is even more specific in assigning the right petal to learning, the left to chivalry. There then follows a long passage, omitted here, that describes in detail the virtues of faith, learning, and chivalry and the way in which chivalry has been dishonored by those who resort to violent warfare or who dissipate their energies in drunkenness. The chapter then concludes with sections 5 and 6 below in which the author makes his own comments on the symbolism of the lilies and the problem of their numbers.

5. "Hec autem tria, scilicet, fides salutaris et sciencia et militaris disciplina, que uno lilii significari posse prediximus, nonnulli tribus integris liliis designant, cuilibet trium predictorum unum lilium integrum adsignantes."

(But these three, that is, salutory faith, knowledge, and military discipline, which we have already said can be represented by one lily, others have designated by three whole lilies, while still others are content to assign the aforesaid three to only one whole flower.)

6. "Quod insignis regis Francie, non solum unum vel tribus, plura lilia sub octodenario scilicet numero depinguntur, hoc forte ad maiorem predictorum expressionem aut potius ad decorem licet, et diligens lector in prefato liliorum numero posset aliquod latens misterium invenire."

(Because the insignia of the king of France are depicted on the eight-penny coins not only by one or three but by a plurality of lilies, it is quite possible that the previous remarks on the greater number of the lilies may rather point to their role as ornament, and the diligent reader can then be left to discover for himself any hidden meaning their numbers might suggest.)

The following French translation is from BN, ms. lat. 13.836, fols. 31–31v. (Chapter heading) "Comment la foy et sapience et chevalerie sont segnefiées par les fleurs de lis qui furent de Dieu envoiées au roy de France."

"Ces .iii. choses, ce est assavoir, foy et sapience et chevalerie, sont coniointes et bien segnefiées par la parole que dit Salemon: Le fouet de .iii. filez est graint peine rompu quant ces .iii. choses dessus dittes sont bien ensamble. Toutes choses sont gardées en amour et se il en y a aucun rompu l'en se doit doubter de guerre et de dissolution. La digneté de foy, de sapience et de chevalerie par les merites Saint Denis .iii. foiz sont données et ottroiées, especiaument ou roiaume de France, qui sont segnefiées en .iii. fleurs de lis qui furent aportées à tres noble et tres excellent homme le roy de France; de quoy dit un vercefieur noble:

> ".ii. fleurs sont en Archare, c'est assavoir
> sapience et chevalerie,
> Le queles Saint Denis si ensivoit, et ou
> roiaume de France sont servies.
> La tierce fleur, si est la foy qui en France
> parfaitement est tenue
> De ces .iii. fleurs la nature est segnefiée
> L'escu des .iii. fleurs de lis."

"Par droiture la fleur de lis qui est dessus senefie la vertu de la foy crestienne qui nous enlumine et envers Dieu nous adresse. Les autres .ii. fleurs de lis qui sont dessous l'autre humblement segnefient sainte sapience et de chevalerie la puissance qui devent estre subietés à la foy et en son obedience. Certes la sapience, la foy et la chevalerie se doivent assembler."

The final portion of chapter 99, reproduced above in sections 5 and 6 of the Latin text, is missing in the French translation, since it was included on the following folio of the manuscript now removed.

# Appendix 3:
# The Symbolism of the Fleur de Lis in *De Alliatis* by Geoffroy de Paris

The text is from BN, ms. fr. 146, fols. 50v–51. The first part of the poem through the first three verses of stanza 7 (fol. 50v), as well as the last six verses of stanza 11 (fol. 51), are published, with an English translation, in Walter H. Storer and Charles A. Rochedieu, *Six Historical Poems of Geoffroi de Paris, Written 1314–1318,* University of North Carolina, Studies in Romance Languages, 16 (Chapel Hill: 1950), 58–60.

7

"Rex, dictus est Philippe lilium;
Vere tu par tunc eris lilio,
Si directum tenet dominium.
Pietatem et in iudicio
Ad populum vultum propicium
Mundiciam in corde regio;
Ista tuum decent imperium
Et te docet eadem ratio.

8

Est lilii radix primaria
Secretorum fides celestium,
Et hastile rectum iusticia,
Distribuens cuiusque proprium,
Viror virans quem servant solia
Et bonorum congaudens gaudium.

160

Sed flos candens vite iudicia,
Exterminans carnale vicium.

9

Iam ascendant in montem Libanum,
Rex, intentes predita lilia.
Unde regni turbitur organum,
Psalterium cum tympanistria;
Cedit corus simul et timpanum,
Verum tamen iustet audacia
Ut probetur per ignis clibanum
A unicorum regni fiducia.

10

Inter spinas non aubsque merito
Convallium lilium legitur;
Te lilium, Regem, non dubito,
Nam lilium armis depingitur.
Iure tamen plures inplicitum
In lilium consurgunt igitur
Tales spine dicuntur debito,
Finis quarum malus ut dicitur."

11

"Sunt silvestres spinarum singuli
Sed lilii clara iocunditas;
Sunt spinarum pungentes stimuli,
Sed tibi, O Rex, benignitas:
Hanc sentiant omnes et singuli,
Non taillias dudum illicitas.
Tui corda conserva populi,
Vultum tuum precedis veritas."

Unlike the *Dit des Alliés,* of which this is the Latin version, in the symbolism of the fleur de lis Geoffroy has here confined himself almost entirely to the single lily. Even more emphatically than in Guillaume de Nangis' *Life of Saint Louis,* it is identified with the king, as in stanza 7, verses 1–2 ("King, thou art called Philip, a lily; / Truly then thou shalt be like a lily") and in stanza 10, verses 3–4 ("There is no doubt thou art the lily, O king, / For the lily is painted on thy coat of arms").

In stanza 8 the botanical lily of the *Vitis mystica* is recalled in the root *(radix)* of the lily plant, followed by the stem *(hastile)* and then the brilliant white flower *(flos candens),* successively symbolizing faith, uprightness, and an unblemished life that eschews the evils of carnality, while in stanza 10 the thorns surrounding the Biblical lily of the valley have become the thorny problems with which the lily king must deal.

Unlike the verses of the *Dit des Alliés,* too, the symbolism of the lily plant in stanza 8 is here the only evidence that the author was acquainted with the far more extended passage on the lily plant in the *Vitis mystica,* and this fact in turn can be seen as one of several indications that the *De Alliatis* was undoubtedly composed sometime before the *Dit des Alliés.*

# Appendix 4:
# The Monarchical Cycle in
# Raoul de Presles' Prologue
# to the *Cité de Dieu*

The following text is transcribed from volume 1 of the Presentation Manuscript, BN, fr. 22.912, fols. 3v–4. For convenient reference, a numbered résumé in English precedes each separate item of the French text.

1. Addressing the king directly, the author reminds Charles V that by birth he is of the lineage of the Roman emperors, whose emblem was the eagle.

"Car premierement, à prendre vostre nativité: il est certain que vous estes filz de roy de France, et qui plus est roy de France, qui est le plus grant, le plus haut, le plus catholique et le plus puissant roy crestien. Et avec ce estes estrait du lignaige des empereurs rommains qui portent l'aigle pour ce que ce fu le premier signe rommain."

2. Charles was baptized with chrism as a Christian and at his coronation he was anointed with the holy oil brought down by a dove at the baptism of Clovis by Saint Remy, archbishop of Reims.

"Secondement, en ce que vous estes le plus digne Roy crestien: car ans ce que est vostre baptesme, vous estes enoint du sainte cresme, comme est un chascun bon crestien. Encore par excellence estes vouz roy consacré et si dignement enoint comme de la sainte liqeur que un coulon, que nous tenons fermement que ce fu le saint esperit mis en celle forme, apporta du ciel en son bec, en une petite empole ou fiole. Et la mist, veant tout le pueple, en la main de monsieur saint Remy, lors arcevesque de Reins, qui tantost en consacra les fons et en enoint le roy Clovis, premier roy crestien. Et en ceste reverence et pour ce tres noble mistere touz les roys de France, qui depuis ont esté à leur premiere creacion, ont esté consacrez à Reins de la liquer de celle sainte empole."

3. Through his consecration Charles, like his predecessors, is imbued with the power to cure scrofula.

"Et ne tienge nous ne autre que celle consecration soit sans tres grant, digne et noble mistere. Car par icelle vos devanciers et vous avez tele vertuz et puissance qui vous est donnée et attribuée de Dieu que vous faites miracles en vostre vie, teles si grans et si apertes, que vous garissez d'une tres horrible maladie qui se appelle les escroelles, de laquelle nul autre prince crestien ne puet gairir fors vous."

4. As a sign of the Holy Trinity, Charles' coat of arms with the three fleurs de lis was sent by an angel to Clovis, the first Christian king, for his encounter with the pagan king Caudat who, after having entered France from Germany, had settled at Conflans.

"Et si portez les armes de trois fleurs de lis en signe de la benoite Trinité, qui de Dieu par son angre furent envoiez au dit Clovis, premier roy crestien, pour soi combatre contre le roy Caudat, qui estoit sarrazin et adversaire de la foy crestienne, et qui estoit venu d'Alemainge à grant multitude de gens es parties de France. Et qui avoit fait, mis et ordené son siege à Conflans."

5. The battle, that began in the valley, ended on the mountain where is now the tower of Montjoie, from which is derived the war cry "Montjoie-Saint Denis!"

"Dont combien que la bataille commencast en la valée, toutevoies fu elle achevée en la monteigne en la quelle est à present la tour de Mont Joie. Et la fu pris premierement et nommé vostre cri en armes, c'est a savoir, 'Mont Joie Saint Denis.' "

6. An angel showed these arms to a hermit who lived next to a fountain in the valley and told him that he should have the three crescents on the arms of Clovis replaced with three fleurs de lis. And with these Clovis would triumph over Caudat.

"Et en la reverence de ceste victoire et de ce que ces armes Notre Seigneur envoia du ciel par un angre et demonstra à un hermite qui tenoit en icelle valée, de costé une fontaine, un hermitage, en lui disant qu'il feist raser les armes des trois croissans que Clovis portoit lors en son escu, feist mettre en ce lieu les trois fleurs de lys et en ycelles se combatist, et il avroit victoire contre le roy Caudat."

7. The hermit revealed the angel's instructions to the wife of Clovis, who substituted the three fleurs de lis for the crescents. A religious house was then founded, known as the abbey of Joyenval, whose armorial shield has long commemorated these events.

"Lequel le revela à la femme Clovis qui reperoit au dit hermitaige et apportoit souvent au dit hermite sa recreation. Laquele les emporta et defassa les croissans et y mist les trois fleurs de lys. Fu fondé un lieu religier qui fu et encore est appelé l'abbaye de Joie en Val, en laquelle l'escu de ces armes a esté par long temps en reverence de ce."

8. Charles, like his predecessors, is wont to take the oriflamme from St-Denis with reverence and devotion.

"Et si portez seul roy et singulierement l'oriflamme en bataille. C'est assavoir, une glaive tout doré ou est attachiée une baniere vermeille, la quelle vos devanciers et vous avez acostumé à venir querre et prandre en l'eglise de monseigneur saint Denis à grant solempnité, reverence et devotion, si comme vous le savez."

9. After being received by the monks in procession, the king is taken to the altar of the martyrs, whose relics and those of Saint Louis are placed on the altar, and the oriflamme is then folded under the corporals. At the conclusion of the mass, it is handed over to its chosen guardian.

"Car premierement la procession vous vient a l'encontre jusques à l'issue du cloitre. Et apres la procession, sont atains les benirs corps saints de monseigneur saint Denis et de ces compagnons, et mis sur l'autel en grant reverence, et aussi le corps saint monseigneur saint Louis. Et puis est mise ceste baniere, ploiée dessoubz les corporaux, ou est consacré le corps de notre seigneur Jesu Crist, le quel vous recevez dignement apres la celebration de la messe. Sit fait celui au quel vous l'avez esleu à baillier, comme au plus prodomme et plus vaillant chevalier."

10. The guardian of the oriflamme holds it while it is being kissed like a relic. He then solemnly swears to guard it, to the honor of the king and his realm.

"Et ce fait le baissiez en la bouche, et un bailles. Et la la tient entre ses mains par grant reverence à fin que les barons assistens la puissent baissier comme relique et chose digne. Et en li baillant por le porter, li faites faire sermment solempnel de la garder et porter en grant reverence et à l'onneur de vous et de votre roiaume."

11. Thus Charlemagne received the oriflamme before going to the aid of the Emperor Constantine of Constantinople against the Saracens.

"Ainsi la prinst ce souverain protecteur et destenseur (defenseur) singulier de l'eglise, monseigneur saint Charles, jadis empereur et roy de France, quant il ala à secours à l'Empereur Constantin qui estoit empereur de Constantinoble, pour delivrer son pais de Sarrasins qui l'occupoient et aussi la terre sainte de Jehrusalem."

12. The Emperor of Constantinople requested his aid because of a vision he had in which an armed and mounted knight appeared at the foot of his bed, holding a golden shaft from which there issued a flame.

"Et lequel empereur de Constantinoble le manda par la vision que il avoit veue devant son lit, qui fut tele selon les croniquers et ancienne hystours: c'est assavoir, que devant icelui empereur, au piez de son lit, il se apparu un chevalier armé de toutes armes et monté à cheval, tenant une hante toute dorée, du bout de la quelle hante yssoit flambe à merveilles grande."

13. In some perplexity as to the significance of the vision, Constantine was visited by an angel, who told him that he whom he had seen would deliver his country from the Saracens.

"Et comme il feust en grant perplexité de savoir quele signification c'estoit et que telle chose signifioit, un angre (ange) s'apparuit à luy, qui li dist que celui qu'il avoit veu, c'estoit celui qui delivreroit le pays de Sarrasins."

14. Having recognized Charlemagne in the vision, Constantine requested his aid; at which the emperor took the oriflamme from St-Denis, went to Constantinople, conquered the Saracens, and destroyed their country.

"Si congnut Constantin parce que il avoit veu que ce estoit le roy Charlemaigne, à present nomme monseigneur saint Charles. Et tantost le manda, qui entendit le mandement et la vision, tantost ala à saint Denys et prist la baniere vermeille en tele reverence, comme vous m'avez oy raconter, mist le coronne sur l'autel, laissa le roiaume de France en la protection de monseigneur saint Denis, et ceste baniere vermeille ainsi reveremment prise et en tele devotion se parti et ala à Constantinoble et vainqui les Sarrasins et detrura le pays."

15. In memory of this vision and Charlemagne's victory, Charles V's predecessors, as well as Charles himself, are accustomed to take the oriflamme, which is so called because of the flame that appeared at the end of the golden shaft.

"Et en ceste reverence, tant de celle sainte vision comme de la noble victoire que il ot, l'ont ainsi acoustumé à prendre vos devanciers et vous. Et si portes hante dorée, et pour ce est il apelé oriflambe pour la flambe qui apparu au bout de la hante dorée."

16. And the banner is red in memory of Saint Denis and his companions who first brought the faith to France and for which they suffered martyrdom.

"Et est la baniere vermeille en la remembrance du glorieux martyr ou martyrs, monseigneur saint Denys et de ses compaignons, qui premier apporta la foy en France, pour la quele il fut martyrés, luy et ses compaignons. Et doit estre atachée ceste baniere, comme dist est, en une hante dorée, pour avoir tous jours vrai recordation et memoire de cele haute et noble vision de notre foy et de leur glorieuse passion."

17. The oriflamme should be deployed only in exceptional circumstances and, once victory is gained, should be returned to St-Denis, following the example of Charlemagne.

"Et ont tenu vos devanciers que celle ne doit point estre desployée sans tres grant necessité. Et qui plus est que, la victoire faite, elle doit estre rapportée à grant devotion et reverence en l'eglise de monseigneur saint Denys et rendue sur son autel en remembrance de la victoire, ainsi comme fist Charlemaigne."

18. These things Raoul de Presles has come to believe because he himself has seen two (standards) on the altar of the martyrs consisting of two small golden shafts, from each of which there hung a red banner. One of them is called the banner of Charlemagne, and this is the one that is carried in procession by a monk of the abbey and is properly called the oriflamme.

"De ce me croy je, car je en ay veu deux de mon temps sur l'autel des glorieux martyrs, de chascune partie de l'autel une. Et estoient en hantes de deux petites hantes dorée, ou pentoient à chascune une baniere vermeille, dont l'une estoit apelée la baniere Challemaigne. Et se portoit par reverence par un des religieux à certaines processions. Et c'est ce que l'en apele proprement l'au(ri)flambe, et dont elle vint de ce qui en peut estre venu à ma petite congnoissance."

# Appendix 5:
# The Origin of the Fleurs de Lis in Étienne de Conty's
# *Treatise on the Monarchy*

The Latin text is from BN, ms lat. 11.730, fols. 31v–32.

"Item: Dicti reges Francie non habent arma sua sicut reges christiani arma talia portant sicut predecessores sui voluerunt ordinare. Sed rex Francie portat arma oridinata a Deo per angelum missa beato Dionisio."

"Unde sciendum, dum beatus Dionisius, parisiensis episcopus, esset in castro quod gallice vocatur Mongoie, quod castrum distat a civitate parisiensis per sex leucas vel circiter, angelus domini apparuit ei, ostendens ei unum scutum cum tribus liliis aureis, dicens ei: 'Quae essent arma regis Francie et suorum successorum, quia sicut lilium inter ceteros flores est dulcerius ad tenendum intus et exterius.' Sic reges Francie semper fuerunt et sunt dulciores, intus et exterius, erga fidem catholicam et, propter praedictam causam, in bellis et aliis factis armorum regum Francie semper prclamatur, 'Mongoie-Saint Denis! Hec de causa quia praedicta arma primitus pro regibis Francie fuerunt tradita beato Dionisio in dicto castro de Mongoie. Ideo sine dubio propter superius declarata, reges Francie merito possunt dici santiores omnibus aliis regibus christianis."

*English translation.* Item: The aforesaid French kings do not bear arms similar to those of other Christian kings, whose coats of arms were marshaled by their predecessors, but the arms of the kings of France were preordained by God and were delivered to the blessed Denis by an angel.

On this wise did it come about. For when the blessed Denis, the bishop of Paris, happened to be staying in a castle called in French "Montjoie," that is situated some seven leagues from Paris, the angel of the Lord appeared to him and showed him a shield with three golden lilies. These, he said, are to be the arms of the king of France and his successors. For just as the lily is a most pleasing flower, both inwardly and outwardly, so the kings of France have proved themselves most pleasing inwardly and outwardly toward the Catholic faith. And this is the reason why in warfare and in the other martial deeds of the French kings it has been customary to cry "Montjoie-Saint Denis!" And for the same reason, ever since the arms were first delivered to the blessed Denis in the castle of Montjoie, as has been related, the kings of France can deservedly be called holier than all other Christian kings.

Excerpts of the Latin text of this passage are reproduced in Jacques Krynen, *Idéal du prince et pouvoir royal en France à la fin du moyan age: 1380–1440*, Paris, 1981, 224f.

# Appendix 6:
# An Illustrated Poem on the Origin of the Fleurs de Lis and the Miracle of the Holy Ampulla in the Bedford Hours

The text is from BL, Add. MS. 18.850, fols. 288v–289v.

| | |
|---|---|
| 1 | "Pour plus tenir foy Xptienne establé |
| | Et des pervers dampner l'iniquité |
| | Fu roy Clovys esleu connestable |
| | Ou hault conseil de sainte Terinité; |
| 5 | Pour anoncier la quelle elleccion |
| | Cest angle par digne affeccion |
| | Au lieu con dit Joyenval descendy |
| | A cest hermite; et du divin tresor |
| | Pour roy Clovys convertir lui tendy |
| 10 | Sur champ asur ces trois fleurs de lis d'or, |
| | Disant; 'Amis, ce present honorable |
| | Signifie foy, force et equité. |
| | Clovys sera victorien notable |
| | Par ces armes d'excellent dignité. |
| 15 | A saincte Clode en fera mencion, |
| | Femme Clovys qui par devocion |
| | Veoir te vient.' Lors encontre elle yssy, |
| | Le fait lui dist; elle respondi: 'Des or |
| | Pandra Clovys quant à dieu plaist ainsi |
| 20 | Sur champ d'asur ces trois fleurs de lis d'or.' |
| | L'escue fist faire à cest present semblable |
| | Et fu au roy par elle presenté |

Qui ou nom Dieu le receut acceptable,
Dont fu Cander, roy des Gothoys, mate.
25 Joyenval a de ce fondacion,
Puis print à Rains regeneracion.
Lors transmist Dieu l'ampole à saint Remy,
Dont fu sacré. Si sont ses hoirs encore
Qui ont porte et portent comme lui
30 Sur champ d'asur ces trois fleurs de lis d'or."

*Illustrations and Subtitles.* Fol. 228v (plate 28). Full-page miniature: The Hermit of Joyenval and the Arming of Clovis. Subtitle at the bottom of the page: "Comment Notre Seigneur par son ange envoya les troys fleurs de lis d'or en un escu d'ascur au roys Clovis."

Fol. 289 (plate 26). Roundel in right margin: Clovis Rides to his Encounter with Candar. First subtitle at the bottom of the page: "Comment le roy Clovys chevaucha à tout son ost pour combastre Candar, roy des Gothoys."

Roundel in lower margin: Combat Between Clovis and Candar. Second subtitle: "Comment le roys Cloys est en`bataille ranget contre le dit Candar et le desconfit à force d'armes."

Fol. 289v (plate 27). Roundel in left margin: Baptism of Clovis. First subtitle at the bottom of the page: "Comment le saint esperit aporte la sainte empolle à saint Remy, de quelle fust sacré le roy Clovys."

Roundel in lower margin: Clovis Supervising the Building of the Abbey of Joyenval. Second subtitle: "Comment le roy Clovys fist faire l'abbaye de Joyenval apres qu'il fust baptisé en l'onneur de Dieu."

# Notes

### 1. The *Signum Regis Franciae*

1. For the general distribution of the fleurs de lis in western Europe and on the coats of arms of Lille and Florence, see Pastoureau, 1978, 256f. and figs. p. 263, and 261, 268, and for the seals of the Norman peasantry, Pastoureau, 1979, 55. The double tressure flory counterflory, to use the language of heraldry, of the Scottish arms first appears on Alexander II's seal of 1215 (Michael Maclagan [text] and Jiří Louda, *Heraldry of the Royal Families of Europe* [New York: 1981], 36).

Although in France, to the very end of the ancien régime, anyone of any social rank whatsoever was entitled to bear arms, the choice of armorials being regulated primarily by custom and prudence, beginning in 1320 to 1340 specific heraldic rules and regulations concerning the bearing of arms, which did not in any way correspond to actual practices, are nevertheless sometimes encountered in the treatises on heraldry and in such political tracts as the *Songe du Vergier* of 1378. See Michel Pastoureau's comments in *SV,* 1: 467f., n.25. And when a king or emperor, as occasionally occurred, bestowed a coat of arms as a mark of his favor, such a gesture in no way impinged on the individual's freedom and right to bear arms.

2. They are described in this way in the coat of arms on the king's banner at the battle of Bouvines of 1214 in the *Gesta Philippi Augusti* by Guillaume le Breton, who was present at the battle (H. François Delaborde, *Oeuvres de Rigord et de Guillaume Le Breton* [Paris: 1882], 1:281–82).

3. Luke E. Demaitre, *Doctor Bernard de Gordon: Professor and Practitioner* (Toronto: 1980), 51–59. For the therapeutic properties of the lily, see Bernard de Gordon, *Lilium medicinae* (Lyons: 1574), 6, 75, 90, 122; Robert T. Gunther, *The Greek Herbal of Dioscorides . . . Englished by John Goodyer A. D. 1655* (Oxford: 1934), 347; Robert T. Gunther, *The Herbal of Apuleius Barbarus from the Early Twelfth-Century Manuscript in the Abbey of Bury St. Edmunds (MS Bodley 130)* (facsimile) (Oxford: 1925), fol. 50v; Franz Unterkircher, *Tacuinum Sanitatis in Medicina* (Commentary on Facsimile edition) (Graz: 1967), 66. For the sources of the medieval herbals, see C. Singer, "The Herbal in Antiquity and Its Transmission to Later Ages," *Hellenic Studies* 47 (1927): 1–52; Luisa Cogliati Arano, *The Medieval Health Handbook: Tacuinum Sanitatis* (New York: 1976), 8f, 11.

4. Piaget, 1936, 351, vs. 1070–71.

5. Pastoureau, 1978, 262, no. 6. Like other seals, that of Prince Louis is dated by the year of the document to which it is appended. The matrix of the seal, however, could have been made earlier within the lifetime of the prince, who was

born in 1187, and the use of the seal, with the arms of France on the shield, could then also have antedated 1211. The arms of Prince Louis are unique for a son of a king of France in that they reproduce his father's coat of arms without brisure, that is, without those heraldic distinctions that differentiate the arms of a cadet member of a family.

6. Yves Delaporte and Etienne Houvet, *Les vitraux de la cathédrale de Chartres* (Chartres: 1926), 457f., plate 238. Fleurs de lis in this present study are regarded as armorial only if they occur on a triangular shield or on a banner, the two forms referred to in the contemporary literature as the bearers of the arms of France, or on such garments traditionally used for the display of heraldic devices as a surcoat or a tabard. For various other forms of the escutcheon and for the use of the term heraldic for emblems placed on the circular ground of the royal seals, see Pastoureau, 1979, 91ff.

7. Pastoureau, 1978, 255. Already in the time of Louis VII and Philip Augustus a particular guardian was entrusted with the king's banner (Contamine, 1973, 215).

8. According to Pastoureau, 1979, 28–32, true armorials do not begin to appear until the decade 1140–1150.

9. Douët d'Arcq, 1: no. 31; Roman, plate 3, fig. 2. The influence of Ottonian Germany on the early French seals is persuasive. The first example of a frontal view in the sigillographic ruler portraits is that of the German emperor Otto I, 962 (Florence Elizabeth Harmer, *Anglo-Saxon Writs* [Manchester: 1952], 95). The orb in Robert's left hand, unique in the extant portraits on the French royal seals, seems also to derive from German precedents. An orb may have appeared on Hugh Capet's lost seal (Pinoteau, 1979, 8, 25n.2).

10. Roman, plate 4, fig. 1; Douët d'Arcq, no. 32. The full-length *majestas* portrait was adopted in imitation of that on the seal of Otto III (983–1002) (Harmer, *Anglo-Saxon Writs*, 95). The first mention of the *majestatis sigillum* is in a charter of 1082 of Philip I (Pinoteau, 1979, 8).

11. On the seals of Louis VII, Philip Augustus, and Louis VIII, the scepter in the king's left hand is surmounted by a diamond-shaped frame enclosing another single fleur de lis (Douët d'Arcq, nos. 36, 38, 40). For this and other innovations in the *sceaux de majesté* portraits, see Germain Demay, *Les costumes au môyen âge d'après les sceaux* (Paris: 1880), 84–85; Roman, 75–77. In all the known seals of the queens of France prior to that of Margaret of Provence, the wife of Louis IX, a single fleur de lis is also generally held in the right hand (Pierre Bony, "An Introduction to the Study of Cistercian Seals," in *Studies in Cistercian Art and Architecture,* ed. Meredith P. Lillich [Kalamazoo, Mich.: 1987], 3:201–40, esp. 206n.11).

12. The arguments for a Marian symbolism of the royal fleur de lis stemming from the reign of Louis VI (1108–37) that have been put forward by Gustav Braun von Stumm ("L'origine de la fleur de lis des rois de France du point de vue numismatique," *Revue numismatique,* 3d ser., 13 [1951]: 43–57) are not as convincing to this writer as they have been to others. It should be emphasized, moreover, that in dealing primarily with the coinage von Stumm fails to take into account the important presence of the stylized lily on the earlier *sceaux de majesté.* For the lily as an emblem of royalty in Carolingian times, as well as in the ancient Near

East and in the Egypt of the Pharaohs, see Jean van Malderghem, "Les fleurs de lis de l'ancienne monarchie française," *Annales de la soc. d'archéol. de Bruxelles* 8 (1894): 180–212.

13. The comparison is embodied in a supposed address of Louis VII to the envoys of Henry II (Giraldus Cambrensis, *De Principis Instructionis Liber,* ed. George F. Warner [London: 1891], 317f; English translation in Friedrich Heer, *The Medieval World* [New York: 1962], 341). Gerald also compares the voracious beasts on the arms and banners of other reigning houses with the simple little flowers of the French king. (Giraldus Cambrensis, *De Principis,* 320f.).

14. "Simplices hujusmodi flores his nostris diebus . . . pardos vincere vidimus atque leones" (Giraldus Cambrensis, *De Principis,* 321).

15. Robert Fawtier, *Les Capétiens et la France: Leur role dans sa construction* (Paris: 1942), 86. See also Robert Folz, *L'idée d'empire en occident du Ve au XIVe siècle* (Paris: 1953), 148.

16. Spiegel, 1978, 32.

17. Georgia Sommers Wright, "A Royal Tomb Program in the Reign of St. Louis," *The Art Bulletin* 61 (1974): 224–43; Elizabeth A. R. Brown, "Tomb Programs and Dynastic Myths in Late Medieval France," unpublished manuscript, 1980.

18. Georgia Sommers Wright, "The Tomb of Saint Louis," *Journal of the Warburg and Courtauld Institutes* 34 (1971), 65–82; Elizabeth A. R. Brown, "The Chapel of Saint-Louis at Saint-Denis," unpublished manuscript, 1978, 1. A summary of the talk on which this manuscript is based is given in *Gesta,* 17. 1 (1978): 76.

19. Spiegel, 1978, 78.

20. The Latin text and French translation of this passage are both reproduced in appendix 1. The Latin title of this work as *Vita Sancti Ludovici, Regis Franciae* in *RHGF,* 20, mistakenly assumes that it was composed after the canonization of the king in 1297, for which there is no evidence in the text. For the Latin and French texts, see also Spiegel, 1978, 102f.

21. The emblem on the 1240 seal (Douët d'Arcq, no. 41; Natalis de Wailly, *Eléments de paléographie* [Paris: 1838], 2:plate D, fig. 2) is known as the Florentine fleur de lis since, like the devise of the city of Florence, it includes two stamens. A similar, nonarmorial Florentine fleur de lis occurs on the two counterseals of Philip Augustus, one of 1180 (Pastoureau, 1978, 261, no. 4), the other of 1209 (Douët d'Arcq, nos. 38, 39). For Louis IX's second counterseal, see Douët d'Arcq, no. 42. Another version of the Florentine fleur de lis is held in the king's right hand on Louis IX's 1240 *sceau de majesté* (see plate 3d).

Philip Augustus was the first king of France to use a counterseal that was a relatively small seal imprinted on the back of the *sceau de majesté* in order to further insure its authenticity. Guillaume de Nangis himself was most likely well acquainted with these royal counterseals and with the early *sceaux de majesté,* since he was charged with guarding and transcribing the abbey's charters (Léopold Delisle, *Mémoire sur les ouvrages de Guillaume de Nangis* [Paris: 1873], 3).

22. Viard, 1:5; Faral, 1949, 333n.1.

23. Léopold Delisle, "La chronique d'Hélinand, moine de Froidmont," in

*Notices et documents publiés pour la société de l'histoire de France* (Paris: 1884), 141–54; Herbert Grundmann, "Sacerdotum, Regnum, Studium,'' *Archiv fur Kulturge-schichte* 34 (1951): 5–22, esp. 8n.6.

24. "Alcuinus, scientia vitaque praeclarus, quia sapientiae studium de Roma Parisius transtulit, quod illuc quodam a Graecia translatum fuerat a Romanis" (Vincent of Beauvais, *Speculum historiale* [*Speculum quadruplex, IV*] [Graz: 1965] [Reprint of Douai edition of 1624], 960). For the *Speculum Historiale* as a source for the *Life of Louis IX,* see Hermann Brosien, "Wilhelm von Nangis und Primat," *Neues Archiv der Gesellschaft fur ältere deutsche Geschichtskunde* 4 (1879): 427–509, esp. 438.

25. A. G. Jongkees, "*Translatio Studii:* Les avatars d'une thème médiévale," in *Miscellanea Mediaevalia in Memoriam Jan Frederick Niermeyer* (Groningen: 1967), 41–50.

26. *Chevalerie* and its order of knighthood are well defined in the French translation of a Latin passage in book 3 of Yves' *Life of Saint Denis,* completed in 1317: "Chevalerie segnefie que tous ceus qui sont rebelles à l'evangile et n'obeissent aus commandemens de sainte eglise et sont obstinez et rebelles contre la foi, illes doivent contraindre et aidier et punir. Et pource ou temps de adonques les chavaliers receivent leur espée de l'autel en recongnoissance que il estoient fils de l'eglise et à l'honneur des prestres et à la deffense des povres et à la vengence des mauves et à la aide du peis" (BN, ms. lat. 13.836, fol. 31v).

27. The fusion of Saint Denis and Dionysius the Areopagite can be traced back to the beginning of the ninth century (R. J. Loenertz, "La légende parisienne de S. Denys l'Aréopagite," *Analecta Bollandiana* 69 [1951]: 217–37).

28. Spiegel, 1978, 113–15. Also stemming from St-Denis are two later versions of the original Latin text in de Nangis' *Life of Louis IX:* a somewhat condensed and modified transcript in his *Chronicon* (*Chronique latine de Guillaume de Nangis, de 1113 à 1300,* ed. Hercule Géraud [Paris: 1843], 1:182f.) composed in major part before 1297 (H. François Delaborde, "Notes sur Guillaume de Nangis," *Bibliothèque de l'école des chartes* 44 [1883]: 192–201) and another version in the French translation of the *Life of Louis IX* composed, not however by de Nangis, toward the end of the thirteenth century or the beginning of the fourteenth (Delisle, *Mémoire,* 9f; see also appendix 1).

29. "Quomodo temporibus Karoli quam plurimum augumentum est in Francia studium litterarum et quomodo per sanctum Dionysium Francie regnum in fide, scientia et milicia regna cetera antecellit" (*Life of Saint Denis,* b. 3, chap. 98: BN, ms. lat. 5285, fol. 174v).

30. The passage in Yves ("multiplicitum augumentatum litterarum studium Parisius per quatuorum monachos, venerabilis Bede discipulos, Alcuinum scilicet et [Ra]banum, Claudium et Johannem Scotum factum [est]; itaque est litterarum studium in diebus Karoli regis ab urbe Roma Parisius sic translatum quod illuc scilicet Roman de Grecia translatum fuerat per Romanos" [BN, lat. 5286, fol. 175]) bears comparison with the text of Helinandus: "Alcuinus . . . sapientiae studium de Roma Parisius transtulit, quod illuc quodam a Graecia translatum fuerat a Romanis. Fueruntque Parisius fundatores huius studii quat-

uor monachi, Bedae discipuli, Rabanus & Alcuinus, Claudius & Joannes Scotus" (Vincent of Beauvais, *Speculum historiale, 960*).

31. Although Charlemagne had already been held responsible for having founded the University of Paris, in view of his new role as the bearer of classical culture that he introduced into France, Saint Denis was now also credited with having been its founder (Jongkees, "Translatio Studii," 49, n.42).

32. "Taller in appearance" *(summa specie).* Since *summa* modifies *Fides,* a double meaning may have been intended here to indicate that *Fides* was both the loftiest of the three attributes and the taller of the three petals. In his original comments on the fleur de lis in his *Life of Louis IX* Guillaume de Nangis fails to note the characteristics that distinguish the petal of *Fides* from the other two. This omission has been rectified in his later *Chronicon* ("Duo enim paria folia sapientiam et militiam significant, quae fidem trinum folium significantem, et altius in medio duorum positam, custodiunt et defendunt" [de Nangis, *Chronique latine,* 182]) and in the French translation of de Nangis' Latin text of the *Life of Louis IX* ("Les II. fuellies de la fleur de liz qui sont oeles [ailes] segnefient sens et chevalerie, qui gardent et deffendent la tierce fuellie qui est ou milieu de elles, plus longue et plus haute, para laquelle foys est entendue et senefié" [see appendix 1]).

33. BN, ms. lat. 15, 966, fol. 7v. For this text, see Barthélemy Hauréau, *HLF* 30 (1888), pt. 2, 398–408, and for its date, see Richard H. Rouse and Mary A. Rouse, *Preachers, Florilegia and Sermons: Studies in the Manipulus florum of Thomas of Ireland* (Toronto: 1979), 99.

34. Sumner McK. Crosby, *The Apostle Bas-Relief at Saint-Denis* (New Haven and London: 1972), 18–23; Blaise de Montesquiou-Fezensac, "Le 'Tombeau des corps-saints' à l'abbaye de Saint-Denis," *Cahiers archéologiques* 23 (1974): 81–95.

35. BN, ms. fr. 6465, fol. 323; Sandro Lombardi, *Jean Fouquet* (Florence: 1983), 156, fig. 254 after p. 202.

36. What reliance can be placed on the accuracy of Fouquet's view of the tabernacle? Although his rendering of the architecture of the apse of St-Denis is far from correct (Suger's original twelfth-century columns are missing from the supports of the apsidal ground-story arcade, and the window of the axial chapel has been erroneously supplied with Gothic tracery), the three gables of the tabernacle's west front are indicated in approximately the same proportions in Francois de Belleforest's 1575 engraving of the church's interior (Montesquiou-Fezensac, "Le 'Tombeau des corps-saints'," fig. 4). The lateral figures of the two martyrs under semicircular arches can be compared to those in a small ivory, circa 1150, probably from St-Denis, now in the Louvre, in which each of the three martyrs stands under the round arch of a triple-arched arcade (Crosby, *Apostle Bas-Relief,* 62f. n.30, fig. 67). In Fouquet's miniature the center arch is obscured by a horizontal band (for an inscription?), and Saint Denis himself seems to be wearing a mitre, indications of a later reworking of this central section, which for this very reason adds validity to the appearance of the tabernacle in the miniature.

37. Montesquiou-Fezensac, "Le 'Tombeau des corps-saints'," 85.

38. The other recipients of the king's fleur de lis were the shrines of Saint Thomas à Becket at Canterbury and Saint Martin at Tours and the church of Notre-Dame at Boulogne-sur-mer that housed a miraculous cult image of the Virgin (Edgar Boutaric, "Notices et extraits de documents inédits relatifs à l'histoire de France sous Philippe le Bel," *Notices et extraits des mss. de la Bibl. Nat. et autres bibliothèques* [Paris: 1862], 20: pt. 2, 233f.).

39. Montesquiou-Fezensac, "Le 'Tombeau des corps-saints'," 85.

40. Blaise de Montesquiou-Fezensac, with Danielle Gaborit-Chopin, *Le Trésor de Saint-Denis, inventaire de 1634,* (Paris: 1973), 1:228, item 73. Although these votive lilies no longer exist, another fleur de lis donated to the abbey has miraculously survived. A masterpiece of the art of the Parisian jewelers, it has been placed in the right hand of the silver gilt statuette of the Virgin and Child offered to St-Denis in 1339 by Jeanne d'Evreux, the widow of Charles IV, and now in the Louvre (Montesquiou-Fezensac and Gaborit-Chopin, *Le Trésor de Saint-Denis, Planches et Notices* [Paris: 1977], 3:30, plates 12b–c). The motif of the fleur de lis in her right hand not only occurs in other votive statues of the Virgin (the lily was after all still her emblem at this time, to be superceded later by the rose), but it can be traced back to the stylized lily held by the seated figure of Mary on the 1146 seal of the chapter of Notre-Dame (Douët d'Arcq, no. 7253). Other images of Mary with a lily without stem are cited on ecclesiastical coins by von Stumm ("L'origine de la fleur de lis," 45f.), the oldest being an obole of Strasbourg, struck before the year 1000 in the name of Otto III (von Stumm, "L'origine de la fleur de lis," fig. 3).

Although von Stumm regards the flower held by the seated Virgin on the Notre-Dame seal as indicative of the Marian symbolism of the royal fleur de lis, this image of Mary may instead have been derived from that of the kings on the earlier *sceaux de majesté* and would thus constitute another not unusual instance of the emulation of monarchical imagery in medieval relgious art.

41. "De ces .iii. fleurs la nature est segnefiée / L'escu des iii. fleurs de lis" (ms. lat. 13.836, fol. 31v). The reference occurs at the end of the translator's extremely free rendering of the allegorical poem on the fleur de lis. See the French translation in appendix 2.

Ms. lat. 5286, from which the Latin excerpts in appendix 2 have been drawn, is the only copy with the complete Latin text of the third book of Yves' work and was made after 1328 but before 1373 according to Spiegel, 1978, 114f. The first two books of the presentation copy, together with a French translation and a complete set of miniatures, survive intact in fr. 2090–92. Lat. 13.836, with the translation of the Latin text in the margin, has been recognized as part of the third book of this same presentation manuscript in Virginia Wylie Egbert, *On the Bridges of Medieval Paris* (Princeton: 1974), 7, n.17. The manuscript, however, is not only incomplete but also bereft of all but one of its miniatures, together with the text on the other side of the missing folios. The contention of Gabrielle Spiegel (Spiegel, 1978, 114) that lat. 13.836 is a fragment of a second complete copy presupposes that there were two fully illuminated copies of all three books of Yves' work, together with the French translation, a conclusion that lacks plausibility in the view of this writer.

2. The Trinitarian Symbolism of the Three Fleurs de Lis

1. Chatillon, 1955, 163. The text of the *Vitis mystica* has been included among the works attributed to Bernard of Clairvaux in the *Patrologia Latina*, ed. J. P. Migne, 184: cols. 635–740.

2. *Patrologia Latina*, cols. 690B–707B.

3. "Flosculus in medio flosculorum aureorum praeeminens, ceteris longior, Divinitatem, signat, quae est super omnia Deus benedictus in saeculi, Amen. Habitantem hic flosculus caput unum triangulum, per quod Trinitas ipsa designatur. Unum enim caput divinae substantiae unitatem figurat: tres vero anguli eminentes, et a se distincti, signant Trinitatis personae" (*Patrologia Latina*, col. 707B).

4. The poem, with English translation, is published in Walter H. Storer and Charles A. Rochedieu, *Six Historical Poems of Geoffroi de Paris, Written 1314–1318, University of North Carolina, Studies in Romance Languages,* 16 (Chapel Hill: 1950), 73–89.

5. Storer and Rochedieu, *Geoffroi de Paris,* v–vi; Armel Diverrés, *La chronique métrique attribuée à Geoffroy de Paris* (Paris: 1956), 14. For Geoffroy as a member of the chancellery and for the manuscript containing the *Dit des Alliés,* see *FG,* no. 231.

6. For a detailed history of these alliances and Geoffroy's attitude toward them, see Elizabeth A. R. Brown, "Reform and Resistance to Royal Authority in Fourteenth Century France: The Leagues of 1314–1315," *Parliaments, Estates and Representation* 1.2, (Dec. 1981): 109–37, esp. 127; Charles-Victor Langlois in Ernest Lavisse, *Histoire de France depuis les origines jusqu'à la Révolution,* 3: pt. 2 (Paris: 1901), 265–72.

7. Storer and Rochedieu, *Geoffroi de Paris,* 74 (stanzas 4, 5), 77 (stanza 13); Langlois, *Histoire de France,* 3: pt. 2, 272.

8. Vs. 157–63.

9. Vs. 164–68. The alternate meanings given "trible" and "triblée" as "riddled" and "broken up" in Storer and Rochedieu's note on verses 165 and 168 do not seem to accord with the general context of these verses.

10. Vs. 169–72.

11. See appendix 3, stanza 8, and my concluding comments.

12. In Chatillon, 1955, 165, the symbolism of the head of the pistil in the *Vitis mystica* has been applied to the fleurs de lis in the later Latin poem on the origin of the arms of France composed at Joyenval in the 1330s, while its primary relevance for the fleurs de lis in the *Dit des Alliés* has to my knowledge remained totally unexplored.

13. "Va, quar victoire t'est sauvé" (V. 180).

14.  Tu doiz estre pierre adurée,
     E(t) glaive asceré et espée,
     Pour maintenir ton tenement,
     Si que ne soit pas mesprisée

> France, en ton temps, ne diffamée,
> Dont tu as le couronnement.

(Vs. 241–46)

15. Perroy, 1945, 49–52; Raymond Cazelles, *La Société politique et la crise de la royauté sous Philippe de Valois* (Paris: 1958), chap. 1, esp. 38.

16. Paul Lehugeur, *Histoire de Philippe le Long, roi de France (1316–1322)* (Paris: 1897), 86n.3. Supposedly dating from legendary Merovingian times, the Salic law debarring women from the French succession is first mentioned circa 1358 (John M. Potter, "The Development and Significance of the Salic Law of France," *English Historical Review* 52 [1937]: 235–53, esp. 247).

17. The results effected by the commissioners dispatched to the provinces by Philip early in 1317 are described in Brown, "Reform and Resistance," 127.

18. Perroy, 1945, 33, 55f.; Cazelles, *La Société politique,* 47–72.

19. Edward himself as Duke of Aquitaine had already paid reluctant homage to Philip VI at Amiens in June 1329 (Michael St. John Packe, *King Edward III* [London and Boston: 1983], 43).

20. Perroy, 1945, 65. For the preparations for this crusade, see also Suryal Atiya, *The Crusades in the Later Middle Ages* (London: 1938), 95f.; Kenneth M. Setton, general ed., *A History of the Crusades,* 2d ed., (Madison: 1975), 3:53.

21. Ronald Nicholson, *Edward III and the Scots: The Formative Years of a Military Career, 1327–1335* (London: 1965), 70.

22. Piaget, 1898, 72–92 (text), 68–72 (résumé of the poem).

23. For the life and works of Philippe de Vitri, see Piaget, 1898, 55–65; *HLF* 24: 483, 29: 505–7, 36: 66f.

24. Direct evidence of his knowledge of de Nangis' *Chronicon* is provided in Hindman and Spiegel, 389, n.31.

25. Stanzas 3, 4.

26. Stanza 5, vs. 25–27.

27. See above, page 35 and n.9.

28.
> ces .111. fleurs, conjoinment,
> S' en yront en la sainte terre
> Pour essaucier la foy et querre
> Nostre general sauvement.

(stanza 116, vs. 785–87)

29.
> Beneurez qui pourront vivre
> L'an mil CCC et .V, et trente!

(stanza 121, vs. 817–18)

These verses can be aptly compared with Daniel, 12:12: "Beatus, qui exspectat, et pervenit usque ad dies mille trecento trigenta quinque."

30. Stanzas 138–55 *passim.*
31. Stanza 156, vs. 1023–26.
32. Stanza 157, vs. 1029–33: stanza 158, vs. 1035–39.
33. Vs. 1076–77.
34. For the end of the great age of the crusades and the later efforts to revive the crusading spirit, see Joseph R. Strayer, *Medieval Statecraft and the Perspectives of History* (Princeton: 1971), 159, 192; Raymond L. Kilgour, *The Decline of Chivalry as Shown in the French Literature of the Late Middle Ages* (Cambridge: 1937), 149.
35. Piaget, 1898, 90, stanza 159.
36. The poet exhorts the *chevaliers* to become true champions in order to deal with rebellions that disturb the populace and

> Pour resister aus nacions
> Estranges, quant invasions
> Encontre le peuple esmouvoient.

> (stanza 81, esp. vs. 88–90)

Later on in the poem, he appeals directly to the saint himself:

> Et le glorieux saint Denis, . . .
> France gard, deffende et delivre
> Qu'erreur ne la puist decevoir.

> (stanza 161, vs. 1055, 1057–58)

And finally he addresses the Deity:

> Soubz tel escu, Diex, par sa grace,
> Gard France et bien regner la face! . . .
> Que le peuple puist vivre en pez.

> (Vs. 1141–42, 1146)

37. Perroy, 1945, 67.
38. Perroy, 1945, 68.
39. Robert Fawtier, *L'Europe occidentale de 1270 à 1380,* pt. 1, *De 1270 à 1328* (*Histoire du moyen âge,* ed Gustave Glotz, 6: pt. 1), (Paris: 1940), 64, 74.
40. BN, ms. lat. 5286, fol. 204; *RHGF* 20: 47, C–D. I am indebted to Professor Elizabeth A. R. Brown for this citation.
41. After hailing Christ as the King of the Franks, he describes the banner of His first advent, that is, His Incarnation: "Vexillum enim adventus Christi fuit depictum cum floribus liliorum." In the red banner of His Second Coming, denoting His fury, can be recognized the oriflamme (Ernest H. Kantorowitz, *The King's Two Bodies: A Study in Mediaeval Theology* [Princeton: 1957], 255n.191). For the life of Guillaume de Sauqueville, see N. Valois in *HLF,* 1914, 34:298–307.
42. The first paragraph of his sermon, *Osianna Filio David,* is reproduced in Hellmut Kämpf, *Pierre Dunois und die geistigen Grundlagen des französischen Nation-*

*albewustseins um 1300, Beitrage zur Kulturgeschichte des Mittelalters und der Renaissance,* 54 (Lepizg and Berlin: 1935), 112.

43. The Latin text is quoted in full in Bloch, 116n.3.

44. Joseph R. Strayer, "Philip the Fair—'A Constitutional King,' " *American Historical Review* 62 (1956): 18–32, esp. 30.

45. Karl Wenck, *Philipp der Schöne von Frankreich, seine Persönlichkeit und das Urteil der Zeitgenossen* (Marburg: 1905), 66f.

46. Joseph R. Strayer, "France: The Holy Land, the Chosen People, and the Most Christian King," in *Action and Conviction in Early Modern Europe: Essays in Honor of E. H. Harbison* (Princeton: 1969), 3–16, esp. 6.

47. Text reproduced in Kampf, *Pierre Dunois,* 99. See also Strayer, "France," 15.

48.  Par ces .iii. fleurs est France forte,
France par els couronne porte
Et est par elles honnourée.

(Piaget, 1898, 72, stanza 3, vs. 16–18)

### 3. The Celestial Origin of the Three Fleurs de Lis

1. A. Dutilleux, "Notice sur l'abbaye de Joyenval," *Mémoires de la Soc. hist. et archéol. de l'arrondissement de Pointoise et du Vexin* 13 (1890): 41–114, esp. 41–45.

2. A French translation of Gregory of Tour's account of the battle is given in Georges Tessier, *Le Baptême de Clovis: 25 décembre* (Paris: 1964), 52f., based on B. Krusch's 1951 edition of the *Historia Francorum,* published in *Monumenta Germaniae historica, Scriptures rerum merovingicarum,* 1:1.

3. Tessier, *Le Baptême de Clovis,* 55.

4. BN, ms. lat. 5286, fol. 131v. While Clovis, his caparisoned charger and his banner, are decorated with fleurs de lis like a contemporary king of France, the emblems of the king of the Alemanni are represented by the eagles of the Empire.

5. Bossuat, 1940, 93–101 (text of the poem), 86–91 (résumé).

6.  Quibus allatis ornatis tribus lilii floribus
Aureis et asuratis ceruleis in partibus.

(stanza 16, vs. 61–62)

7.  Tunc, reversus de prelio, loquebatur cum uxore
De trium florum lilie, de asurate colore,
Quid signaret misterio, . . .
Uxor respondet: 'Ideo tibi dat santa Trinitas
Victoriam, Clodoveo, ut trium florum unitas
Auri sint tuo clipeo, quod dabit perpetuitas
Ut dominatu aureo tua regnet auctoritas.'

(stanza 19, vs. 73–74; stanza 20)

8. Chatillon, 1955, 105. Each of these twenty-three stanzas from 1 to 23 begins with a letter of the medieval alphabet from *A* to *Z*. For this type of alphabetical scheme in medieval poetry, see Bossuat, 1940, 88f.

9. The second part of the poem, stanzas 28 to 50, also comprises twenty-three similarly alphabeticized quatrains (Bossuat, 1940, 98–101; Chatillon, 1955, 108f.). But in order to complete fifty quatrains in all, or two hundred verses, four additional quatrains comprising stanzas 24–27 were inserted between the two alphabetized parts (Chatillon, 1955, 106f.). In stanza 24 Clovis presents himself to Saint Remi of Reims, thus linking these additional verses to the last stanza (23) of part 1, in which Clovis prepares himself for his baptism. The other three additional stanzas laud his later piety and end by mentioning the war cry "Montjoie-Saint Denis!" derived from his castle of Montjoie. That both parts of the poem, as well as the four added stanzas, were indeed composed by the canons regular of the abbey is suggested in verse 198, stanza 50, at the very end of the poem: "fundavit Bartholomeus / Locum quo sumus coloni" (Bartholomew founded the place where we are the settlers).

10. Dutilleux, "Notice sur l'abbaye de Joyenval," 62; Bossuat, 1940, 92.

11. Formerly a favorite summer residence of the bishops of Paris, Conflans-Ste-Honorine is now a working-class new town some twenty miles northwest of Paris. Its present mayor, Michel Rocard, is, as of this writing, the premier of France.

12. Destroyed in the seventeenth century, the tower, just south of Poissy, is mentioned in a letter of 1358 as Montjoie Saint Denis (Faral, 1962, 101n.2).

13. See my *The Portal of the Saints of Reims Cathedral*, Monographs on Archaeology and the Fine Arts, 13 (1965): 37f. for the beliefs concerning the holy ampulla.

14. Bossuat, 1940, 100, stanza 45.

15. Stanzas 46–50.

16. Bossuat, 1940, 86. But the correct date is not 1331, as given by Bossuat, but 1333 according to *Gallia christiana,* 8:col. 1334.

17. The poem is dated not before the second quarter of the fourteenth century in Faral, 1949, 337 and between 1328 and 1335 in Chatillon, 1955, 182–190.

18. BN, ms. lat. 13.836, fol. 31v. See also appendix 2.

19. Bossuat, 1940, 94, v. 7.

20. As can be inferred from the first two verses of the poem:

> Aggredior opusculum jussu obediencie,
> Quod non latere populum debet pie memorie.

(Bossuat, 93)

(I approach this little work by order, in obedience [i. e., to his superior, the abbot] / So that the pious memory [of the legend] should not be hidden from the people.)

21. Chatillon, 1955, 188; Bossuat, 1940, 85.

22. The text of the poem is published in Piaget, 1936. The author's name is misspelled "Digueville" in Hindman and Spiegel, 390, and again in other publications of the early 1980s. Thus do errors proliferate.

23. For his life and works, see Faral, 1962.

24. A more detailed résumé is given in Faral, 1962, 89–95.

25. This is in spite of the doubts expressed by Faral (1962, 104) who claims any knowledge of the legend of Joyenval on the part of Digulleville is highly improbable, and who had already stated his belief that the Latin poem probably stems from circa 1350! This date for the Latin poem is repeated in Hindman and Spiegel, 391.

26.  Et ad sanctum Remigium supplex, devotus, humilis,
    Implorabat officium.

(Bossuat, 1940, 97, vs. 93–94)

27. Piaget, 1936, 351, vs. 1070–71, and 1080–81.

28. Michael St. John Packe, *King Edward III* (London and Boston: 1983), 79.

29. Desmond Seward, *The Hundred Years War: The English in France 1337–1453* (London: 1978), 35. See also G. P. Cuttino, "The Causes of the Hundred Years War," *Speculum* 31 (1956): 463–77, esp. 469, 472.

30. Piaget, 1936, 334f, vs. 439–50.

31. According to recent studies on the question of the double-headed eagle, summarized in Pastoureau, 1979, 148f., though occasionally used under the Hohenstaufen, it did not become the definite heraldic emblem of the emperor until the beginning of the fifteenth century. But according to Felix Hauptman in his early work on heraldry (*Wappenkunde* [Munich and Berlin: 1914], 21), it was Ludwig who established the double-headed eagle as the emblem of the empire, a theory that is given some support in the length to which Digulleville has gone in deriding the monstrous characteristics of this double-headed freak of nature, and thereby mocking the emperor himself (Piaget, 1936, 336–39, vs. 499–619).

32. Henry Stephen Lucas, *The Low Countries and the Hundred Years War: 1326–1347* (Ann Arbor: 1929), 290–93; Paul Johnson, *The Life and Times of Edward III* (London: 1973), 61.

33. Faral, 1949, 331.

34. *Chronique de Richard Lescot religieux de Saint-Denis,* ed. Jean Lemoine (Paris: 1896), 47, 215–28. See also John Bell Henneman, *Royal Taxation in Fourteenth Century France* (Princeton: 1971), 129.

35. According to Froissart, a tailor of Ghent immediately fashioned a tunic for the king adorned with the new emblems (Lucas, *The Low Countries,* 364f., n.205).

36. Packe, *King Edward III,* 88.

4. The Prologue to the *Cité de Dieu*

1. Bloch, 138.

2. Uncertainty exists as to whether Jean Golein's translation dates from 1372 or 1374 (Contamine, 1973, 204, n.2). The treatise has been published in Jackson from the original text of the presentation manuscript of the *Rational des Divins Offices,* BN, ms. fr. 437, fols. 43v–55v. Brief extracts are given in Bloch, 478–89.

3. Ms. fr. 437, fol. 48. In the margin, opposite Jean Golein's reference to the

Dionysian origin of the fleurs de lis, is a notation: "Non, car Dieux les envoia par miracle à Montjoie." Marc Bloch has suggested that this marginal correction, in an impersonal hand, might have been dictated by Charles V to a secretary, though granting there is no proof whatsoever for such a conclusion (479). In Jackson (315n.75), however, in a misreading of Bloch, this correction has been attributed to Charles V himself, an error repeated in Hindman and Spiegel (393, n.43).

4. "Mais ces .ii. banieres de France sont baillés, l'une par le saint hermite de Joyenval des .iii. fleurs de lys, et l'autre par revelacion de angelz en merveilleuse vision et clere apparicion" (Ms. fr. 437, fol. 52v; see also Jackson, 322). The second banner mentioned was the oriflamme that in a vision an angel is said to have revealed to the emperor of Constantinople. This legend is also included in the treatise (Jackson, 320f).

5. Etienne de Conty (c. 1350–1413) was the chief benefactor of the library at Corbie (Léopold Delisle, "Recherches sur l'ancienne bibliothèque de Corbie," *Bibliothèque de l'Ecole des Chartes* 21 (1860): 421–26, esp. 421f.

6. "et propter praedictam causam in bellis et aliis factis armorum regum Francie semper proclamatur 'Mongoie-Saint Denis!' Hac de causa quia praedicta arma primitus pro regibus Francie fuerunt tradita beato Dionisio in dicto castro Mongoie" (BN, ms. lat. 11.730, fol. 32. See also appendix 5).

7. S. O. Dunlap Smith, "Illustrations of Raoul de Praelles' Translation of St. Augustine's City of God Between 1375 and 1420" (Ph.D. diss., New York University, 1974), 1:32. For the life of Raoul de Presles, see Antoine Lancelot, "Mémoire sur la vie et les ouvrages de Raoul de Presles," *Mémoires de l'Académie des Inscriptions et Belles-Lettres* 13 (1740): 607–24 and 617 (bis)-665; Robert Bossuat, "Raoul de Presles," *HLF* 40 (1974): 113–86. Another work, a treatise on the oriflamme, wrongly attributed to Raoul de Presles by Bossuat ("Raoul de Presles," 157 f., 158n.1), is in fact the text of a sermon delivered in 1414 by an abbot of St-Denis (Charles J. Liebman, Jr., "Un sermon de Philippe de Villette, abbé de Saint-Denis . . .," *Romania* 78 [1944–45]: 444–72).

8. Charles V's experiences in Paris before his accession, when he was regent for his father while he was imprisoned in London, are matched by those of Raoul de Presles, as he has described them in his *Compendium Morale* of c. 1360. See Robert Bossuat, "Raoul de Presles et les malheurs du temps," in *Studi in onoro di Italo Siciliano* (*Biblioteca dell' Archivum Romanicum*, ser. 1) (Florence: 1966), 86: pt. 1, 117–22.

9. BN, ms. fr. 22.912, fol. 4v.

10. For Charles' reputation as *Karolus Sapiens,* see Desmond Seward, *The Hundred Years War: The English in France 1337–1453* (London: 1978), 103f.

11. As indicated in a note at the end of the second volume of the presentation copy, BN, ms. fr. 22.913, fol. 449. Léopold Delisle, *Recherches sur la librarie de Charles V* (Paris: 1907), 1:109f.

12. The commentary on the Salic law, from book 3, chap. 21, is reproduced in Lancelot, "Mémoire sur la vie," 642–44.

13. The idea of Clovis as the very first Christian king is already implicitly

present in verses 179 and 180 of the Latin poem: "In ecclesia Remensium ubi rex primus illico / Accepit baptisterium in sermone veridico" (Bossuat, 1940, 100).

14. Viard (1920), 1:65–67.

15. A. Van de Vyver, "L'unique victoire contre les Alamans et la conversion de Clovis en 506," *Revue belge de philologie et d'histoire* 17 (1938): 793–813, esp. 801.

16. Bloch, 232n.1; Albert Stimming, "Die geschwänzten' Engländer," in *Studi letterari e linguistici dedicati a Pio Rajna* (Milan: 1911), 475–90; P. Richard, *Britain in Medieval French Literature, 1100–1500* (Cambridge: 1956), 165f.

17. The proposals made by François Chatillon ("Le roi Caudat," *Mélanges à la mémoire d'Istvan Frank* [Saarbrucken: 1957], 141–54) that Caudat is derived from *condate,* the Roman word for the confluence of two rivers, or else from the symbolic serpent *(Deos conflatiles)* mentioned in Exodus 34:17, do not seem as convincing to this writer as does the derivation from *caudatus.*

18. BN, ms. lat. 14.663, fols. 35–36v, fol. 38–38v; Lancelot, "Mémoire sur la vie," 635f.

19. Chatillon, 1955, 134f.

20. The presence of the fleurs de lis on the arms of Joyenval can be inferred from the conclusion of the legend in the Prologue: "Fu fondé un lieu religier qui fu et encore est appelé l'abbaye de Joie en Val, en laquelle l'escue de ces armes a esté par lonc temps en reverence de ce" (appendix 4.7). But nothing seems to be known about the abbey's actual coat of arms. Four nonarmorial fleurs de lis appear on the 1364 counterseal of the abbot of Joyenval (Douet d'Arcq, no. 8776), but none on the 1245 seal of the community (Douet d'Arcq, no. 8250). See Bloch, 231n.2. Other than the sparse foundations of the abbey church, these two seals are, as far as I know, the sole existing material remains of the abbey.

21. This last portion of the Prologue, written retrospectively, was probably added later on, after Raoul de Presles had finished his translation, and it leads logically to an analysis of the major divisions of the text and then, beginning on folio 6 of fr. 22.912, to a list of the chapter headings for book 1.

22. BN, ms. fr. 437, fol. 54. Jackson, 324.

23. Delisle, "Recherches sur l'ancienne bibliothèque de Corbie," 421. For other aspects of Etienne de Conty's life, see Philippe Contamine, "Une interpolation de la 'Chronique Martinienne': le 'Brevis Tractatus' d'Etienne de Conty, official de Corbie (t 1413)," *Annales de Bretagne et des pays de l'Quest* 87. 2 (1980): 367–86.

24. Marion Schnerb-Lièvre (*SV* 1:lxxxv f.) has tentatively identified the author of the *Somnium* as probably Evard de Trémaugon, a canon and doctor of civil law, as well as a counselor to the king.

25. Another instance of the use of the word *Saracen* in the general sense of *pagan* occurs in the second quarter of the thirteenth century in Villard de Honnecourt's *Sketchbook* where the drawing of a Gallo-Roman funerary monument is described as "li sepouture dun sarrazin" (Carl F. Barnes, Jr. and Lon B. Shelby, "The Preliminary Drawing for Villard de Honnecourt's 'Sepulchre of a Saracen,' " *Gesta* 25 [1986]: 135–38).

26. Black crescents on a light field also occur on the banner of a group of pagans in a battle scene included in a copy of *Le Roman de Godefroi de Bouillon,*

dated 1337 and thus approximately contemporary with the Latin poem on the fleurs de lis (BN, ms. fr. 22.495, fol. 265v; Pastoureau, 1979, 248, fig. 267).

27. "Nam, ut narrant historiae, cum antiquitus reges Franciae ante commissionem consueverunt tres buffones marinos deferre, dicti tres buffones in tria lilia mirabiliter sunt conversi" (*Somnium Viridarii,* book 1, chap. 173 in Melchior Goldast, ed. *Monarchia Sancti Romani Imperii* [Hanover: 1611], 1:58–229, esp. 129).

28. Toads cling to the boiling cauldron in the lowest right inner voussoir of the Last Judgment portal of Notre-Dame, Paris, 1220–30 (Willibald Sauerländer, *Gotische Skupturen in Frankreich 1140–1270* [Munich: 1970], 112, plate 73) and in a relief from the destroyed choir screen of the cathedral of Bourges, c. 1260, Paris, Musée du Louvre (Sauerländer, *Gotische Skupturen,* plate 294). Toads nursing at the breasts of Luxuria occur in the "Enfer de Braine," a relief composed of fragments, probably from the destroyed choir screen, now in the church at Braine and dated before 1216 (Jeoraldean McClain, "A Modern Reconstruction of the West Portals of Saint-Yved at Braine," *Gesta* 24.2 [1985]: 105–19; Sauerländer, *Gotische Skupturen,* 112, plate 73) and on the tympanum of the Last Judgment on the west central portal of the cathedral of Bourges, c. 1250 (Sauerländer, *Gotische Skupturen,* 184). Three toads cling to the head of the Leviathan on the Last Judgment tympanum of the church of St-Eugène (Aisne), after 1250 (?) (Edouard Fleury, *Antiquités et monuments du départment de l'Aisne* [Paris: 1882], 4:26, fig. 555; photo by Robert Branner, Photographic Collection, Dept. of Art History, Columbia University).

29. Oxford Bodleian Library, MS douce 180. The close stylistic relationships between some of the miniatures and fresco and panel painting in Westminster Abbey point to the Westminster court school as the source of the manuscript (Peter Klein, *Commentary on the Facsimile of the Douce Apocalypse* [Graz: 1983], 1:37, 49).

30. Douce 180, fol. 56 (p. 87), based on the text: "And when the thousand years are expired, Satan shall be loosed out of prison, and shall go out to deceive the nations of the earth, Gog and Magog, to gather them together to battle" (Revelations 20:7–8).

31. "Et vidi de ore draconis, et de ore bestiae, et de ore pseudoprophetae spiritus tres immundos in modum ranarum." The demonic nature of frogs has likewise been alluded to in the writings of the Church Fathers (Alexander C. Hassal, *The Douce Apocalypse* [London: 1961], 8). The emblems in the Douce Apocalypse are erroneously referred to as toads in Michel Pastoureau ("L'héraldique, une discipline méconnue," *L'histoire,* no. 9, Feb. 1979, 112–13) and by Marion Schnerb-Lièvre in a note to book 1, chap. 80, 8, of the *Songe du Vergier (SV,* 1:449), who also mentions three toads on a banner in a window in Chartres cathedral, as cited in W. Smith (*Les drapeaux à travers les âges et dans le monde entier* [Paris: 1976], 131). This, however, must be a misquotation. Although this French publication has not been available to me, in what is apparently the original English edition (Whitney Smith, *Flags Through the Ages and Across the World* [New York: 1975]), an illustration of a banner with three toads on page 131 is described as stemming from "a tapestry in the Cathedral of Reims." This can only refer to the banner of Clovis in one of the fifteenth-century Clovis tapestries described above, now at Reims. (See also plate 44a.) Nor have I found any other basis for

Schnerb-Lièvre's claim that a tradition of toads as the emblems of the pagan Clovis antedated the crescents of the legend of Joyenval by many decades (*SV,* 1:449f).

32. Hassal, *The Douce Apocalypse.* As suggested by the full text of Apocalypse 16:14 ("Sunt enim spiritus daemoniorum, facientes signa, et procedunt ad reges totius terrae, congregara illos in proelium ad diem magnum omnipotentis Dei"), the mission of the demonic spirits in gathering together the kings of the earth was similar to that of Satan himself in Apocalypse 20:7–8 (Klein, *Commentary,* 224).

33. *SV,* 1:449.

34. This explanation presupposes that at this time the creatures in the reliefs on the portals and the choir screens were indeed thought to be toads, even though originally they may have been intended to represent, not toads, but frogs, as in the Douce Apocalypse.

35. For the dating of the French and Latin texts, see *SV,* 1:xx, xxviii; *FG,* no. 282. According to Schnerb-Lièvre (*SV,* 1:lxxxvff.), the author of the French translation was definitely not Evard de Trémaugon who may, nevertheless, have had a hand in certain of the emendations.

36. Book 1, chap. 80, 8; *SV,* 1:133.

## 5. The Shield and the Crown

1. BN, ms. fr. 22.912, fol. 3. But there is no conclusive evidence that supporting angels were solely the result of the legend in the Prologue. Two angels also support the royal shield charged with multiple lilies on the frontispiece of Charles V's copy of the *Grandes chroniques* (BN, fr. 2813, fol. 4), executed between 1375 and 1379 (*FG,* no. 284) and the shield bearing the arms of Jeanne, dame de Plasnes et de la Mouche of 1376, cited in Germain Demay (*Les costumes au môyen âge d'après les sceaux* [Paris: 1880], 212). A single angel supports the escutcheon with fleurs de lis of Jeanne II of Navarre, of 1330 (Pinoteau, 1979, 25n.23).

2. Léopold Delisle, *Recherches sur la librairie de Charles V* (Paris: 1907), 1:61.

3. "Lilia quidem signum regni Francie, in quo florent flores; ymo flores lilii non tantum duo, sed tres, ut in se tipum gererent Trinitatis." Often reproduced, this well-known passage of the preamble is quoted by, among others, Antoine Lancelot and Foncemagne (*Mémoires de l'academie des Inscriptions et Belles-lettres* [1740], 23:634; [1753], 20:593) and by Vallet de Viriville (*Mémoires de la société des antiquaires de France* [1865], 28:243).

4. The author of the charter, however, may have had in mind the obverse of a silver coin, the "Blanc au K," issued under Charles V on 20 April 1365 (Lafaurie, no. 373, plate 16), in which two nonarmorial fleurs de lis on the circular field of the coin flank a large initial *K* under a crown, the latter a motif that was incorporated into the initial *K* of the charter.

5. See above, 87f.

6. "ut sicut Pater, Verbum et Spiritus Sanctus hi tres unum sunt."

7. MS. 3142, fol. 229; Jean Bodel, *La chanson des Saxons,* ed. Francisque Michel (Paris: 1839), 1:lii.

8. Max Prinet, "Armoiries couronnées figurées sur des sceaux français de la fin du XIIIe et du commencement du XIVe siècles," *Revue archèologique,* 4th ser., 14 (1909): 370–79, esp. 371, fig. 1. The seal of Bordeaux was followed by numerous later seals displaying the crowned arms of France belonging to other French communes and to the royal courts of law, and finds an echo in three nonarmoiral fleurs de lis, surmounted by a crown, on a minor seal of John le Bon, of 1343 (Douët D'Arcq, no. 55).

9. Hervé Pinoteau and Claude Le Gallo, *L'héraldique de Saint Louis et de ses compagnons, Les Cahiers Nobles,* 27 (Paris: 1966), 6; Natalis de Wailly, *Eléments de paléographie* (Paris; 1838), 2: plate G, no. 6. Since the *sceau de majesté* was the most precious of the royal seals, its matrix was not allowed to be removed from the chancellery. Hence, beginning with Philip VI, another type of seal, the so-called secret seal, was used when the king was traveling in the provinces (Roman, 20f., 31).

10. Hervé Pinoteau, "Quelques reflexions sur l'oeuvre de Jean du Tillet," *Archives héraldiques suisses* 70 (1955): 2–25, esp. 8; de Wailly, *Elément de paléographie,* plate H, no. 1. For the use of the counterseal, see above, chap. 1, p. 10, n.21.

11. *FG,* no. 319. Charles V's aversion for the old royal palace on the Ile de la Cité due to the tragic and violent events he experienced there as regent for his father later led him to choose the Hotel St-Paul on the right bank as his domicile (Roland Delachenal, *Histoire de Charles V* [Paris: 1909], 2:207, [Paris: 1916], 3:105f).

12. Claire Richter Sherman, *The Portraits of Charles V of France (1338–1380), Monographs on Archaeology and the Fine Arts,* 20 (New York: 1969), 38f., figs. 25, 26.

13. Sherman, *Portraits of Charles V,* 39f., fig. 27.

14. Max Prinet, "Les variations du nombre des fleurs de lis dans les armes de France," *Bulletin monumental* 75 (1911): 467–88. Since the arms of France with three fleurs de lis occur almost as early as those with multiple lilies, I have therefore avoided as misleading the terms generally used in heraldry of "France ancient" for the arms with multiple lilies and "France modern" for those with triple emblems.

15. Of four instances of triple fleurs de lis on royal seals before the reign of Charles V, the earliest occurs on the reverse of Philip III's regency seal, 1285 (de Wailly, Elément de *paléographie,* 1:352), followed by two seals of Philip VI of 1333 and 1334 (Pinoteau, 1979, 26n.28) and, according to François Le Blanc (*Traité historique des monnoyes de France* [Amsterdam: 1692], cited by Pinoteau [1979, 9]), on a seal of John the Good attached to a charter of 1355. Among the coins, the earliest instance of the arms of France charged with three fleurs de lis prior to the reign of Charles VI occurs on the obverse of the gold "Angelot" of 1341 (Lafaurie, no. 258). According to Le Blanc (*Traité historique*) as cited by Pinoteau, the royal shield with triple lilies is also found on the silver "Tournois" of John the Good. But among the silver coinage of his reign described in Lafaurie (51–58), the only emission that figures a shield with three fleurs de lis, the "Blanc à l'écuson" (Lafaurie 58, no. 324, plate 15), cannot, according to Lafaurie, be dated with any certainty as early as the reign of King John. Moreover, since Lafaurie (xiii) has called attention to errors in Le Blanc's treatise, its reliability in this instance might well be questioned.

16. Prinet, "Les variations," 472.

17. Hervé Pinoteau, "Les origines de l'héraldique capetienne," *Communicationes y conclusiones al iii congreso internacional de genealogia y heraldica,* Madrid, 1955, 485–511, esp. 487.

18. Multiple lilies still prevail, however, in a later historiated charter granted by Charles V in 1366 to the cathedral of Rouen for commemorative masses (Sherman, *Portraits of Charles V,* 48, fig. 40).

19. See Wagner, 1956, 65. By the middle of the fourteenth century, professional heralds were already entering into the service of the major powers, while their free-lance counterparts were leading a more precarious existence due to the increasing official hostility towards tournaments (Paul Adam-Evan, "Les fonctions militaires des héraus d'armes, leur influence sur le développement de l'héraldique," *Archives héraldiques suisses* 71 [1957]: 2–23, esp. 4).

20. Wagner, 1956, 43.

21. Perroy, 1945, 113f., 133; Delachenal, *Histoire de Charles V* (Paris: 1928), 4:144.

22. Text published in Jones, 221–52. Once thought to be the earliest surviving treatise on heraldry, Bartolo's work is now considered to have been preceded by the Anglo-Norman *De Heraudie,* thought to have been written around 1300. See Dennys, 45, and Pastoureau 1979, 236.

23. "Quant aucun porte lez armes d'autruy ou le signe sanz luy faire prejudice, ce n'est mie chose qui soit contre rayson." The author then gives the example of a German knight who bears the same arms as a French knight he meets at a tournament in France. "Certes, pour tant, il ne fait aucune injure au chevalier Francoys . . . pour la tres grant distance laquelle est entre leurs maysons . . . Mez quant un voysin prent lez armes d'un aultre voysin, ou le signe aussi, ce luy puet estre chose prejudiciable en plusieurs manieres." *SV,* 1:289, book 1, chap. 148, paragraphs 1, 2. This passage may be compared to a similar one in Bartolo's treatise, summarized in Wagner, 1956, 30f.

24. "quant aucun prent lez armes d'autruy à l'esclandre et à la decepcion du pueple, car, en tel cas, il appartient au souverain pourvoir que le pueple ne soit deceüz . . . et se ilz sont teulx que ilz ne recognoissent souverain, celluy qui est tellement injurié puet contre l'autre mover justement guerre, juques à tant que il ait deposées et demisés sez armes, car au prince appartient mouver guerre." (*SV,* 1:289f., book 1, chap. 148, paragraph 3).

25. "c'est tres grant prejudice au roy de France que le roy d'Angleterre porte lez armes et le nom du roy de France, et puet estre en esclandre du pueple, car, subz umbre de ce que il porte lez armes, et se dit roy de France, aucuns simples subjés du Roy pourroient estre deceuz, ou aultres, qui n'ont mie bone volanté à la couronne de France, se voudroient excuser de seremens fais au Roy et à la couronne de France" (*SV,* 1:290, book 1, chap. 148, paragraph 4).

26. It may well have been at the request of the king himself that the passage dealing with the fleurs de lis on the English coat of arms was included in the *Songe du Vergier,* since it does not appear in the corresponding passages on heraldry in the earlier *Somnium Viridarii,* book 1, chap. 126 and 127 in Melchior Goldast, ed. *Monarchia Sancti Romani Imperii* (Hanover: 1611), 1:104f.

27. Douët d'Arcq, no. 64; Roman, 77, plate VI. For the use of the secret seal, 187/see above, see above, 187n.9.

28. The province of the Dauphiné had been given to Charles in 1349 as the eldest son and heir of John the Good (Perroy, 1945, 86).

29. This opinion can be traced back at least to the seventeenth century in Johannes Mabillon (*De re diplomatica* [Paris, 1681]): "Carolum V, qui ea [i.e., "lilia"] in trium numerum redegit," and was still being reiterated with greater precision by Marion Schnerb-Lièvre in the 1982 edition of *Le Songe du Vergier:* "Le nombre (des fleurs de lys) fut variable jusqu'en 1376, date à laquelle Charles V le fixa à trois" (note on book 1, chap. 80, 8, *SV* 1:450).

30. BN, ms. fr. 2813, fol. 4. See the notice on this manuscript by François Avril in *FG,* no. 284, fig. p. 330. An analysis of the text and comments on the illustrations are given in Anne Dawson Hedeman, "Valois Legitimacy: Editorial Changes in Charles V's *Grandes Chroniques de France,*" *Art Bulletin* 66 (1984): 97–117.

31. Vol. 1, BN, fr. 22912, fol. 303v, 342v, 384; Vol. 2, fr. 22913, fol. 2v, 225, 329v, 370.

32. François Avril, *Manuscript Painting at the Court of France: The Fourteenth Century (1310–1380)* (New York: 1978), 29, 109, plate 35; Douët d'Arcq, no. 69.

33. The following account is based mainly on Jean Lafaurie's detailed and comprehensive study of French coinage from Hugh Capet to Louis XII.

34. The introduction of gold into French currency at this time coincided with its initial appearance in the coinage of Florence (1252) and England (1257) and heralded an important change in the monetary systems of western Europe. Marie-Madeleine Gauthier, "L'or et l'église au Moyen Age," *Revue de l'art* (1975): 64–77, esp. 65, n.15.

35. Lafaurie, no. 197, plate VII.

36. Lafaurie, no. 213. For the other three portraits, see Lafaurie, nos. 211, 212, 214, plate VIII.

37. Lafaurie, no. 254, plate X. In the coin the interior of the pavilion, seeded with fleurs de lis, is derived from the similarly decorated cloth draped behind the king on Philip V's *sceau de majesté* (Douët d'Arcq, no. 51).

38. Lafaurie, no. 258, plate XI.

39. For the triple lilies on the shield of a silver coin that may have been minted under John the Good, see above, 113f., n.15.

40. However, in an article by Sabine Bourgey, "Les émissions des pièces d'or en France pendant la Guerre de cent ans," (*L'Estampille,* no. 119 [1980]: 38–42), as kindly reported to me by Georgia Wright, crown and spear seem not to have deterred the author from identifying the angel as both Saint Michael and the angel of Joyenval! Otherwise, her conclusions as to the significance of the coins seem to parallel those in Dr. Wright's *Royal Imagery in 14th Century French Coins,* a talk given at Kalamazoo in 1985 at the 20th Congress on Medieval Studies, a transcript of which she has kindly sent me.

41. Lafaurie, nos. 260, 260A, plate XI.

42. In the first campaign the French candidate for the vacant dukedom of Brittany was pitted against his rival, backed by the English. The second cam-

paign sought to contain the incursions of the Gascons and English into Languedoc (Perroy, 1945, 89, 93).

43. Lafaurie, no. 297, plate XIII.

44. Lafaurie, no. 370, plate XVI.

45. Five emissions of the coin occurred between 11 March 1385 and 2 November 1411 (Lafaurie, no. 378, plate XVI). Beginning on the same date to 10 May 1417, five emissions of a silver coin, the "Guénar," displaying the arms of France with three fleurs de lis, but omitting the crown, were also issued (Lafaurie, no. 381).

46. Lafaurie, no. 378. See also Arthur Engel and Raymond Serrure, *Traité de numismatique du Moyen Age* (Bologna: 1892–1905), 3:973.

47. Prinet, "Les variations," 484f. But like the coinage, beginning c. 1385–86 with Charles VI's second counterseal, in which a shield with triple fleurs de ls is supported by a single angel (*FG*, 351; Douët d'Arcq, 68; best illustrated in Henri Omont, *Portraits des roi de France du recueil de Jean du Tillet* [Paris: 1907], plate 27), the multiple lilies are now also permanently banished from the king's seals in favor of the shield with triple fleurs de lis.

For a much amplified exposition of the significance of the royal seals, including the second counterseal of Charles VI, see Brigitte M. Bedos Rezak, "Mythes monarchiques et thèmes sigillaires du sceau de Louis VII aux sceaux de Charles VII," *XV Congreso Internacional de las Ciencias Genealogica y Heraldica,* Madrid, 1982, 199–213.

48. Guenée and Lehoux, 13.


6. The Rival Claims to the Origin of the Fleurs de Lis

1. Léon Mirot, *Les insurrections urbains au début du règne de Charles VI, 1380–1383* (Paris: 1905), viif., 219f.

2. A detailed account of the revolt is given in Harold F. Hutchison, *The Hollow Crown: A Life of Richard II* (London: 1961), 48–78.

3. The truce was to run from the end of the existing truce in 1398 and hence for 20 years in all (Palmer, 1972, 172).

4. The text is reproduced from Edward Bysshe's seventeenth-century edition in Jones, 95–143.

5. This is indicated in the author's introduction to the treatise in which he states that he had written it at the insistence of the queen, lately deceased (Jones, xvii, 95).

6. Jones, xxxii–xxxiv.

7. Jones (xlii) claims that Johannes de Bado Aureo can be read as John Trevor: (ref = town = tun = *badus:* or = *aureus*). But the author of the treatise has also been called Johannes de Vado Aureo (Jones, xxiv), which translates more readily as John Guild *(aureus)*-ford *(vadus)*. For this otherwise unknown Guildford, see also the *Encyclopedia Brittanica* (15th ed., 1982) under "heraldry," where, however, confusion is compounded by the author of the article who, while opting for John Guildford, refers to his Latin name as Johannes de Bado Aureo!

8. The author states that his treatise follows in part the "dogmata ac traditiones excellentissimi Doctoris et Praeceptoris mei magistri Francisci de Foveis" (Jones, 95).

9. Jones, 245–47; *SV*, 1:291f., book 1, chap. 148, paragraphs 13–15. The metals, colors, and furs used in medieval heraldry are described in Dennys, 46–48; Pastoureau, 1979, 100–121.

10. "Adhuc et aliam rationem assignat meus magister Franciscus, quae est ista: color azoreus ideo praeferatur omnibus coloribus mediis, et specialiter colori aureo, quia color iste fuit a Deo missus per angelum Karolo Magno regi francorum tamquam pro subiecto et fundamento armorum suorum. Detulit quidem angelus scutum cum campo azoreo et tribus floribus aureis. Et sic ibi color aureus fuit inferior colore azoreo, quia fuit accidentalis et ideo non substantia. Et si velitis, sic Gallice, 'Il porte d'azour treys flordelys d'ore." (My master Francois gives still another reason why the color azure is to be preferred above all other colors, and especially the color gold, since this was the color sent by God through his angel to Charlemagne, king of the French, as the basis and foundation of his arms. For the angel brought down a shield with azure field and three golden flowers. And thus this color gold was inferior to the color azure, since the color gold was used only accidentally and not as the essential element of the coat of arms. And if you wish, you can say thus in French: 'He bears azure three fleurs de lis or' [*Tractatus de Armis*, I; Jones, 103]). Rodney Dennys wrongly attributes to Johannes de Bado Aureo and to François de Fossés the Heraldic colors listed in the later *De Studio Militari* of the Englishman Nicolas Upton (68, 81).

11. See above, p. 40 and chap. 3, 72n.18.

12. Robert Folz, "Aspects du culte liturgique de Saint Charlemagne en France," in *Karl der Grosse: Lebenswerk und Nachleben,* ed. Wolfgang Braunfels and Percy Ernst Schramm (Düsseldorf: 1967), 4:77–83.

13. Blaise de Montesquiou-Fezensac and Danielle Gaborit-Chopin, *Le Trésor de Saint-Denis, Planches et notices* (Paris: 1977), 3:80; *FG,* no. 202. The sceptre is probably that represented (without the lily on which the statuette now rests and which may have been added later) in the scene of Charles' coronation in the *Livre du Sacre*; BL, Cottonian MS Tiberius B. VIII, fol. 64 (François Avril, *Manuscript Painting at the Court of France: The Fourteenth Century (1310–1380)* [New York: 1978], plate 28).

14. S. O. Dunlap Smith, "Illustrations of Raoul de Praelles' Translation of St. Augustine's City of God Between 1375 and 1420" (Ph.D. diss., New York University, 1974), 37n.6.

15. "vous (Charles V) avez voulu ensuivre monseigneur saint Charles qui entre tous les livres que il estudioit et veoit volentiers, il lisoit les livres de monseigneur saint Augustin. Et sur tous les autres, le livre de la *Cité de Dieu*" (BN, ms. fr. 22.912, fol. 4v). "Historia et antiquorumque gesta libenter audiebat, in libros diurnis perpetue beati Augustini qui *De Civitate Dei* intitulantur non mediocriter delectatus" (Yves, *Life of Saint Denis,* book 3, chap. 17; BN, ms. lat. 5286, fol. 174v).

16. Folz, "Aspects du cult liturgique," 79f.

17. Jones, 13, 151. From internal evidence the Welsh version seems indeed to have been the work of John (Zion) Trevor (Dennys, 67, 70f).

18. Nicolas Upton, *De Studio Militari,* ed. E. Bissaeus (London: 1654). For a short biography of the author and copies of his work, see Dennys, 76–86.

19. The facts concerning the career of Jean Goleim are reviewed in the introductory comments in Jackson, 305. For Thomas of Ireland and Etienne de Conty, see above, chap. 1, 15; chap. 4, 51f.

20.
> Lilii flores Dionysius olim
> Franciae fertur domui dedisse,
> Cujus obtentu precibus dignis
> Lilia crescant.

(Denis is said to have once given the fleurs de lis to the House of France. Through his intercession and worthy prayers may the lilies continue to grow.) (Jean Gerson, *Oeuvres complètes,* ed. Mgr. Glorieux, vol. 4, *L'oeuvre poétiques* [Paris: 1962], 114, no. 151.)

21. Gerson, vol. 1, *Essai biographique* (1960), 109.

22. For the text of the sermon, see Gerson, vol. 5, *L'oeuvre oratoire* (1963), 151–68.

23.
> Lilii flores decorasti ample,
> Remigi necnon Ludovice sancti,
> Jugiter vestro petimus favore
> Lilia crescant.

(Gerson, vol. 4, *L'oeuvre poétiques,* 114)

24. "Quid autem si ternarium liliorum in scute suo regio et divino rex noster ad mores retorquere considerando volebat? . . . Haec tria sunt quae lilia ut crescant exigunt: ros, humor, claustra." (But what if our king wished to return to the custom of contemplating the triple lilies on his royal and divine shield? . . . These three things are needed in order that the lilies may grow: moisture, earth, protection.) (Gerson, vol. 5, *L'oeuvre oratoire,* 156f.)

25. "Et poteram, o doctissimi et sapientes viri, poteram latius ista deducere ex ejusdem regis celebri chronica si vacaret." (And I would, O most learned and wise men, I would quote more extensively from the chronicles of this famous king if there was time.) (Gerson, vol. 5, *L'oeuvre oratoire,* 157.)

26. For the Latin and French texts of the passages on the fleurs de lis, see appendix 1 and *Chronique latine de Guillaume de Nangis de 1113 à 1300,* ed. Hercule Géraud (Paris: 1843), 182f. The French text of the *Life of Saint Louis* has been paraphrased in at least one copy of the *Grandes Chroniques de France,* BL, Roy. MS. 16G. VI (Viard [1953], 10:1–2, 10–12). The manuscript is dated probably before 1350 in Warner and Gilson, 2:209ff.

27. Gerson, vol. 5, *L'oeuvre oratoire,* 156.

28. These eleven copies can be identified among the forty-nine manuscripts of the *Cité de Dieu,* or parts thereof, listed by Robert Bossuat (*HLF,* 40 [1974]: 171–

73), as follows: Amiens, BM, 216; Angers, BM, 162; BRB, 1153; The Hague, Bibl. Roy., Y 390; London, Charles Butler Library; Paris, Bibl. de l'Arsenal, 5060, and BN, fr. 23–24; 170–71; 172–73; 174; 20.105–20.106. (Corrigendum to Bossuat's list: the manuscript under "Vente Hamilton" is now Strasbourg, Bibl. Nat. et Universitaire, 523–24. Addenda: Baltimore, The Walters Art Gallery, W 770, Ex. Coll. Cheltenham; Philadelphia, Musuem of Art, books 1–4, c. 1410, Ex. Colls. Marques of Lothian and Cortland Bishop.)

29. The Chanson is dated no earlier than the third quarter of the fourteenth century and is attributed to a jongleur from Picardy in Robert Bossuat ("Saint Honoré, saint Honorat?," *Recueil de travaux offert à M. Clovis Brunel* [Paris: 1956], 163–73). Bossuat (" 'Charles le Chauve': Etude sur le declin de l'epopée française," *Les lettres romans* 7 [1953]: 107–32, esp. 130) suggests that it may have been written after 1360 (Battle of Poitiers). A résumé of the poem is in L. F. Flutre, " 'Dieudonné de Hongrie,' chanson de geste du XIVe siècle (alias 'Roman de Charles le Chauve')," *Zeitschrift für romanische Philologie* 68 (1952): 321–400.

30. This is quoted from the only manuscript of the poem, dating from the very end of the fourteenth century (BN, fr. 24.372, p. 1). See also Bossuat, " 'Charles le Chauve,' " 109.

31. Bossuat. "Théseus de Cologne," *Le Moyen Age* 14 (1959): 293–320, esp. 313f. Georges Tessier (*Le Baptême de Clovis: 25 décembre,* [Paris: 1964], 145, n.2), in a misreading of the text of the poem, attributes the gift of the three fleurs de lis to Saint Denis. The full citation of this passage reveals the error:

> La couronne de France vint de Dieu proprement,
> Qui les 111 fleurs de lis envoia dignement
> Au noble roy Clovis qui reigna loiaulment.

Bossuat, "Théseus de Cologne," 539–77, esp. 552f. A mural of the adventures of Theseus in the Hotel St-Pol, Paris, executed c. 1361 at the earliest, and a tapestry of Theseus belonging to Charles V, mentioned in a 1379 inventory, attest to the popularity of this "chanson de geste" at the French court (Bossuat, "Théseus de Cologne," 304–6).

32. See the editor's introduction to the prose version of the chronicle in *La Chronique de Messire Bertrand du Guesclin,* ed. Gabriel Rachou (Paris: 1879), 2f.

33. Cuvelier, *Chronique de Bertrand du Guesclin,* ed. E. Charrière (Paris: 1839), 2:268, vs. 21576–77. At the entrance of du Guesclin's army into Poitiers, the populace cries out:

> Hé noble fleur de lis, honnourer vous doit-on,
> Car vous estes la fleur de consolacion
> Que Dieux transmist sà jus (en bas) à Clovis le baron.

(Cuvelier, *Chronique de Bertrand du Guesclin,* vs. 21189–91)

34. The versified version of this *Roman* survives in three fifteenth-century manuscripts. The copy here used (BN, fr. 12.482) is the one preferred in the

analysis of the text in Rudolph Ruths, "Die französischen Fassungen der Roman de la belle Helaine" (Ph.D. diss., University of Greifswald, 1897), 94. Clovis' well-known devotion to Saint Martin of Tours, the son of "la belle Helaine," would seem to account for his inclusion in the poem (Emile Roy, "Philippe le Bel et la légende des trois fleurs de lis," *Mélanges . . . offerts à M. Antoine Thomas* [Paris: 1927], 383–88).

35. Fr. 12.482, fol. 131v. Chartres is here called Crante. The enemy horde assembled in Chartres is also referred to as "Les serrafins" (the Saracens or pagans) (fr. 12.482, fol. 133).

36.    Une expiration luy est du corps entrée,
En la vertu de Dieu si à son cuer plantée,
Tant qu'il dist doulcement, 'Doulce vierge, savée
Qui du corps Jhesu Crist feus si noble portée.
Vray dieu, au vendredi fut ta char lapidée,
Or me soyez aidant huy en ceste journée.
Doremais en avant est ta loy à moustrée,
Exaucie par moy et très bien gouvernée,
Car bien que Clotaire, qui est mon espousée,
Ytrevoit bien fermement de cuer et de pensée.

                  (fr. 12.482, fol. 132)

37.    Luy envoya Jhesu, qui fist ciel et rousée,
Un ange beneoit de sa gloire loée,
Qui luy a prestement sa targe transmuée,
Qui estoit de fin or moult tres bien couloree,
A trois serpentaux d'or de guise desquisée.
C'estoient trois crapaux, portrais d'oeuvre dorée.
Maix Dieu vault qu'il n'eust plus telz armes portées,
Ayant luy envoyé par miracle ordonnée
Trois flours de lis d'or fin en champaigne asurée
De par Jhesus luy fut cest eneigne ordonnée.

                  (fr. 12.482, fol. 132)

38.    Si dist, 'Glorieux Dieu, pere de paradis . . .
Il m'a faicte grand grace, il en soit beneys!
Et se je puis veoir l'eure que soye revertis,
Moy et trestout mon peuple serons ja convertis . . .
Or, avant, bonnes gentz! Ne soyez huy faintis.
Cellui nous aidera qui en la croix fus mis,
Donc ce noble blason m'est donnée et furnis.'

                  (fr. 12.482, fol. 132v)

39. BN, ms. fr. 2606, fol. 2. The miniature is reproduced in Godefroid Kurth, *Clovis* (Tours: 1896), 313, and was probably painted by "Rémiet" who was responsible for illuminating Guillaume de Digulleville's *Pèlerinages* (BN, ms. fr. 823) in 1393 (*FG*, no. 294). See Anne Dawson Hedeman, *"The Illustrations of the Grandes Chroniques de France from 1274 to 1422"* (Ph.D. diss., Johns Hopkins University, 1984), 379.

The miniature thus provides a general terminal date for this redaction of the poem in the last decade of the century at the very latest. Although in Alexandre Haggerty Krappe, "La belle Hélène [sic] de Constantinople," *Romania* 63 (1937): 324–52, the poem is merely termed "une compilation tardive," probably based on a "chanson de geste" of the twelfth century, to which were added accessory episodes, because of the reference to the toads on Clovis' shield, this particular episode cannot have been composed before the *Songe du Vergier* of 1378 that apparently first replaced the crescents with the "crapauds" in the story of the miraculous origin of the fleurs de lis. See above, 62f. Marion Schnerb-Lièvre's conclusions (*SV*, 1:449f.) that the legend of Clovis and the fleurs de lis in *La belle Helaine* is coeval with the original composition of the poem that, according to Schnerb-Lièvre, can probably be dated toward the end of the thirteenth century, or even around 1260, are not shared by this writer.

40. Among the later illustrations of the battle against the Alemanni, the only exception to the black toads on a light field known to me occurs in a miniature in a copy of the *Grandes Chroniques*, dated by Colophon 1471, of the school of Tours(?), in which the banner of Clovis displays three gold "crapauds" on a black field (BN, ms. fr. 2609, fol. 18).

41. Compare Clovis' reference to Clotilda's devotion to the Lord in the description of the battle in the *Grandes Chroniques*, "Diex tres puissanz que la reine Crotilde coutive et aoure de cuer et de pensée" (Viard [Paris: 1920], 1:66), and the corresponding passage in *La belle Helaine*, "Car bien que Clotaire, qui est mon espousée, / Ytreoit bien fermement de cuer et de pensée" (BN, ms. fr. 12.442, fol. 132).

## 7. The Leopards and the Fleurs de Lis

1. "Sunt insuper alii qui portant flores arborum vel herbarum, ut hic. Et portat de azoreo cum tribus floribus aureis. Et dic quod portare flores ut rosas et tales est signum instabilitatis, quia non sunt per annum duraturi, nec per totum annum permanent. Merito ergo fuerunt arma ista ad regem Francorum missa a Deo, quia ut credo, cum Deus ipsa arma misit per angelum deferens, per ea inconstantiam et instabilitatem in Francia illis temporibus esse monstravit. . . . Haec Franciscus de terra sua loquitur." (Besides these, there are others who bear the flowers of the trees and plants, such as the one who bears a shield with azure field and three golden flowers. And I say, that to bear flowers, such as roses, is a sign of instability, since they are not destined to last through the year, nor are they permanent for a whole year. Deservedly, therefore, these arms were sent to the king of France by God since, as I believe, when God sent these same arms that the

angel brought down, he pointed out by means of them that inconstancy and instability existed at that time in France. . . . These things François says concerning his own native land.) (Jones, 135.)

2. "Plus que faire n'avons de ce liepart felon; / Voit faire ailleurs son ni, plus de lui volons" (Cuvelier, *Chronique de Bertrand du Guesclin,* ed. E. Charrière [Paris: 1839], 2:268, vs. 21192–93).

3. In two instances Richard II's arms are impaled with the mythical blazon attributed to Edward the Confessor (who of course lived long before the age of heraldry), one on the back of the Wilton diptych, painted probably after Richard's death in 1400, the other on the vaulting of the canopy above the head of the king's effigy in Westminster Abbey (Francis Wormald, "The Wilton Diptych," *JWCI* 27 [1954]: 191–203, esp. plate 27, fig. b, opp. p. 192; plate 33, fig. 3, opp. p. 200).

4. The roses refer to the emblems on the shield of Saint Mercurius previously mentioned by the author that was also the gift of an angel (Jones, 103).

5. The conclusions I have given gain added plausibility from the fact that in both of the later versions of the *Tractatus de Armis,* namely, the second Latin text and the Welsh translation (see the chronology of these works in Jones, xlviii, xlvix) this entire passage on the significance of floral emblems has been omitted, since with the conclusion of the treaty in 1396 such warnings would no longer have been considered necessary.

6. The letter, dated 15 May, is published in Kervyn de Lettenhoven, ed., *Oeuvres de Froissart* (Brussels: 1871), 15:388–90 (English summary in Palmer, 1972, 180).

7. Although England had sided with Rome against the French schismatics, Richard II eventually showed himself favorable to the Avignonese papacy (Edouard Perroy, *L'Angleterre et le Grand Schism d'Occident* [Paris: 1933], esp. 3–6).

8. "en multipliant par la vertu de la croix la sainte foy catholique par toutes les parties de l'Orient" (Lettenhoven, *Oeuvres de Froissart,* 390).

9. Palmer, 1972, 186.

10. The French text with English translation is given in *Philippe de Mézières, Letter to King Richard II,* ed. G. W. Coopland (Liverpool: 1975).

11. *Philippe de Mézières,* 103.

12. *Philippe de Mézières,* xxxii, 143–45.

13. Roy. MS. 20. B. VI. This is the only existing copy of the *Epistre.*

14. Fol. 2 is illustrated in color, *Philippe de Mézières,* frontispiece.

15. The design of the banner is again reproduced on fol. 36v (Aziz Suryal Atiya, *The Crusade in the Late Middle Ages* [London: 1938], plate opp. p. 128). The arms of La Chevalerie de la Passion are described in the Rules of the Order in Abdel Hamid Hamdy, "Philippe de Mézières and the New Order of the Passion," pt. 3, "La sustenance de la Chevalerie de la Passion de Jhesu Crist en françois," *Bulletin of the Faculty of Arts, University of Alexandria,* 18 (1964): 43–105, esp. 86.

16. "la terre seinte à nous acquis par le précious sanc de l'aignelet occis pur les brebis" (Lettenhoven, *Oeuvres de Froissart,* 390). A similar expression in reference to Jerusalem occurs in the French text of the Rule of the Order: "nostre region et propre heritage, acquis par le precieux sanc de l'Aignelet ochis" (Hamdy, *Philippe de Mézières,* 46).

17. Roy. 20. VII, fol. 1v. Atiya, *Crusade in the Late Middle Ages,* plate opp. p. 6.

18. Above Charles' crown is EN BIEN; above Richard's crown, SANS DEPAR-TIR (Warner and Gilson, 2:363).

19. "par la bonté de Dieu transmuez de rigour en douleour, de cremour en amour, et de crueuse proie en l'amour de Mont Joye" (Coopland, *Philippe de Mézières,* 137).

20. Nicolae Jorga, *Philippe de Mézières 1327–1405* (Paris: 1896): 471–76.

21. "Nisi discencio inveterata inter lilia et animalia ferocia varietate coloris adornata prius a Deo sopiatur" (Jorga, *Philippe de Mézières,* 474f., 475n.2).

22. "Pax firma confirmetur: agnus et leo, leopardus et lilium insimul pascan-tur et nutriantur" (Jorga, *Philippe de Mézières,* 475n.4).

23. Palmer, 1972, 204f., 211, 213–222.

24. John J. N. Palmer, "The Anglo-French Peace Negotiations, 1390–1396," *Transactions of the Royal Historical Society,* 5th ser., 16 (1966): 81–94, esp. 61; John J. N. Palmer, "English Foreign Policy 1388–99," in *The Reign of Richard II: Essays in Honor of May McKisack* (London: 1971): 75–107, esp. 79, 107.

25. See under "John Trevor," *Dictionary of National Biography,* 19:1147.

26. A member of the parliamentary commission, he may even have composed the sentence himself (*Annales Ricardi II et Henrici IV (1392–1406)* in *Chronica Jo-hannes de Trokelowe,* ed. H. T. Riley, Rolls series [London: 1866], 278). See also Jones, xxxiv, and for these events in general, Harold F. Hutchison, *The Hollow Crown: A Life of Richard II* (London: 1961), 216–30.

27. Perroy, 1945, 213–19. An analysis of the treaty is given in Jean de Pange, *Le roi très chrètien* (Paris: 1949), 16–19. For the historical setting of the treaty and the events leading up to it, see James Hamilton Wylie and William Templeton Waugh, *The Reign of King Henry the Fifth* (New York: 1968), 3:196–206; Margaret Wade Labarge, *Henry V: The Cautious Conqueror* (London: 1975), 145–57.

28. The profound and widespread grief over the unexpected death of Henry V extended to the followers of the Dauphin Charles, his deadliest foes (Griffiths, 11). On the other hand, Charles VI, abandoned by all, died unlamented and alone, but for a few servants, in the Hotel St-Paul (Perroy, 1945, 236).

29. Ralph E. Giesey, *The Royal Funeral Ceremony in Renaissance France, Travaux d'humanisms et renaissance,* 37 (Geneva: 1960), 126–35. The proclamation of Henry VI at St-Denis immediately after the prayers for the dead king set an enduring precedent for the later recognition of the kings of France (Ernest H. Kantorowitz, *The King's Two Bodies: A Study in Mediaeval Theology* [Princeton: 1957], 388ff., 412). At Windsor on 28 September 1422, homage and fealty had already been sworn to the little Henry as King of England (Griffiths, 13).

30. Perroy, 1945, 216, 221, 226.

31. Disciplinary ordinances against recognizing the rights of the Dauphin to the crown of France were published by Bedford in December, 1423 (Benedicta J. H. Rowe, "King Henry's Claims to France in Picture and Poetry," *The Library,* 4th ser., 12 [1932–33]: 77–88).

32. See the excerpts from the poem (Rowe, "King Henry's Claims," 84, 86). Laurent Calot was to become notorious for the sinister role he played during the

trial of Joan of Arc (Régine Pernoud, *Joan of Arc: By Herself and Her Witnesses* [London: 1964], 213).

33. The claim of John W. McKenna ("Henry VI of England and the Dual Monarchy: Aspects of Royal Political Propaganda, 1422–1432," *JWCI* 28 [1965]: 145–62, esp. 151) that copies of both the picture and the poem were posted together in the major churches in northern France does not seem to be warranted by the evidence derived from a single incident that occurred in Reims in 1425. According to the account given by Vallet de Viriville ("Notice de quelques manuscrits precieux," *Gazette des Beaux Arts,* 1e periode, 20 [1866]: 453–66, esp. 457), two canons of the cathedral quarreled over a genealogical chart similar to that in the Shrewsbury manuscript that hung in one of the capitulary halls. See also Rowe, "King Henry's Claims," 82.

34. BL, Roy. MS. 15. E. VI, fol. 3. Rowe, "King Henry's Claims," 79–81; Paul Durrieu, "Les souvenirs historiques dans les mss. à peinture de la dominion anglaise en France," *Annuaire-bulletin de la soc. de l'hist. de France* 41 (1905): 111–35, esp. 129–31.

35. The Valois line is headed by its founder, Charles of Valois, the brother of Philip IV and the father of Philip VI. The reader may wish to compare this illuminated copy of Calot's chart with the genealogical chart of the descendants of Louis IX at the beginning of this book.

36. The chart is supported on the left by Humphrey Duke of Gloucester, at the right by Richard Duke of York, each flanked by the arms of England (quartered, of course, with those of France). The ornaments are, above, at the left the arms of France, at the right Saint George's cross within a Garter; below, the arms of Margaret of Anjou and a crowned initial *M,* each circled with the riband of the Garter. In the right border, a banner with, again, the arms of Margaret of Anjou. Its staff is wrapped with a scroll inscribed "Dieu est [sic] mon droit" and is supported by an antelope gorged with a crown and chain (the royal device) (Warner and Gilson, 2:179). John Talbot, Earl of Shrewsbury, the great adversary of Joan of Arc and the donor of the manuscript, was particularly proud of his membership in the Order of the Garter, which probably accounts for the three appearances of the Garter in the ornaments of the miniature.

37. Rowe, "King Henry's Claims," 83; McKenna, "Henry VI of England," 151f.

38.          Le doulx Jhesus plain de misericorde,
             Prince de paix, voiant le grant discorde
             D'entre les Roix de France et Angleterre

                                    (quoted in Rowe, "King Henry's Claims," 145)

39. *Philippe de Mézières,* 145.

40. These analogies may have been still more striking in the original design of the chart, as is suggested by the caption to Calot's poem: "Le roys Louis portant la couronne d'espines et les claux en sa main destre" (Rowe, "King Henry's Claims," 82n.1), since the caption may well have referred to the actual appearance of Saint Louis at the top of the chart in the original poster. But Rowe's suggestion that

someone impersonating Saint Louis at Henry VI's later French coronation was delegated to hold these sacred relics, while reciting Calot's poem, does not seem plausible.

41. Lafaurie, 90–92; McKenna, "Henry VI of England," 146.

42. McKenna, "Henry VI of England," 147f., plate 26 opp. p. 145, figs. c–g.

43. Henry's seal is illustrated in Wolffe, fig. 10, b, opp. p. 49 and that of Charles VI in *FG,* no. 351.

44. Above the crown and beneath a sunburst is a horizontal scroll inscribed AVE (McKenna, "Henry VI of England," plate 26, fig. h).

45. Their celestial origin and the Trinitarian symbolism of the three fleurs de lis were also introduced into English poetry during this same decade of the 1420s by John Lydgate in his ballad on the English coronation of Henry VI (Thomas Wright, ed., *Political Poems and Songs Relating to English History* [London: 1861], 2:141–45, esp. 142).

46. For the Christological symbolism of the lily of the Annunciation, see Gertrude Schiller, *Iconography of Christian Art,* trans. Janet Seligman (New York: 1971), 1:51. A fleur de lis also occasionally replaces the natural lily in the vase in the scene of the Annunciation, as in the Psalter of Blanche of Castille, of the second quarter of the thirteenth century, Paris, Bibl. de l'Arsenal, ms. 1186, fol. 16 (*Saint Louis à la Sainte Chapelle,* Exh. cat. [Paris: 1960], no. 168, plate 10; Robert Branner, *Manuscript Painting in Paris During the Reign of Saint Louis* [Berkeley-Los Angeles-London: c. 1977], 30, 204), and also on the 1304 counterseal of Robert Courtenay, archbishop of Reims (Jean van Malderghen, "Les fleurs de lis de l'ancienne monarchie française," *Annales de la soc. d'archéol. de Bruxelles* 8 [1894]: 180–212, fig. p. 206), and on the contemporary seal of the priory of Montrouge, Pinoteau, 1979, 6.

47. McKenna, "Henry VI of England," plate 26 opp. p. 145, fig. J. Only the "Salut d'or" of the second emission of 6 September 1423 has survived (Lafaurie, 93f., no. 447, plate XX).

48. The supposed uniqueness of the Virgin on the left in the Anglo-Gallic "Salut d'or" has led McKenna ("Henry VI of England," 149) to interpret the message of the coin as implying that the angel (England) announces to the Virgin (France) the birth of the Savior (the infant Henry VI), an interpretation repeated in Wolffe, 53.

49. Jean Taralon, *Treasures of the Churches of France* (New York: 1966), 278, colored plates 144–45; *FG,* no. 340, with illustration. Although rare in France in the fourteenth century, between 1415 and 1420 four instances of the Annunciation from the right occur in Parisian manuscript painting of the Boucicaut Master and his workshop (Millard Meiss, *French Painting in the Time of Jean de Berry: The Boucicaut Master* [London: 1968], 29, figs. 128–30), and from that time forth this more unusual orientation was evermore frequently favored in French pictorial art (Don Denny, *The Annunciation from the Right from Early Christian Times to the Sixteenth Century* [New York and London: 1977], 55ff).

50. The reduction of the lilies on the English escutcheon so as to conform to their number on the French coat of arms, thus further emphasizing the English

claims to the crown of France, may have been prompted by the renewal of the war between 1404 and 1406, when the efforts of the French under the duc d'Orléans, the brother of Charles VI, to take Bordeaux in Guyenne were successfully repulsed by the English and their allies (J. L. Kirby, *Henry IV of England* [London: 1970], 124f., 210f).

### 8. The Fleurs de Lis and the Holy Ampulla

1. Wolffe, 48–51. But there are grave doubts, in spite of Wolffe's claim, that any of the Lancastrian kings were ever anointed at their coronations with the famous Becket oil, supposedly donated by the Virgin Mary to Thomas à Becket. The question has been exhaustively studied in T. A. Sandquist, "The Holy Oil of St. Thomas of Canterbury," in *Essays in Medieval History Presented to Bertie Wilkinson,* ed. T. A. Sandquist and M. R. Powicke (Toronto: 1969), 330–44. The legend probably arose as a belated counterpart to that of the Reims ampulla and is related in detail, but with some scepticism, in the *Chronique du religieux de Saint-Denys contenant le règne de Charles VI de 1380 a 1422,* ed. M. L. Bellaguet, vol. 2 (Paris: 1840).

2. Alain Renoir, *The Poetry of John Lydgate* (London: 1967); Derek Pearsall, *John Lydgate* (Charlottesville: 1970).

3. For Lydgate's role in the development of the mumming and as the speaker at the mumming at Windsor, see Robert Withington, *English Pageantry* (London: 1918), 1:106; Pearsall, *John Lydgate,* 185f.

4. I have modernized the spelling from the original text in Henry Noble MacCracken, *The Minor Poems of John Lydgate* (London: 1934), 2:692–94, esp. 694, vs. 82–87, 90–91.

5. MacCracken, *Minor Poems of John Lydgate,* 692f., vs. 31–35.

6. Piaget, 1936, 352f., vs. 1128–64.

7.  Et le bon roy Clovis don je vous signifie
   Fut baptisiez à Rains en la esglise jolie.
   La fut à Saint Remi ly ampolle envoyé
   De quoy il fut sacré

(BN, ms. fr. 12482, fol. 133v)

8. Henry resided in the great castle of Rouen where, soon after his arrival, Joan of Arc was imprisoned after her capture 23 May 1430 and there awaited her trial. The immense keep of the castle, known as La Tour de Jeanne d'Arc, is still extant.

9. That the book was donated to Henry VI with the consent of Anne's husband is attested to in a Latin inscription by Henry VI's own physician on fol. 256 of the Book of Hours, BL, Add. MS. 18,850 (Richard Gough, *An Account of a Rich Illuminated Missal Executed for John Duke of Bedford* [London: 1794], 19f). The portraits of the Duke and Duchess among the illustrations and the armorials and mottoes have led to the assumption that the manuscript was originally ordered

by the Duke, but the fact that the text is for the use of Paris, which Anne would have preferred, rather than following the Sarum usage of her husband's liturgical books, is the main reason for concluding that the manuscript was intended as a present for Anne (Eleanor P. Spencer, "The Master of the Duke of Bedford: The Bedford Hours," *The Burlington Magazine* 107 [1965]: 495–502).

10. The battle, based on Gregory of Tours and Aimon, is included in the *Grandes Chroniques de France,* chap. 22 (Viard [Paris: 1920], 1:80–83). A reversion to the triple symbolism of the three fleurs de lis favored by Philippe de Vitri (Piaget, 1898, 72, vs. 19–21) and the earlier Dionysian writers occurs in the words of the angel to the hermit:

> "ami, ce present honorable
> Signifie foy, force et equité."

(appendix 6, vs. 11–12)

11. 
> L'escu fist faire a cest present semblable
> Et fu au roy par elle presenté,
> Qui ou nom de Dieu le recent acceptable.

(appendix 6, vs. 21–22)

12. Appendix 6, vs. 26–28.

13. The opening lines in Lydgate's recitation, "For in the high heavenly consistory / By full accord of the Trinity" (MacCracken, *Minor Poems of John Lydgate,* 692, vs. 8–9) are echoed at the beginning of the Bedford poem, "Ou hault conseil de sainte Terinité [*sic*]" (appendix 6, v. 5). The heavenly shield in Lydgate is called "a treasure of great price" (MacCracken, *Minor Poems of John Lydgate,* 694, v. 89); in the Bedford poem it is said to have come from the divine treasury ("du divin trésor," v. 8) and is called "ce present honorable" (v. 11, Benedicta J. H. Rowe, "Notes on the Clovis miniature in the Bedford Book of Hours," *Journal of the British Archaeological Association,* 3d ser. 25 [1962]: 56–65).

14. While in Paris he was commissioned by the earl of Warwick to compose an English translation of Calot's French poem that accompanied Henry VI's genealogical chart (Griffiths, 219).

15. Of the sixty-eight verses that comprise the legend of Joyenval in Lydgate's recitation, thirty deal more or less exclusively with Clotilda; in the Latin poem, of the thirty-one stanzas out of fifty, which constitute the legend itself, ten are concerned with her pious deeds.

16. The specific reference to the founding of Joyenval by Clovis in the subtitle at the bottom of the second page, fol. 289v ("Comment le roy Clovis fist faire l'abaye de Joyenval apres qu'il fust baptisé en l'honneur de Dieu") is, however, only implied in the Latin poem:

> Qui destructor ydolorum loca plantans ecclesiam,
> Alumpnis canicorum exercens alimoniam,
> Nutriens (et) monarchorum multam gessit abbaciam.

(Who founded a church in the place where he [Clovis] had destroyed the idols, and provided support for the novices among the canons and nourishment for a large body of monks under his care.) (Stanza 43, vs. 169–71, Bossuat, 1940, 100.) On the other hand, in the reference in his prologue to the founding of Joyenval, Raoul de Presles gives no indication as to the name of its founder.

17. Add. 18.850, fol. 288v.

18. In the descriptive subtitle below the miniature, however, the celestial gift takes the form of a shield: "Comment notre seigneur par son ange envoya les troys fleurs de lis d'or en un escu d'ascur au roys Clovys." In what manner the arms of France were delivered to the hermit by the angel, whether on a shield or a banner, is not indicated in the verses of the poem itself. See appendix 6.

19. As far as I know, the armorial colors and emblems on the tabards of the two squires have not been identified and may be purely fanciful. See also Rowe, "Notes on the Clovis Miniature," 57f.

20. According to Rowe ("Notes on the Clovis Miniature," 56–61) the courtier represents Philip the Good presiding over the transfer of the lilies of France to Henry V, impersonated by Clovis, and the whole scene is thus a Burgundian allegory of the Treaty of Troyes. In support of this theory Rowe ("Notes on the Clovis Miniature," 57) calls attention to the minute device on the tiny shield placed over the gatehouse of the castle, which, under a magnifying glass, she identifies as the lion of Flanders, the emblem of Philip's most important province! However, one might well question whether such impersonations were as prevalent in the art of the period as has sometimes been claimed. Charles V in his portrait statue in the Louvre, at least, can now no longer be justifiably considered as impersonating Saint Louis. See FG, no. 68.

21. Paris, Musée Jacquemart-André, ms. 2, fol. 65v. The manuscript is dated most likely between 1405 and 1408 by Millard Meiss (French Painting in the Time of Jean de Berry: The Boucicaut Master [London: 1968], 132) who has also demonstrated the stylistic influence of the Boucicaut master on the Bedford master and his workshop (30f., 35, 70).

22. The two miniatures of the story of Noah (Building the Ark, fol. 15v, and the Exit from the Ark, fol. 16v) are part of a later insertion comprising folios 13 to 18 that also includes three full-page miniatures of the Story of Adam and Eve, fol. 14, the Bedford Armorial Tree, fol. 15, and the Tower of Babel, fol. 17v. The complete contents of Add. 18.850 is given in Jeanette Backhouse, "A Reappraisal of the Bedford Hours," The British Library Journal 7 (1981): 47–69. According to Eleanor Spencer ("The Master of the Duke of Bedford," 479) all of these insertions, including the Old Testament scenes toward the beginning of the manuscript and the illustrated poem at the end, were added in 1430. Since, however, the folios with the portraits of the Duke and Duchess of Bedford were also later additions, Spencer has suggested that the original portion of the book was given to Anne, not by Bedford, but by Anne's brother Philip the Good who had ordered the manuscript before the signing of the marriage contract in 1423. But as Millard Meiss (The De Levis Hours and the Bedford Workshop [New Haven: 1972], 25, n.67) has pointed out, Spencer has overlooked the mottoes of Bedford and Anne on the

scrolls in folio 138 that are part of the original manuscript. In wishing to subscribe to Spencer's theory of a donation by Philip the Good, but well aware that the page with the mottoes belongs to the original folios, Backhouse ("Reappraisal of the Bedford Hours," 63) has proposed that the mottoes were added later to the initially empty scrolls!

23. Backhouse ("Reappraisal of the Bedford Hours," 55, 58) has suggested that the four Old Testament scenes, though unrelated to the existing text of the manuscript, may have been part of a cycle illustrating the *Speculum Humanae Salvationis* and would have been so explained in the now blank pages between the miniatures.

24. Rowe, "Notes on the Clovis miniature," 56.

25. Jules J. Guiffrey, *Histoire générale de la tapisserie* (Paris: 1885), 3:19.

26. Wolffe, 53f.

27. Wolffe, 59.

28. Enguerrand de Monstrelet, *Chronique, 1400–1444*, ed. L. Douët d'Arcq (Paris: 1861), 5:1–4. See also Guenée and Lehoux, 64–70.

29. Desmond Seward, *The Hundred Years War: The English in France, 1337–1453* (London: 1978), 222; August Longnon, *Paris pendant la domination anglaises (1420–1436): Documents extraits des registres de la Chancellerie de France* (Paris: 1878), xviif.

30. For Henry's French coronation and the banquet that followed, see Wolffe, 61f.

31. "Et fut ledit roy sacré par le cardinal Wincestre [i.e., Beaufort], qui chanta la messe. Dont l'evêque de Paris ne fut point bien content, et dist qu'à lui appertenoit à faire ycelui office" (Monstrelet, *Chronique,* 5:5).

32. Seward, *The Hundred Years War,* 223; Wolffe, 62.

33. "l'endemain de Noël, jour Saint Etienne, le roy se departy de Paris . . . oncques personnes, ne à secret ne en appert, on n'en ouy louer. Et si ne fist on oncques à Paris autunt de honneur à roy, comme on lui fist à sa venue" (*Journal d'un bourgeois de Paris: 1409–1449,* ed. Alexandre Tuetey [Paris: 1881], 279, item 597).

34. According to Griffiths, 193, the crossing to Dover was made on 29 January; according to Wolfe, 63, Henry landed in Dover 9 February 1432.

35. "et aussi tost que le roy entra dedens la ville ilz lui mirent ung grant ciel d'azur sur la teste, semé de fleurs de lis d'or, et le portèrent sur lui les 1111 eschevins tout en la fourme et maniere c'on fait à Nostre Seigneur à la Feste-Dieu" (*Bourgeois de Paris,* 274, item 586). See also *Monstrelet, Chronique,* 5:3.

36. Guenée and Lehoux, 13f., 16f. According to Guenée and Lehoux, 14, all three of the canopies used for Charles VI in the Midi were covered on top with cloth of gold. The sides of one of the canopies were of blue silk, those of another of white satin, both seeded with fleurs de lis. The sides of the third canopy were formed of fringes and entirely lacked any royal emblems. In spite of the meticulousness of Guenée and Lehoux's admirable monograph on the royal entrances, the significance of Henry VI's canopy of 1431 in introducing the "ciel" (though mentioned in Guenée and Lehoux, 20) seems to have eluded the authors' attention.

37. A detailed description of Henry's London entrance is given in Wolffe, 63f.

38. Lydgate's poem "On the Coming of the King out of France to London" is

published in *Chronicles of London,* ed. Charles L. Kingsford (Oxford: 1905), 97–116. For the verses on the genealogical trees, see *Chronicles of London,* 111.

39. Ralph Griffith's claim that the Becket oil was used at the ceremony in Notre-Dame (222) is as dubious as that of Bertram Wolffe in his account of the Westminster coronation (200n.1).

40. A full description of the coronation is given in Jean de Pange, *Le roi très chrétien* (Paris: 1949), 432–37.

### 9. The Burgundian Illustrations of the Legend of Joyenval

1. Richard Vaughan, *Valois Burgundy* (London and Hamden: 1975), 53.

2. Johan Huizinga, "L'état bourguignon, ses rapports avec la France et les origines d'une nationalité néerlandaise," *Le moyen age* 40 (1930): 171–93, esp. 184.

3. Olivier de la Marche, *Mémoires,* ed. Henri Beaune and J. d'Arbaumont (Paris: 1883), 1:240.

4. "Et prist le duc Phelippe le Hardy les armes de Bourgoinge . . . et les escartela de France, en chief, semé de fleurs de lis; car j'ay sceu . . . que tous les filz de France doivent porter semé de fleurs de liz, et n'appertient à nulz de porter les trois fleurs de lis, sinon à celluy qui est Roy de France ou l'heritier apparent" (La Marche, *Mémoires,* 73f). The new Burgundian arms were in actuality officially assumed by Philip the Bold, the son of John the Good and the first Valois Duke, on 2 June 1364, long before the number of the fleurs de lis had been permanently reduced to three, and consisted of the arms of France with multiple lilies quartered with the ancient Burgundian arms of the former Capetian Dukes (François Salet, "Histoire et héraldiques: La succession de Bourgogne de 1361," in *Mélanges offerts à René Crozet* [Poitiers: 1966], 2:1307–16).

5. As one example, the arms of Charles the Bold on his secret seal, taken by the Swiss at Granson in 1476, display three fleurs de lis (Pinoteau, 1979, 92). For another instance of the Burgundian arms with triple lilies, see Amadée Boinet, "Um bibliophile du XVe siècle: le Grand Bâtard de Bourgogne," *Bibliothèque de L'école des chartes* 67 (1906): n.6.

6. The Burgundian arms of the Grand Bâtard are represented in three miniatures, in one instance with three fleurs de lis, in the other two with multiple lilies, in A. Boinet, "Un bibliophile," 255–69, esp. plate, p. 260 and 2 plates after p. 264.

7. In volume one of a two-volume copy (BRA, ms. 9005, fol. 3). Camille Gaspar and Frederic Lyna, *Les principaux mss. à peintures de la bibliothèque royale de Belgique* (Paris: 1945), 2:43f. No. 30 in Laborde, 2:318–23.

8. The upper part of the miniature has suffered considerably from water damage.

9. For these analogies with the eagle, see the transcript of the Prologue in Laborde, 1:63.

10. Yves Delaporte and Etienne Houvet, *Les vitraux de la cathédrale de Chartres* (Chartres: 1926), 439ff. (Baie CII), plate CCVIII. See also Contamine, 1973, 220, fig. 1 opp. p. 208.

11. Referred to as "la banniere Charlemaine" in the Prologue to the *Cité de Dieu*. See appendix 4.18. The other identical banner seen by Raoul de Presles on the altar was probably a copy of the original and would thus have been the actual banner flown on the battlefield, while the original remained in the safekeeping of the abbey (Contamine, 1973, 217, n.2).

12. G. Hulin de Loo, "Gui Guilbaut," *Bulletin de la soc. d'hist. et d'archéol. de Gand* 19 (1911): 329–41, esp. 332, 334.

13. Gaspar and Lyna, *Les principaux mss.*, 44.

14. The miniatures in Guilbaut's *Cité de Dieu* are attributed to this master in Friederich Winkler, *Die flämische Buchmalerei des XV and XVI Jahrhunderts* (Leipzig: 1925), 162; in Gaspar and Lyna, *Les principaux mss.*, 43; and in Patrick M. de Winter, "Mss. à peintures produits pour le mécenat lillois sous les règnes de Jean Sans Peur et de Philippe le Bon," *Actes du 101e Congrès national des soc. savantes, Lille, 1976, Section d'archéol. et d'hist. de l'art: Archéol. militaire: Les Pays du Nord,* BN, 1978, 233–56, esp. 240.

15. According to Winkler (*Die flämische Buchmalerei,* 29), Guillebert de Mets not only received a Parisian training but also probably visited Italy, since a direct Italian influence can be detected in the drawing of rinceaux and in the use of green in the flesh tones, a practice derived from Bolognese painting.

16. BRA, ms. 9015, fol. 1. No. 38 in Laborde, 2:341–45. Both the frontispiece of this first volume and that of vol. 2 (ms. 9016) have been attributed to Jan van Eyck in L. Fourez, "L'évêque Chevrot de Tournai et sa *Cité de Dieu*," *Revue belge d'archéol. et d'hist. de l'art* 13 (1954): 73–110, in spite of the fact that Jan van Eyck died in 1441, some four years before the manuscript was finished.

17. These verses, explaining the sacramental mysteries and taken from Scripture, Saint Ambrose, and Peter Lombard, are displayed on the scrolls held by angels above each of the seven scenes depicting the sacraments (Erwin Panofsky, *Early Netherlandish Painting* [Cambridge, Mass.: 1964], 283n.2). The triptych is assigned to Roger van der Weyden himself and his assistants and dated c. 1453–55 in James Snyder, *Northern Renaissance Art: Painting, Sculpture and the Graphic Arts from 1350 to 1575* (Englewood Cliffs, and New York: 1985), 129, and fig. 124, p. 130.

18. Elizabeth Dhanens, *Hubert and Jan Van Eyck* (New York: 1980), 369; fig. 228, p. 363; colored plate 213, p. 345. The Carthusian monk, the donor of the painting, has been tentatively identified as Jan Vos, who was prior of the Carthusian monastery of Genadedal near Bruges from 30 March 1441 to 1450, and the painting is thought to have been that dedicated by the visiting Irish bishop, Martin of Mayo, on 3 September 1443 and to have been begun by Jan Van Eyck shortly before his death in 1441 (Snyder, *Northern Renaissance Art,* 155; fig. 114, p. 116). As in Dhanens, *Hubert and Jan Van Eyck,* 369, however, I see no evidence of Jan's participation in this work.

19. The uninterrupted view of Old St. Paul's in Anthonis van den Wyngaerde's panoramic drawing of London, executed before the fall of the cathedral spire in 1561, and reproduced in plate 39 from W. Bentham and C. Welch, *Mediaeval London* (London and New York 1901), fig. 3, is no longer available in an original photograph, since the drawing, now in the Ashmolean Museum, Ox-

ford, was cut into separate sections some twenty years ago as a conservation measure, according to Noëlle Brown of the museum's Photo Archive. The flying buttresses supporting the tower appear to be a peculiarly English feature, since they also support the central tower of Salisbury Cathedral, some of them concealed inside the clerestory.

The modern engraving in plate 40, in spite of its gratuitous embellishments, clarifies the essential features of the cathedral and its tower and raises the question of whether or not the city itself in the two paintings also reflects the actual appearance of London at that time. The view in the paintings was presumably taken from the opposite bank of the Thames at Southwark, since in the Frick painting the river is shown flowing beneath the city walls. Panofsky (*Early Netherlandish Painting,* 430f., n.2) has suggested that the view of Old St. Paul's in both paintings was based on a sketch by Jan Van Eyck himself.

20. Frederich Lyna ("Les Van Eyck et les 'Heures de Turin et de Milan,' " in *Miscellanea Erwin Panofsky* [Brussels: 1955], 7–20) has concluded that either there is a probable identity between the author of the frontispiece and "Hand G" or at least that both artists belonged to the same atelier. See also the favorable comments by Elizabeth Dhanens (*Hubert and Jan Van Eyck,* 350, 353) on Lyna's conclusions. The miniatures assigned to "Hand G" are described in Panofsky (*Early Netherlandish Painting,* 233f.) and are dated c. 1435 or later in Snyder (*Northern Renaissance Art,* 96).

21. The photographs of the destroyed Turin miniatures are reproduced in Paul Durrieu, *Heures de Turin: Quarante-cinq feuillets à peintures provenant des Très Belles Heures de Jean de France, Duc de Berry* (Paris: 1902) and are reprinted from the original negatives in a new edition of the *Heures de Turin* by Albert Chatelet (Turin: 1967), reviewed by James Marrow, *Art Bulletin* 50 (1968): 203–9.

22. Jeffrey Chipps Smith, "The Artistic Patronage of Philip the Good, Duke of Burgundy (1419–1467)" (Ph.D. diss., Columbia University, 1979), 347f.

23. Turin, Biblioteca Nazionale, MS. L.1. 6, fol. 1; no. 49 in Laborde 2:371–87. The left edge of the frontispiece, including the portrait of Saint Augustine, was damaged in the 1904 fire of the Turin library. For the appearance of the miniature before the fire, see Laborde, plate XLII. The second volume of this two-volume copy of the *Cité de Dieu* is in the library of the State Archives of Turin, ms. b. III. 12 J.

24. William R. Tyler, *Dijon and the Valois Dukes of Burgundy* (Norman, Okla.: 1971), 91.

25. BL, Roy. MS. 14. D. I, fol. 1; no. 47 in Laborde, 2:365–68.

26. Warner and Gilson, 2:138. In Laborde, 2:366, the arms are identified as those of the Dukes of Guelders.

27. The influence of Liédet and his workshop is most evident in the features of Saint Augustine that can be compared to those of several heads in book 3 of a copy of the *Chroniques de Hainaut* illuminated by Liédet c. 1468; BRA, ms. 2944, fols. 28, 136; Facsimile of miniatures, with preface by P. Cockshaw, in *Les Miniatures des Chroniques de Hainaut (15ème siècle)* (Mons: 1979).

28. The grisaille miniatures comprise nine illustrations, beginning with fol. 41v, and can be compared to a four-part miniature in a *Life of Christ* of 1478, now in

Cracow (Marja Jareslawiecka-Gasiorowska, *Les principaux mss. à peinture du Musée des Princes Czartoryski a Cracow, Bull. de la soc. fr. de reproduction de mss. à peintures,* 18 [Paris: 1935], 105–9, plate XXIII). See also K. G. Boon, "Naar aanlieiding van tekeningen van Hugo van der Goes en sijn school," *Nederlandisch Kunsthistorisch Jaarboek* 3 (1950–51): 83–101, and fig. 16, p. 97; Ira Moskowitz, ed., *Great Drawings of All Time* (New York, 1962), no. 471; J. L. Schrader, *The Waning Middle Ages*, Exh. Cat., University of Kansas Museum of Art, 1969, 25f., no. 23. Still another illustration, "The Taking of Rome," on fol. 7 of Roy. 14. D. I, is apparently by the same artist responsible for the frontispiece.

29. Roy. MS. 17. F. III, in 2 vols. (Warner and Gilson, 2:262). The frontispiece of vol. 1 is embellished with a presentation scene in a different style from the pictographic frontispiece of Roy. 14. D. I. According to a communication kindly sent me by Janet Backhouse, the latter *Cité de Dieu* "may have been among the books collected by Edward IV," implying "a date in the 1470s."

30. Smith, "Artistic Patronage," 39–54.

31. Dated after 1434 by François Salet (*L'art gothique* [Paris: 1963], 173); c. 1440, as indicated by the costumes, and stemming from an Arras atelier in M. Godbillon-Sartor, *Les tapisseries, toiles peintes et broderies de Reims* (Reims: 1912), 45, 58f; woven in Tournai, probably during the 1450s (Smith, "Artistic Patronage," 55).

32. Godbillon-Sartor, *Les tapisseries,* 61–64; fig. 9 opp. p. 60 and fig. 10, p. 63. Part of the luggage of the Emperor Charles V that was lost at the siege of Metz, the tapestries were later given to the cathedral of Reims in 1573 by Charles de Guise, Cardinal of Lorraine (Godbillon-Sartor, *Les tapisseries,* 59f).

33. Louis Paris (text) and Casimir Leberthais (illustrations), *Toiles peintes et tapisseries de la ville de Reims* (Paris: 1843), 2:1059–79; plates 29–32.

34. On the occasion of the marriages of Charles the Bold to Margaret of York, the sister of Edward IV (Jean, Sire de Haynin et de Louvignies, *Mémoires, 1465–1477*, ed. D. D. Browers [Liège: 1906], 2:22ff., 25).

35. The huge size of these hangings can be gauged by the fact that all six measured 4.9 m (almost 16') in height according to a Brussels inventory of 1536 and that the first chronologically of the two surviving tapestries measures 8.80 m. (29'4") in length and the second, 9.50 m (31'8") (Smith, "Artistic Patronage," 59f).

36. Viard, 1:54–83.

37. The same general chronology of events has been followed in the Sire de Haynin, *Mémoires* (25) in the description of the tapestries, with one exception. The Taking of Soissons, which comes after the Coronation of Clovis on the first of the surviving tapestries, has been mistakenly placed after the Baptism.

38. This lost tapestry may have included the defeat of the Goths at the battle of Poitiers and the death of Alaric at the hands of Clovis, as suggested by Smith ("Artistic Patronage," 62), since the last previous event on the fourth tapestry (the second now at Reims) depicts Clovis about to cross the river Vienne in pursuit of Alaric.

39. "On distingue sur ce fragment, malgré son mauvais état, le religieux de l'abbaye de Joyenval, debout sur le seuil de son église, levant les yeux au ciel, d'ou descend vers lui un ange tenant un étandard bleu aux trois fleurs de lis d'or.

Clovis et Clotilda, non loin de là, semblent attendre l'hommage céleste que va leur faire le saint ermite. L'armée de Clovis est près de là, n'ayant encore d'autre enseigne que celle aux trois crapauds" (Paris and Leberthais, *Toiles peintes et tapisseries,* 1084). A more general description is given in the Sire de Haynin, *Mémoires:* "comment langle aporta à lermite le drap dasor à iii fleur de lis dor, lequel ermite les bailla à la roine et la roine audit Roy Clois pour porter comme ses armes, en lieu quil les porter dor à iii crapaus de sable" (25).

40. " 'et depuis tout le cours de sa vie [Clovis] triumpha victorieusement et tant fist que la haulte renommée de luy dure en mémoire jusqu'à present' " (Paris and Leberthais, *Toiles peintes et tapisseries,* 1085). Although Smith ("Artistic Patronage," 62) places the legend of Joyenval on the fifth tapestry, according to Louis Paris the last lines of the inscription, quoted above, are indicative that the tapestry illustrating the legend must have been the sixth and final one of the series, a conclusion that agrees with the description of the hangings by the Sire de Haynin, for whom the legend of Joyenval is the last of the events he describes.

41. La Marche, *Mémoires,* 1:52.

42. In the preface to the first volume Philip is addressed as "mon dit redoubté et très puissant seigneur descendus . . . du hault noble et excellent sang des Troyens" (BRA, ms. 9242, fols. 1–2, quoted by P. Crockshaw in the preface to *Chroniques de Hainaut,* 6).

43. La Marche, *Mémoires,* 1:49.

44. Raoul de Presles, Prologue to the *Cité de Dieu,* (see appendix 4.4); Eustache Deschamps, *Ouvres complètes,* (Paris: 1878), 1:306, no. 172; Jouvenel des Ursins, quoted in Jean de Pange, *Le roi très chrétien* (Paris: 1949), 20f. See also Léopold Pannier and Paul Meyer, eds., *Le débat des hérauts d'Armes de France et d'Angleterre . . .* (Paris: 1878), 12, item 34; *Chronique abregée jusqu'à Louis XII,* BN, ms. fr. 4954, fols. 22v–23, quoted in G. du Fresne de Beaucourt, *Histoire de Charles VII* (Paris: 1891), 6:450.

45. Sire de Haynin, *Mémoires,* 1:25; La Marche, *Mémoires,* 1:51.

46. BL, Yates-Thompson, MS. 32, fol. 5, quoted in Smith, "Artistic Patronage," 57.

## 10. The Frontispiece of the Mâcon *Cité de Dieu*

1. Mâcon, BM, ms. 1, fol. 2; no. 57 in Laborde, 2:448–57; plate CV. See also André Malraux, Preface, in *Les mss. à peintures en France du XIIIe au XVIe siècle,* Exh. Cat., BN, 1955, no. 268.

2. The Mâcon *Cité de Dieu* in two volumes is dated c. 1480 in Laborde, 456; c. 1475 in Malraux, *Les mss. à peintures.*

3. Nicole Reynaud, "Un peintre cartonnier de tapisseries au XVe siècle: Henri de Vulcop," *Revue de l'art* 22 (1973): 6–21, esp. fig. 27 and n.47; Paul Durrieu, *Bulletin de la société des antiquaires de France* (1921): 301–17.

4. Durrieu, *Bulletin,* 305.

5. Durrieu, *Bulletin,* 307. Although Alexandre Delaborde has attempted to decipher the lettering in the Mâcon frontispiece, he concludes that the inscription is a product of the artist's fantasy (Laborde, 2:453n.2).

6. For illustrations of the cartoons with cryptic inscriptions, see Frits Lugt, *Musée du Louvre: Inventaire générale des dessins des écoles du Nord: Maîtres des anciens Pays-Bas nés avant 1550* (Paris: 1968), nos. 53 ("Mort de Penthésilée: Trahison d'Anténor"), 54 ("Prise de Troie"), plate 27; Reynaud, "Un peintre cartonnier," 6, fig. 2; 8, fig. 3.

Nicole Reynaud, moreover, has proposed that the tapestries for which the cartoons were originally intended were made for Charles VII's younger son, Charles of France, "quoique l'hypothèse reste sans preuve" ("Un peintre cartonnier," 15). Circumstantial evidence, however, strongly indicates that the very first edition of these Trojan War tapestries was that which the citizens of Bruges are known to have given Charles the Bold of Burgundy in 1472 to commemorate his marriage four years earlier to Margaret of York (Jean-Paul Asselberghis, "Les tapisseries tournaisiennes de la Guerre de Troie," *Revue belge d'archéol. et de l'hist. de l'art* 39 [1970]: 93–183, esp. 172f).

The exploits of Hercules, from whom the Valois dukes claimed descent and who was said to have captured Troy on two occasions, and the deeds of Jason that were recalled in the Order of the Golden Fleece instituted in 1430, all resulted in a new interest in the Trojan War at the Burgundian court. The most concrete manifestation of this interest resided in the sixteen manuscripts on the Trojan legend in the Burgundian library that during the reign of Philip the Good were added to the single copy on Troy surviving from his father's reign and that, out of a total of c. one thousand volumes amassed during Philip's lifetime, constituted the library's most important single group (Alphonse Bayot, *La légende de Troie à la cour de Bourgogne, Soc. d'émulation de Bruges, Mélanges,* 1 [Bruges: 1908], 25–30, 34f.). Furthermore, the boat on which Margaret of York sailed from England for her wedding to Charles the Bold was named "The new Ellen." And it was she who later encouraged the merchant William Caxton to translate into English *Le Recueil des Hystoires de Troyes* of Raoul de Fevre that subsequently around 1474 was to be the subject of the first printed book in the English language (Bayot, *La légende de Troie,* 14f).

7. BL, Roy. MS. 19C. IV, fol. 2. Claire Richter Sherman, *The Portraits of Charles V of France (1338–1380), Monographs on Archaeology and the Fine Arts* (New York; 1969), 30f., fig. 13.

8. Generally these bands seem to have been three in number. See Sherman, *Portraits of Charles V,* 19n.13, figs. 1, 53, and the portrait of Jean duc de Berry, brother of Charles V, in the historiated initial of his marriage contract of 1398, exhibited in the Musée de l'Histoire de France, Paris, Archives nationales, a reference I owe to Professor Elizabeth A. R. Brown.

9. BN, ms. fr. 6272, fol. 3. Malraux, *Les mss. à peintures,* 80f., no. 3.

10. Warner and Gilson, 2:334.

11. Viard, 1:67f.

12. Bloch, 357f.

13. P. S. Lewis, "Two Pieces of Fifteenth-Century Political Iconography," *JWCI* 27 (1964): 317–20, esp. 318.

14. At least this is the region of the sores indicated in Bloch, 28.

15. Bloch, 357n.2.

16. "Scimus ex Historiographis & Chronicis authenticis ac probatis, quibus fides adhibetur, quis fuit Clodoveus ille Christianissimus Rex, ad quem a coele lilia transmissa fuere, sacraque unctio, & alia quae divinitus recepit . . . tum in sacra unctione, tum in miraculis dietim coruscantibus, tum in curatione vulnerum, & quae vulgariter *escroüelles,* latine vero scrophilae nuncupantur, tum in vexillo auriflameo ad Francorum Reges coelitus emisso." (We know from authentic and reliable histories and chronicles, in which one can place one's trust, why Clovis was the most Christian king of France; for it was he on whom the heavens bestowed both the lilies and the holy unction and other gifts which he received as celestial favors through his holy unction, in being able to cure wounds and what are called in the vernacular "escrouelles," and in Latin, *scrofula,* and finally, through the reception of the standard of the oriflamme sent from heaven for the use of the kings of France.) (Luc d'Achery, *Spicilegium* [Paris: 1723], 3:821, col. 2).

17. Although known to have been in England by the seventeenth century, the manuscript was earlier in the possession of the French king Henry II and his queen, Catherine de Medici (A. N. L. Munby, *Connoisseurs and Medieval Miniatures: 1750–1850* [Oxford: 1972], 2f.).

18. The fictitious arms of Charlemagne are first described c. 1275 in the *Enfances Ogier* by Ardenet le Roi (Louis Carolus-Barre, "Contributions à l'étude de la légende carolingienne. Les armes de Charlemagne dans l'héraldique et l'iconographie médiévale," in *Mémorial du voyage en Rhénanie de la soc. nat. des antiquaires de France* [Paris: 1953], 289–308, esp. 289).

19. Viard (Paris: 1923), 3:166.

20. Colette Beaune, "Saint Clovis: Histoire, religion royal et sentiment national en France à la fin du Moyen Age," in *Le métier d'historien au Moyen Age,* ed. Bernard Guenée (Paris: 1977), 139–56, esp. 145, 147.

21. Beauner, "Saint Clovis," 139.

22. Beauner, "Saint Clovis," 145.

23. Bernard Guenée, "Etat et Nation en France au Moyen Age," *Revue historique* 237 (1967): 17–30, esp. 29.

24. Of the two earlier versions of the origin of the oriflamme, one claimed that it had been given by the pope to Charlemagne, the other that it had been made by Dagobert, who gave it to St-Denis (Contamine, 1973, 190f). The oriflamme is already described as a divine gift to Clovis in a treatise by Robert Blondell of 1449 and again c. 1453 to 1461 in *Le débat des héraulx d'armes de France et Angleterre* (Contamine, 1973, 240f, 241 nos. 1, 2). In the 1459 address of the French ambassadors, the oriflamme is sent from heaven for the kings of France (see above, n.16), as it is in a treatise of 1464 on the Salic law, where it is one of the three "dons singuliers" bestowed by heaven on the French king, along with the fleurs de lis and the holy ampulla (John M. Potter, "The Development and Significance of the Salic Law of France," *English Historical Review* 52 [1937]: 235–53, esp. 251n.3).

25. The banner actually preserved at St-Denis, however, appears to have been only a copy of the original, which must have long since disappeared (Contamine, 1973, 239f.).

26. For the white cross, see Philippe Contamine, *Guerre, Etat et Société à la fin du Moyen Age: Etudes sur les armées des rois de France, 1337–1494* (Paris and The Hague: 1972), 668–76; Henri Stern, "Un fragment des tapisseries des Victoires de Charles VII au chateau de Fontainbleu," *Mémoires de la soc. nat. des antiquaires de France,* 1899, 6th ser., 10 (1901): 174–88, esp. 179.

27. Pierre Roger Gaussin, *Louis IX: Un roi entre deux mondes* (Paris: 1976), 419.

28. Robert Brun, *Le livre français* (Paris: 1969), 13–17.

29. Brun, *Le Livre français,* 33.

30. Legitimized by Charles VIII in 1486, the Grand Bâtard died at Bruges in 1504 at the ripe old age of 83 (Laborde, 2: 373–75; Amadée Boinet, "Un bibliophile du XVe siècle: le Grand Bâtard de Bourgogne," *Bibliothèque de l'école des chartes* 67 [1906]: 255f).

### 11. Pierre le Rouge's Double Illustration in *La Mer des Histoires*

1. Volume 2 of the first edition of *La Mer des Histoires* that contains the woodcut appeared in Paris in February 1489 (1488 old style); volume 1 had already appeared in July 1488 (Francois Courboin, *Histoire illustrée de la Gravure en France, première partie, Des Origines à 1660* [Paris: 1923], 36, plate 53; Henri Monceaux, *Les Le Rouge de Chablis, calligraphes et miniaturistes,* vol. 1, *Graveurs et imprimeurs* [Paris: 1896], 150f.).

2. Courboin, *Histoire illustrée,* 36.

3. I am preparing a comprehensive survey of the baptism of Clovis in Medieval and early Renaissance art that will include other instances of this double theme.

4. Bloch, 283–85.

5. This episode is undoubtedly based, not on Raoul de Presles, but on the original Latin poem of Joyenval when Clotilda attempts to persuade her husband to forsake Jove, Mercury, and his other gods (Bossuat, 1940, 95, stanza 9) who are represented in the woodcut by the small figures set on columns behind the king. Another reversion to the Latin poem occurs in the scene of the baptism in the woodcut when Clovis kneels before the bishops, thus echoing lines 93 and 94 of the poem: "Et ad sanctum Remingium supplex, devotus, humilis, Implorabat officium" (Bossuat, 1940, 97).

6. Of the representations of the battle against the Alemanni known to me, in only two is their leader not threatened by Clovis. In a *Grandes Chroniques* dating before 1350 (BL, Roy. MS. 16, G VI, fol. 15; Warner and Gilson 2:209–12) the mounted Clovis chases the enemy's fleeing horseman, and in a *Chronique abrégée* of the 1470s (Baltimore, Walters Art Gallery, MS W 306, fol. 14v; Hindman and Spiegel, fig. 6) the dismounted Clovis at the moment of his conversion kneels at the left, facing the army of the king of the Alemanni.

7. Hermann Wiesflecker, *Kaiser Maximilian I* (Munich: 1971), 1:190f.

8. Jackson, 322, col. 2.

9. Joseph M. Tyrrell, *Louis XI* (Boston: 1980), 162–78.

10. The following account of the war is mainly based on Wiesflecker, *Kaiser Maximilian I,* 200–205.

11. Monceaux, *Les Le Rouge de Chablis,* 22; Robert Brun, *Le livre français* (Paris: 1969), 27.

12. Now in the Réserve of the Bibliothèque nationale in Paris.

13. For fourteen weeks, from 5 February to 16 May (Wiesflecker, *Kaiser Maximillian I,* 210).

14. The best known of these variants on Pierre le Rouge's woodcut is that of Jean du Pré in the Lyons edition of *La Mer des Histoires* of 1491 (A. Claudin, *Histoire de l'imprimerie en France au XVe et XVIe siècle* [Paris: 1904], 491, 497). Jean de Pré's version of the baptismal scene, with the baptism below and the crowning of the king in the upper section, is repeated in the small woodcut on the frontispiece of Robert Gaguin's 1518 copy of *La Mer des Croniques* (plate 54). Other more or less free copies of Pierre le Rouge's original engraving in later editions of *La Mer des Hystoires* dating from 1503 to 1536 are noted in Ruth Mortimer, *Harvard College Library: Department of Printing and Graphic Arts, Catalogue of Books and Manuscripts,* part 1, *French 16th Century Books,* vol. 2 (Cambridge, Mass.: 1964), nos. 372, 467, 468, 469.

15. Tyrrell, *Louis XI,* 184f.

16. As in the Mâcon *Cité de Dieu,* the legend of Joyenval is here illustrated in five separate scenes. Although this copy of the *Abrégée,* of which the miniature is the frontispiece, is now ms. 3430 of the Bibl. de l'Arsenal, Paris, the arms of France in the initial at the beginning of the text indicates that originally it may have been in the royal library.

17. Baltimore, Walters Art Gallery, ms. W 306, fol. 11; first published in Hindman and Spiegel, fig. 1, along with a second similar frontispiece in another copy of the *Chronique Abrégée,* BN, ms. fr. 2598, fol. 1 (Hindman and Spiegel, fig. 2).

18. The passage occurs in the left-hand column of the text: "Pour ce que moust de gens, mesmement les haulx hommes et les nobles, qui souvent viennent en l'eglise monsiegneur Saint Denis de France, ou grant partie des vaillans roys de France gisent en sepulture." This passage, however, and its bearing on the subject matter of the miniature have been overlooked in Hindman and Spiegel. As a consequence the bearded figure seated at the lower left and wearing a triple crown, like a pope's tiara, has been thought to be Charlemagne (Hindman and Spiegel, 397f.). Since Charlemagne was buried at Aachen, however, should the figure indeed represent a Carolingian ruler, he must be Charles the Bald who was buried at St-Denis where his silver tomb effigy was at the center of the program of royal tombs in the abbey church.

19. See above, chap. 2, pp. 32–35. In the frontispiece to the second copy of the *Chronique Abrégée* (Hindman and Spiegel, fig. 2), in a different arrangement of the floral leaves, three large petals hang from the fully opened flower. The central petal being longer than the other two, they are thus made to correspond more nearly to the three unequal petals of the fleur de lis.

For the Walters Art Gallery manuscript and the style of its miniatures, see also John Plammer, *The Last Flowering: French Painting in Manuscripts, 1420–1530,* Exh. Cat., The Pierpont Morgan Library (New York: 1982), 39, no. 52, where the manuscript is said to stem from the Loire valley or Bourges, c. 1475, and its miniatures are attributed to the circle of the Coëtivy Master.

# Selected Bibliography

## Heraldry, Sigillography, and Numismatics

Adam-Evan, Paul. "Les fonctions militaires des héraus d'armes, leur influence sur le développement de l'héraldique." *Archives héraldiques suisses* 71 (1957): 2–33.

Demay, Germain. *Les costumes au môyen âge d'après les sceaux*. Paris: 1880.

Dennys, Rodney. *The Heraldic Imagination*. New York: 1975.

Douët d'Arcq, Louis. *Archives de l'Empire . . . Collection de sceaux*. 3 vols. Paris: 1863–68.

Jones, Evan John. *Medieval Heraldry: Some Fourteenth Century Heraldic Works*. Cardiff: 1943.

Lafaurie, Jean. *Les monnaies des rois de France: Hugues Capet à Louis XII*. Paris and Basle: 1951.

Pastoureau, Michel. "La fleur de lis: emblème royal, symbole marial ou thème graphique?" In *La monnaie, miroir des rois*. Exh. Cat., Hotel de la Monnaie, 251–71. Paris: 1978.

———. *Traité d'héraldique*. Paris: 1979.

Pinoteau, Hervé. *Héraldique Capétienne*. Paris: 1979.

Prinet, Max. "Armoiries couronnées figurées sur des sceaux français de la fin du XIIIe et du commencement du XIVe siècles." *Revue archéologique,* 4th ser. 14 (1909): 370–79.

———. "Les variations du nombre des fleurs de lis dans les armes de France." *Bulletin monumental* 75 (1911): 467–88.

Rezak, Brigitte M. Bedos. "Mythes monarchiques et thèmes sigillaires du sceau de Louis VII aux sceaux de Charles VII." *XV Congreso Internacional de las Ciencias Genealogica y Heraldica,* 199–213. Madrid: 1982.

Roman, Jules. *Manuel de sigillographie française*. Paris: 1912.

Salet, François. "Histoire et héraldiques: La succession de Bourgogne de 1361." In *Mélanges offerts à René Crozet*. 2:1307–16. Poitiers: 1966.

Stumm, Gustav Braun von. "L'origine de la fleur de lis des rois de France du point de vue numismatique." *Revue numismatique,* 3d ser. 13 (1951): 43–57.

Wagner, Arthur Richard. *Heralds and Heraldry in the Middle Ages*. 2d ed. Oxford: 1956.

Wailly, Natalis de. *Eléments de paléographie*. 2 vols. Paris: 1838.

## History

Atiya, Aziz Suryal. *The Crusade in the Late Middle Ages*. London: 1938.

Beaune, Colette. "Saint Clovis: Histoire, religion royale et sentiment national en

France à la fin du Moyen Age." In *Le métier d'historien au Moyen Age,* edited by Bernard Guenée. 139–56. Paris: 1977.

Bloch, Marc. *Les rois thaumaturges.* Strasbourg and Paris: 1924.

Brown, Elizabeth A. R. "Reform and Resistance to Royal Authority in Fourteenth Century France: The Leagues of 1314–1315." *Parliaments, Estates and Representation* 1. 2 (Dec. 1981): 109–37.

Cazelles, Raymond, *La société politique et la crise de la royauté sous Philippe de Valois.* Paris: 1958.

Contamine, Philippe. *Guerre: Etat et Société à la fin du Moyen Age: Etudes sur les armées des rois de France, 1337–1494.* Paris and The Hague: 1972.

———. "L'oriflamme de Saint-Denis aux XIVe et XVe siècles." *Annales de l'Est,* 5th ser. 25e année, no. 3 (1973): 179–244.

Delachenal, Roland. *Histoire de Charles V.* 5 vols. Paris: 1909–31.

Durrieu, Paul. "Les souvenirs historiques dans les manuscrits à peintures de la dominion anglaise en France." *Annuaire-bulletin de la société de l'histoire de France* 41 (1905): 111–35.

Dutilleux, A. "Notice sur l'abbaye de Joyenval." *Mémoires de la Société historique et archéologique de l'arrondissement de Pontoise et du Vexin* 13 (1890): 41–144.

Griffiths, Ralph A. *The Reign of King Henry VI.* Berkeley and Los Angeles: 1981.

Guenée, Bernard, and Françoise Lehoux. *Les entrées royales françaises de 1328 à 1515.* Paris: 1968.

Huizinga, Johan. "L'état bourguignon, ses rapports avec la France et les origines d'une nationalité néerlandaise." *Le moyen age* 40 (1930): 171–93.

Hutchison, Harold F. *The Hollow Crown: A Life of Richard II.* London: 1961.

Kämpf, Hellmut. *Pierre Dunois und die geistigen Grundlagen des französischen Nationalbewustseins um 1300, Beiträge zur Kulturgeschichte des Mittelalters und der Renaissance,* 54. Leipzig and Berlin: 1935.

Kantorowitz, Ernest II. *The King's Two Bodies: A Study in Mediaeval Theology.* Princeton, 1957.

McKenna, John W. "Henry VI of England and the Dual Monarchy: Aspects of Royal Political Propaganda, 1422–1432." *Journal of the Warburg and Courtauld Institutes* 28 (1965): 145–62.

Packe, Michael St. John. *King Edward III.* London and Boston: 1983.

Palmer, John J. N. "The Anglo-French Peace Negotiations, 1390–1396." *Transactions of the Royal Historical Society,* 5th ser. 16 (1966): 81–94.

———. *England, France and Christendom, 1377–99.* Chapel Hill and London: 1972.

———. "English Foreign Policy 1388–99." In *The Reign of Richard II: Essays in Honor of May McKisack,* 75–107. London: 1971.

Perroy, Edouard. *L'Angleterre et le Grand Schisme de l'Occident.* Paris: 1933.

———. *La guerre de cent ans,* Paris: 1945.

Setton, Kenneth M., general ed. *A History of the Crusades.* 2d ed. 5 vols. Madison: 1969–77.

Seward, Desmond. *The Hundred Years War: The English in France 1337–1453,* London, 1978.

Strayer, Joseph R. "France: The Holy Land, the Chosen People, and the Most

Christian King." In *Action and Conviction in Early Modern Europe: Essays in Honor of E. H. Harbison*. Princeton: 1969. 3–16.

————. *Medieval Statecraft and the Perspectives of History*. Princeton: 1971.

————. "Philip the Fair—'A Constitutional King,' " *American Historical Review* 62 (1956): 18–32.

Tessier, Georges. *Le Baptême de Clovis: 25 décembre*. Paris: 1964.

Vaughan, Richard. *Valois Burgundy*. London and Hamden: 1975.

Wenck, Karl. *Philipp der Schöne von Frankreich, seine Persönlichkeit und das Urteil der Zeitgenossen*. Marburg: 1905.

Wiesflecker, Hermann. *Kaiser Maximilian I*. 2 vols. Munich: 1971.

Wolffe, Bertram, *Henry VI*. London: 1981.

Literature

Bossuat, Robert. " 'Charles le Chauve': Etude sur le declin de l'épopée française." *Les lettres romans* 7 (1953): 107–32.

————. "Poème latine sur l'origine des fleurs de lis." *Bibliothèque de l'école des chartes* 101 (1940): 80–101.

————. "Raoul de Presles." *Histoire littéraire de la France* 40 (1974): 113–86.

————. "Saint Honoré, saint Honorat?" In *Recueil de travaux offert à M. Clovis Brunel*, 163–73. Paris: 1956.

————. "Théseus de Cologne." *Le Moyen Age* 14 (1959): 293–320, 539–77.

Chatillon, François. "Lilia crescunt." *Revue de moyen age latin* 11 (1955): 87–200.

Cuvelier. *Chronique de Bertrand du Guesclin*. Edited by E. Charrière. 2 vols. Paris: 1839.

Delisle, Léopold. *Recherches sur la librairie de Charles V*. 2 vols. Paris: 1907.

Faral, Edmond. "Guillaume de Digulleville, moine de Châalis." *Histoire littéraire de la France* 39 (1962): 1–132.

————. "Le roman de la fleur de lis de Guillaume de Digulleville." In *Mélanges de philologie romane et de la littérature médiévale offerts à Ernest Hoepffner*, 327–38. Paris: 1949.

Gerson, Jean. *Oeuvres complètes*. Edited by Mgr. Glorieux. 5 vols. Paris: 1960–63.

Giraldus Cambrensis. *De Principis Instructionis Liber*. Edited by George F. Warner. London: 1891.

Golein, Jean. "The 'Traité du Sacre' " (ed. Richard A. Jackson). *Proceedings of the American Philosophical Society* 113: (1969): 305–24.

Guillaume de Nangis. *Chronique latine de Guillaume de Nangis, de 1113 à 1300*. Edited by Hercule Géraud. 2 vols. Paris: 1843.

————. *Vita Santi Ludovici, Regis Franciae. Recueil des historiens des Gaules et de la France* 20 466–539.

Hamdy, Abdel Hamid. "Philippe de Mézières and the New Order of the Passion." pt. 3, "La sustenance de la Chevalerie de la Passion de Jhesu Crist en françois." *Bulletin of the Faculty of Arts*, University of Alexandria 18 (1964): 43–105.

Jongkees, A. G. "*Translatio Studii:* les avatars d'une thème médiévale." In *Miscellanea Mediaevalia in Memoriam Jan Frederick Niermeyer*, 41–50. Groningen: 1967.

Jorga, Nicolae. *Philippe de Mézières 1327–1405*. Paris: 1896.

*Journal d'un bourgeois de Paris: 1405–1449*. Edited by Alexandre Tuetey. Paris: 1881.

Krappe, Alexandre Haggerty. "La belle Hélène de Constantinople." *Romania* 63 (1937): 324–52.

La Marche, Olivier de. *Mémoires*. Edited by Henri Beaune and J. d'Arbaumont. 4 vols. Paris: 1883–88.

Lancelot, Antoine. "Mémoire sur la vie et les ouvrages de Raoul de Presles." *Mémoires de l'Académie des Inscriptions et Belles-Lettres* 13 (1740): 607–24, 617 (bis)–665.

Lydgate, John. "On the Coming of the King out of France to London." In *Chronicles of London*, edited by Charles L. Kingsford, 97–116. Oxford: 1905.

MacCracken, Henry Noble. *The Minor Poems of John Lydgate*. 2 vols. London and New York: 1911–34.

Monstrelet, Enguerrand de. *Chronique, 1400–1444*. Edited by L. Douët d'Arcq. 6 vols. Paris: 1857–62.

Pearsall, Derek. *John Lydgate*. Charlottesville: 1970.

*Philippe de Mézières, Letter to King Richard II*. Edited by G. W. Coopland. Liverpool: 1975.

Piaget, Arthur, " 'Le chapel des fleurs de lis' par Philippe de Vitri." *Romania* 27 (1898): 55–92.

———. "Un poème inédit de Guillaume de Digulleville, 'Le roman de la fleur de lis.' " *Romania* 62 (1936):317–58.

Ruths, Rudolph. "Die französischen Fassungen der Roman de la belle Helaine." Ph.D. diss., University of Greifswald, 1897.

Sire de Haynin et de Louvignies, Jean. *Mémoires, 1465–1477*. Edited by D. D. Browers. 2 vols. Liège: 1906.

*Somnium Viridarii*. In *Monarchia Sancti Romani Imperii*, edited by Melchior Goldast, 58–229. Hanover: 1611.

*Songe du Vergier, édité d'après le manuscrit Royal 19 C IV de la British Library, Le* (ed. Marion Schnerb-Lièvre). 2 vols. Paris: 1982.

Spiegel, Gabrielle M. *The Chronicle Tradition of Saint-Denis: A Survey*. Brookline, Mass. and Leyden: 1978.

Storer, Walter H., and Charles A. Rochedieu. *Six Historical Poems of Geoffroi de Paris, Written 1314–1318. University of North Carolina, Studies in Romance Languages, 16*. Chapel Hill: 1950. 73–89.

Viard, Jules, ed. *Les Grandes Chroniques de France*. 10 vols. Paris: 1920–53.

*Vitis mystica*. In *Patrologia Latina*, edited by J. P. Migne. 184, cols. 635–740.


Unpublished or Only Partially Published Texts

Charter of the Foundation of the Celestine Abbey of Limay, January 1377; Versailles, Archives des Yvelines et de l'Ancien Départment de Seine-et-Oise, 41 H 48.

Etienne de Conty. *Treatise on the Monarchy*; Paris, Bibliothèque nationale, ms. lat., 11.730, fols. 31v–32.

Geoffroy de Paris. *De Alliatis*. Paris, Bibliothèque nationale. MS. fr. 146, fols. 50v–51.

*Illustrated Poem on the Origin of the Fleurs de Lis and the Miracle of the Holy Ampulla,* with Subtitles to the Illustrations: "The Hours of the Duke of Bedford." London, British Library. Add. MS. 18.850, fols. 288v–289v.

Raoul de Presles. Prologue to the *Cité de Dieu*. Paris, Bibliothèque nationale. ms. fr. 22.912, fols. 3–5v.

*Roman de Charles le Chauve* (also known as *Dieudonné de Hongrie*). Paris, Bibliothèque nationale. ms. 24. 372, fol. 1.

*Roman de la Belle Helaine*. Paris, Bibliothèque nationale. ms. fr. 12.482, fols. 131v–133v.

Yves of St-Denis. *Vita Sancti Dionysii*. Paris, Bibliothèque nationale. ms. lat. 5286.

———. *Vita Sancti Dionysii*, an incomplete and fragmentary copy of Book 3, with French translation. Paris, Bibliothèque nationale. ms. lat. 13.836.

Art

Avril, François. *Manuscript Painting at the Court of France: The Fourteenth Century (1310–1380)*. New York: 1978.

Backhouse, Jeanette. "A Reappraisal of the Bedford Hours." *The British Library Journal* 7 (1981): 47–69.

Boinet, Amadée. "Un bibliophile du XVe siècle: Le Grand Bâtard de Bourgogne." *Bibliothèque de l'école des chartes* 67 (1906): 255–69.

Brun, Robert. *Le livre français*. Paris: 1969.

Denny, Don. *The Annunciation from the Right from Early Christian Times to the Sixteenth Century*. New York and London: 1977.

Dhanens, Elizabeth. *Hubert and Jan Van Eyck*. New York: 1980.

Durrieu, Paul, *Heures de Turin: Quarante-cinq feuillets à peintures provenant des Très Belle Heures de Jean de France, Duke de Berry*. Paris: 1902.

*Fastes du Gothique, Les: Le siècle de Charles V*. Exh. Cat., Grand Palais. Paris: 1981.

Godbillon-Sartor, M. *Les tapisseries, toiles peintes et broderies de Reims*. Reims: 1912.

Gough, Richard. *An Account of a Rich Illuminated Missal Executed for John Duke of Bedford*. London: 1794.

Guiffrey, Jules J. *Histoire générale de la tapisserie*. 3 vols. Paris: 1878–85.

Hindman, Sandra, and Gabrielle M. Spiegel. "The Fleur-de-Lis Frontispieces to Guillaume de Nangis's *Chronique Abrégée*." *Viator* 12 (1981): 381–407.

Laborde, Alexandre de. *Les manuscrits à peinture de la "Cité de Dieu" de Saint Augustin*. 2 vols. Paris; 1909.

Lyna, Frederich. "Les Van Eyck et les 'Heures de Turin et de Milan.' " *Miscellanea Erwin Panofsky*, 7–20. Brussels: 1955.

Malderghem, Jean van. "Les fleurs de lis de l'ancienne monarchie française." *Annales de la société d'archéologie de Bruxelles* 8 (1894): 180–212.

Meiss, Millard. *The De Levis Hours and the Bedford Workshop*. New Haven: 1972.

———. *French Painting in the Time of Jean de Berry: The Boucicaut Master*. London: 1968.

*Miniatures des Chroniques de Hainaut (15 ème siècle), Les.* (Facsimile of miniatures, with preface by P. Cockshaw). Mons: 1979.

Monceaux, Henri. *Les Le Rouge de Chablis, calligraphes et miniaturistes.* vol. 1, *Graveurs et imprineurs.* Paris: 1896.

Montesquiou-Fezensac, Blaise de. "Le 'Tombeau des corps-saints' à l'abbaye de Saint-Denis." *Cahiers archéologiques* 23 (1974): 81–95.

Panofsky, Erwin. *Early Netherlandish Painting.* Cambridge, Mass.: 1964.

Reynaud, Nicole. "Un peintre cartonnier de tapisseries au XVe siècle: Henri de Vulcop." *Revue de l'art* 22 (1973): 6–21.

Rowe, Benedicta J. H. "King Henry's Claims to France in Picture and Poetry." *The Library.* 4th ser. 12 (1932–33): 77–88.

———. "Notes on the Clovis Miniature in the Bedford Book of Hours." *Journal of the British Archaeological Association,* 3d ser. 25 (1962): 56–65.

Sherman, Claire Richter. *The Portraits of Charles V of France (1338–1380). Monographs on Archaeology and the Fine Arts,* 20. New York: 1969.

Smith, Jeffrey Chipps. "The Artistic Patronage of Philip the Good, Duke of Burgundy (1419–1467)." Ph.D. diss., Columbia University, 1979.

Smith, S. O. Dunlap. "Illustrations of Raoul de Praelles' Translation of St. Augustine's City of God Between 1375 and 1420." Ph.D. diss., New York University, 1974.

Spencer, Eleanor P. "The Master of the Duke of Bedford: The Bedford Hours." *The Burlington Magazine* 107 (1965): 495–502.

Warner, George F., and Julius P. Gilson. *British Museum: Catalogue of Western Manuscripts in the Old Royal and Kind's Collections.* 4 vols. London: 1921.

Winkler, Friederich. *Die flämische Buchmalerei des XV and XVI Jahrhunderts.* Leipzig: 1925.

Winter, Patrick M. de. "Manuscrits à peintures produits pour le mécenat lillois sous les règnes de Jean Sans Peur et de Philippe le Bon." *Actes du 101e Congrès national des sociétés savantes, Lille, 1976, Section d'archéologie et d'histoire de l'art: Archéologie militaire: Les Pays du Nord.* Bibliothèque nationale, Paris: 1978, 233–56.

# Index

Abbeville *Cité de Dieu. See Cité de Dieu* (Raoul de Presles): Abbeville edition of

Alcuin, 7–8

Alexander II (king of Scotland), 171n.1

Ampulla, holy, 25, 34, 66–75, 77, 200n.1, 210n.24; in the Bedford Hours, 68, 69, 70, 71, 72–73, 168–69, *pls. 26–27;* in the *Cité de Dieu* (Raoul de Presles), 34, 79, 88–89, *pls. 33, 48;* and the "Histoire du fort roy Clovis," 84; in *Life of Saint Denis* (Yves), 23, *pl. 6;* in *La Mer des Histoires,* 96, *pl. 53;* in the Mumming at Windsor (Lydgate), 67–68; in *Roman de la fleur de lis* (Guillaume de Digulleville), 29

"Angelot," 47, 187n.15, *pl. 17d*

Anne of Bohemia, 50

Anne of Burgundy, 68, 70, 72, 83, 200–201n.9, 202–3n.22

Annunciation, the 65, 99, 199 nn. 46, 49, *pl. 25*

Antecedents of fleurs de lis, 2, 4. *See also* Crescents as heraldic emblems; Fleurs de lis; Origin of fleurs de lis; Toads as heraldic emblems

Antoine de Bourgogne, 204n.6, 211n.30; and the *Cité de Dieu* (Raoul de Presles), 78, 82, 83, 93, 94, *pl. 41*

Arras, Treaty of, 77, 97

Augustine, Saint, 86, 87; in the Abbeville *Cité de Dieu,* 94, *pl. 52;* in the Burgundian *Cité de Dieu,* 79, 80, 81, 83, 94, *pls. 33, 41; Civitas Dei,* 34, 37, 51. *See also Cité de Dieu* (Raoul de Presles)

Barthelemi de Roie, 24, 26, 27

Bartholomew. *See* Barthelemi de Roie

Bartolo di Sassoferrato: *Tractatus de Insigniis et Armis,* 43, 50, 188n.22

Barton, Philippe: *Chroniques de Bourgogne,* 85

Beaufort, Cardinal, 73

Bedford, Duke of, 62, 68, 88, 200–201n.9, 202–3n.22

Bedford Hours, the, 68–73, 80, 83,